THE FIRST JIHAD

THE
FIRST
JIHAD

*The Battle for
Khartoum and the
Dawn of Militant Islam*

By
DANIEL ALLEN BUTLER

CASEMATE
Philadelphia

Published by
CASEMATE

© 2007 Daniel Allen Butler

ISBN (10): 1-932033-54-8
ISBN (13): 978-1-932033-54-0

Cataloging-in-Publication Data is available from the
Library of Congress.

10 9 8 7 6 5 4 3 2 1

MANUFACTURED IN THE UNITED STATES OF AMERICA

CONTENTS

For
Eily

who was there
from the beginning

INTRODUCTION

For over a hundred years, the siege of Khartoum has been considered a modern military epic. It was there, on the banks of the Nile, that a few thousand Egyptian soldiers led by British General Charles Gordon held off the massed hordes of the Mahdi, a Moslem holy man waging *jihad*, for three hundred and seventeen days. For nearly all of this time the most enduring image of the siege has been that of the indomitable Gordon, with his apparently inexhaustible courage, exhorting the citizens and garrison alike to hold out just a few days longer as help was on the way.

Yet as central to the story of Khartoum as is Gordon, just as vital, and perhaps more so, is the Mahdi. It could even be said, with considerable justification, that without the Mahdi, Gordon would be remembered as little more than a minor footnote in the history of Victorian Britain. Of even greater significance is the force that the Mahdi unleashed on the world, one that would grow in intensity and malignancy as the decades passed. It was the power of militant Islam, with the Moslem religion harnessed as the violent driving force of revolutions, a power to be reckoned with in and of itself, rather than being used, as it had been so often in the past, as an ecclesiatical camouflage for temporal and material ambitions.

The victor of Khartoum, born Muhammed Ahmed ibn-Abdullah, was an *imam* whose messiah-like delusions led him to style himself "The Mahdi"—"The Expected One." More than one hundred twenty years ago, he united the Islamic peoples of the Sudan in a bloody revolt, denouncing all who did not follow his vision as heretics and infidels. He declared that foreign influences had corrupted and defiled the true Moslem faith, and proclaimed a *jihad*, a holy war, to purify Islam and remake the "true faith" by cleansing it in a torrent of foreign blood. The Mahdi's followers annihilated Egyptian expeditions sent to crush them, and then challenged the military might of the world's greatest power, the British Empire. It was at a heretofore insignificant city sitting astride the confluence of the White Nile and the Blue Nile—Khartoum— that this confrontation came to a head, as the British general Charles "Chinese" Gordon defended the city and made it a household word around the globe.

What is startling today about the story of the Mahdi is the immediacy of the mysterious desert mullah to the incarnation of modern worldwide terrorism. It is a significant and striking relevance, for those dangerous fanatics who seek to impose their vision of Islam on an unwilling world are only echoing the declamations and proclamations issued by the Mahdi more than a century ago. Militant Islam is not a late 20th-century phenomenon, but rather its roots run deep in certain still-powerful segments of the Moslem world. To the majority of people in the West—preoccupied through most of the century with global wars, hot and cold—militant Islam first reared its head in the Munich tragedy of September 1972 at the Olympic Games, and peaked with the horrors of September 11, 2001. Yet the frightening truth is that such terrible acts were steps in what parts of the Moslem world have long seen as an ancient and honorable determination to achieve worldwide Islamic hegemony by any means possible.

Many elements of the story of the siege and fall of Khartoum will seem eerily familiar: the refusal of the governments involved to recognize the threat the Mahdi presented; the influence of the press in shaping public opinion and shifting public policy; the disavowal of responsibility by the government charged with the safety of Khartoum; the search for scapegoats as the specter of failure loomed; the seemingly ponderous and unwieldy military reaction; and above all, the Mahdi's refusal to be deflected or diverted from what he regarded as his divine calling, no matter what its price in misery and bloodshed.

Some aspects of the story that follows are less precise than many scholars prefer their histories to be, but that is an unfortunately inescapable consequence of the subject, due in part to the vagueness of the available records, and on the Muslim side to the fact that even the most "objective" Arab-written "life of the Mahdi" is more hagiography than biography. Dates are frequently imprecise (there are, for example, three separate dates given for when the telegraph line between Khartoum and Cairo was cut), spellings of names are often subjected to the whims of the person recording them at the time or at the mercy of translators (in Great Britain "Sudan" was spelled "Soudan" until well into the 20th century), and geographic features are often known by a variety of local and regional names. Equally frustrating is the simple lack of records and archives from the Sudan for most of the 19th century, and the fact that those that do exist are frequently suspect as to accuracy.

Nevertheless, the story that appears is fascinating, not only for its appeal as a classic Victorian adventure, but because of its chilling immediacy. Today a powerful Imam in Iraq style his militia "The Mahdi Army," civil war in the Sudan pits Moslem Arabs from the north against Christian and animist black Africans in the south, and Moslem fundamentalists of the most extreme shade and hue proclaim *jihad* in a desire to "cleanse" Islam from what they perceive to be the corruptions and decadence of the non-Moslem world. All have roots in the Mahdi's revolt in the Sudan in the early 1880s, which reached its climax at the city of Khartoum.

The story that follows is a straightforward historical narrative, though its implications and relevance become obvious with the telling. There are no simple resolutions to the troubles caused by Islamic extremism to be found in the history of the great duel between the Mahdi and Gordon at Khartoum. What is to be found instead is the reminder, often overlooked but all the more necessary for that, of the truth that militant Islam is a challenge to the very existence of Western society, one that has endured for generations, and one that will continue to strike at any and all that it perceives as enemies, Moslem and Christian alike, until and unless the West and Islam join hands to ensure its eradication.

"Fuzzy Wuzzy"
(Soudan Expeditionary Force)

RUDYARD KIPLING

WE'VE fought with many men acrost the seas,
  An' some of 'em was brave an' some was not:
The Paythan an' the Zulu an' Burmese;
  But the Fuzzy was the finest o' the lot.
We never got a ha'porth's change of 'im:
  'E squatted in the scrub an' 'ocked our 'orses,
'E cut our sentries up at Suakim,
  An' 'e played the cat an' banjo with our forces.
    So 'ere's to you, Fuzzy Wuzzy, at your 'ome in the Soudan;
    You're a pore benighted 'eathen but a first class fightin' man;
    We gives you your certificate, an' if you want it signed
    We'll come an' 'ave a romp with you whenever you're inclined.

We took our chanst among the Khyber 'ills,
  The Boers knocked us silly at a mile,
The Burman give us Irriwaddy chills,
  An' a Zulu impi dished us up in style:
But all we ever got from such as they
  Was pop to what the Fuzzy made us swaller;
We 'eld our bloomin' own, the papers say,
  But man for man the Fuzzy knocked us 'oller.
    Then 'ere's to you, Fuzzy Wuzzy, an' the missis and the kid;
    Our orders was to break you, an' of course we went an' did.
    We sloshed you with Martinis, an' it wasn't 'ardly fair;
    But for all the odds agin' you, Fuzzy Wuz, you broke the square.

'E 'asn't got no papers of 'is own,
  'E 'asn't got no medals nor rewards,
So we must certify the skill 'e's shown
  In usin' of 'is long two'anded swords:
When 'e's 'oppin' in an' out among the bush
  With 'is coffin 'eaded shield an' shovelspear,
An 'appy day with Fuzzy on the rush
  Will last an 'ealthy Tommy for a year.
    So 'ere's to you, FuzzyWuzzy, an' your friends which are no more,
    If we 'adn't lost some messmates we would 'elp you to deplore;
    But give an' take's the gospel, an' we'll call the bargain fair,
    For if you 'ave lost more than us, you crumpled up the square!

'E rushes at the smoke when we let drive,
  An', before we know, 'e's 'ackin' at our 'ead;
'E's all 'ot sand an' ginger when alive,
  An' 'e's generally shammin' when 'e's dead.
'E's a daisy, 'e's a ducky, 'e's a lamb!
  'E's a injiarubber idiot on the spree,
'E's the on'y thing that doesn't give a damn
  For a Regiment o' British Infantree!
    So 'ere's to you, FuzzyWuzzy, at your 'ome in the Soudan;
    You're a pore benighted 'eathen but a firstclass fightin' man;
    An' 'ere's to you, FuzzyWuzzy, with your 'ayrick 'ead of 'air—
    You big black boundin' beggar—for you broke a British square!

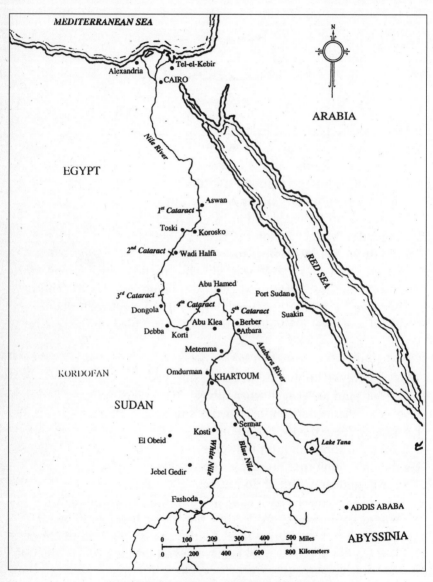

EGYPT AND THE SUDAN IN 1884

PROLOGUE

It was January 26, 1885.

The city had fallen.

For more than three hundred days it had held out, defended by a slowly dwindling garrison, once numbering some eight thousand but now with fewer than a thousand left, led by a charismatic British general named Charles Gordon. They were all that stood between the forty thousand men, women, and children of the city and the massed rabble that called itself an army, more than a hundred thousand strong, that had pledged itself to their destruction and death.

The rabble were the followers of the Mahdi, a Sudanese Arab holy man who had come to believe himself to be the Islamic messiah. The Mahdi had a vision: a dream of a world driven at his command to embrace Islam, an Islam he had purged of its corruption and heresies. It was a vision that he was prepared to carry out at the point of a sword—Islam would be cleansed and the infidels would either be converted or ruthlessly killed.

In the quiet grayness before dawn, as the garrison and inhabitants of Khartoum uneasily slept, their defiance was undone in a single act of betrayal. One of the garrison's officers, whether bribed or a true turncoat, opened the gates to the city and the Mahdi's forces rushed in. In a few hours of shrieking chaos, Khartoum was overrun. Gordon and the rest of the garrison were slaughtered without mercy, while men, women, and children, Moslem and Christian, Egyptian and Sudanese alike, were put to death in an orgy of murder, rape, and plunder. By nightfall nearly thirty thousand would die. For the hand-

1

ful of women and young boys and girls who were spared, death might have been preferable, for they were fated to be sold into slavery.

They died even though they had not taken up arms against the Mahdi or his followers; even though they had not opposed his message or his faith; and even though they did not live on land unfairly taken from the Sudanese. Their slayers were not a repressed people yearning to worship as they wished or trying to achieve their freedom. They died because their vision of the world and their profession of their faith differed from that of the Mahdi. The Mahdi had no interest in glory, land, wealth, or power: for him, all of life was a mission to impose his vision of Islam with the sword.

That morning was witness to more than the fall of Khartoum. It was witness to the birth of a religious movement which would cast a shadow of death across the next century and beyond.

It was more than the triumph of the Mahdi—it was the dawn of militant Islam.

CHAPTER I

THE LAND AND THE PROPHET

If it could ever be said that a land and a religion were made for each other, it would be true of the Sudan and Islam. The seemingly endless and almost empty, unforgiving landscape of the sub-Saharan region of Africa known as the Sudan found its spiritual reflection in Islam, born in the equally vast wastes of the Arabian Peninsula, with its starkly declared doctrines governing the most mundane aspects of daily life, and its sternly decreed punishments for transgressions against those doctrines. Simple, subtle, remorseless, utterly lacking in grace, though not in beauty, the Sudan and Islam mirrored one another as if "they were anon twin halves of one august event." It was a union pregnant with import and fraught with danger, for austerity is often the cradle of fanaticism and zealots.

It would prove to be so with the Sudan and Islam, when in the last quarter of the 19th century a Moslem holy man would declare his divinity, raise an army of ferociously loyal followers, and in the name of the Prophet Muhammed challenge the power of the greatest empire of his time. More than a century later his spiritual descendants still seek to terrorize the world by bringing senseless death and mutilation to countless thousands. Which was the greater influence, the land or the Prophet, is a question that can never be settled, but it is certain that without one the other would have never produced the charismatic and bloody persona of Muhammed Ahmed ibn Abdullah, known to history as the Mahdi.

It would be incorrect to speak of the Sudan of the mid-19th century as a country, as it possessed few of the attributes normally asso-

3

ciated with nationhood; rather, it was more of a geographical notion. Its borders were vague and fuzzy; the only firm political boundary was the one that existed to the north, between the Sudan and Egypt. The Red Sea and the mountains of Abyssinia provided a rough and ready—though in the hills a highly imprecise—demarcation of the Sudan's eastern marches, while in the south any sense of where the land began and ended was confined to a handful of Egyptian-garrisoned forts clustered along the Nile River, roughly level in latitude with the Tropic of Cancer. To the west was only void, as the emptiness of the Sudan spilled into the vast wastes of the Sahara Desert. Only along the Nile, which bisects the country as it meanders from south to north through the desert, is there to be found any relief from the apparently endless desolation.

It is only along the Nile, in fact, that there is any real vitality to the Sudan. For a few miles inland from either of its banks the country is fertile and green; the few towns and cities of any size to be found in the Sudan are sited on the river's banks. Unless a traveler chose to journey by caravan, the only reliable transportation in the country was found on the river. In essence this meant that whoever controlled the Nile controlled the Sudan. As a consequence, the towns along the river often assumed a significance out of proportion to their size. But once away from the fertile ribbon of the Nile's banks, the abiding impression of the Sudan is not one of hostility to human existence, but utter indifference to it.

And yet people lived there, some ten million in 1880, although that number could have fluctuated either way by as much as a million, so imprecise were the land's borders and so inept was its administration. Save for small numbers of merchants, who eked out their existence by maintaining a loose network of trading posts at the oases scattered across the Sudanese landscape, the people were herders, living a nomadic existence as they moved to and fro across the county in search of adequate grazing for their flocks.

Archeologists and anthropologist have found evidence that humans have lived in the Sudan for at least nine million years. It may well be that the valley of the Nile, which wanders more than 4,000 miles from the lakes of central Africa to the Mediterranean, is the real cradle of civilization rather than the Euphrates. If that is so, then in a strange juxtaposition, technology, the handmaiden of civilization, has never really come to the Sudan at all: in some ways the country carries on in the beginning of the 21st century much as it did a half-dozen millennia ago. About five centuries before Christ, the ox-driven water wheel, which is still an essential part of the Sudan's mainly agrarian economy, was introduced along the banks of the Nile. At the same time came camels, brought by the Persians when Cambyses, the son of Cyrus the Great, invaded Egypt in 525 B.C.

Homer knew of the Sudan, as the Greeks came there to trade, bartering cloth, wine and trinkets for gum arabic, spices and slaves. In Roman times the Emperor Nero sent a legion to explore far up the Nile, but the commander's experience with the "sudd"–the Arabic word for "obstruction" from which the country derived its name—a vast and impenetrable papyrus swamp in the southern Sudan, quickly put paid to any thought of conquest. When he returned to Rome, he reported a patchwork of petty kingdoms and principalities scattered across the land, populated mostly by Arabs in the north, by Negroes in the south. It was during the reign of Justinian that many of these northern Sudanese kingdoms converted to Christianity and churches began to appear along the sweep of the Nile—until the spread of Islam in the territory during the 16th century.

The history of the southern half of the Sudan before the 19th century is obscure, and it appears as little more than a large blank space on contemporary maps. European explorers, venturing into the heart of central Africa for the first time in the 1850s, found primitive, post-Neolithic cultures that literally had no awareness of a world beyond their own horizons. In inexplicable contrast, from remote antiquity until the 16th century A.D., the northern region of the Sudan, known as Nubia, was well known throughout the Mediterranean world. Having taken the shape of an independent kingdom some three millenia before Christ, Nubia began to fall under Egyptian sway during the period of Egypt's Old Kingdom, about 2600–2100 B.C. By 1550 B.C., under the 18th Dynasty, Nubia had been reduced to a vassal state. A Nubian revolt in the 8th century B.C. brought Egyptian overlordship to an end, but the land between the Nubian Desert and the Nile River still remains strewn with monuments and ruins dating from the centuries of Egyptian dominance. A succession of independent kingdoms subsequently took the place of the deposed Egyptians. The most powerful of these, Makuria, was founded in the 6th century, centered at Old Dunqulah, near the site of modern Khartoum.

As Christianity spread south into Africa, first into Abyssinia and then into Egypt, it soon made its way into Nubia. Most of the people had converted to Coptic Christianity by the end of the 6th century A.D., and by the 8th century the petty kingdoms reported to Rome by Nero's centurions were flourishing. Strong enough to resist repeated incursions from Egypt, which had fallen under Muslim rule in the 7th century, these small kingdoms were eventually undone by peoples from the north—mostly Egyptians and Arabs–who came as traders and craftsmen and who brought Islam with them. They gradually began to outnumber the Christian population until, between 1300 and 1500, the Christian states collapsed and Nubia became Muslim.

During the 16th century, a people who called themselves the Funj formed a powerful Islamic state in what had been Nubia, and the city of Sennar became one of the great cultural centers of Islam. The glory of the Funj kingdom lasted a little more than two hundred years, as in the closing decades of the 18th century religious dissension among the Funj tribes left the kingdom weak and divided. In 1820, Egypt, which by this time was part of the Ottoman Empire, again invaded the Sudan, and by 1822 the land was conquered by armies led by the Ottomans' Egyptian viceroy, Muhammad Ali. This Turkish-Egyptian rule, which would be marked by increasingly heavy-handed administration as the Egyptians continued to expand southward, would endure for the next sixty years before it was undone by revolution in Egypt and revolt in the Sudan.

It was the introduction of Islam in the 15th century, and its subsequent domination of the land, which would eventually cause the Sudan to cease being an obscure backwater and bring it briefly to a position of prominence in the eyes of the world. Islam is a religion distinctly Arab in origin, the name itself derived from the Arabic word "salaama," which has a two-fold meaning: peace, and submission to God. Anyone who follows Islam is known as Moslem, a term that comes from the Arabic word signifying a person totally devoted to the will of God. Likewise, the Moslem word "Allah," meaning "the one True God," is also of Arabic origin.

The history of Islam centers around the Prophet Muhammed, the Messenger of God. It was sometime around 610 A.D. that one man's mystic vision in the Arabian desert forever changed the world. In what is now Saudi Arabia, in a cave outside the city of Mecca, a 39-year old trader named Muhammed is said to have had a life-changing religious experience. Just why he was in the cave in the first place, and how long he stayed there, is unknown, but when he emerged he claimed to have had a visitation from the angel Gabriel. The angel told him he was to become a prophet and revealed to him the first few words of what would become the holy book of Islam, the Koran.

Muhammed spent the next two years meditating and thinking, allowing his vision and the thoughts it inspired to coalesce and take shape as a coherent body of religious thought and teaching. At the time the people of the Arabian peninsula were largely animistic, worshiping trees, rocks, wells, springs, and caves; some tribes practiced idolatry, others sorcery. Eventually Muhammed began taking his teachings to the streets, telling the Arabs of Mecca that they should no longer worship idols and objects but devote their faith and belief to "Allah," the "one true God." This teaching became the core of Islamic doctrine–"There is no God but Allah." Outside of his wife and a handful of family members, Muhammed made few converts, instead becoming the object of severe persecution by local tribes in and around Mecca. This became so severe that he and his followers fled to the nearby city of Medina in 622.

The flight to Medina, the "hejira," became the pivotal point of the nascent religion that Muhammed was creating. The date became the first year of the Islamic calendar, while all Islamic history traces back to Muhammed's arrival in Medina. It also marked the beginning of a profound change in how Muhammed proclaimed his message, as began to choose a more dynamic and often outright violent method of proclaiming that Allah was the one true God, Islam the one true faith, as he coerced his hearers into accepting the beliefs he taught. A skilled swordsman and a fierce fighter, Muhammed trained his handful of followers as fighting men, and began to raid the caravans and settlements of his enemies, literally waging war on them, demanding that they renounce their idolatrous beliefs and embrace his teachings under pain of death. One recorded incident tells of Muhammed slaughtering seven hundred men in one caravan and selling their wives and children as slaves. Within ten years Muhammed and his followers were the masters of Arabia.

The precedent set by Muhammed in these early years—he did not make his converts by his teaching or example, but literally with the point of his sword—would have a far-reaching effect on Islam, and its consequences would still be felt in the 21st century. When Jesus Christ was arrested before His crucifixion, he rebuked one of his disciples who tried to resist; the founder of Islam, however, chose to kill rather than be persecuted. Thus the concept of "conversion by the sword" became one of the early fundamentals of Islamic doctrine. There are passages in the Koran which condemn aggression, but others openly exhort acts of violence against those who are perceived to be persecuting or oppressing Moslems. In Surah 2:191 it says "to be persecuted is worse than committing murder." (Some translations record it as saying persecution is worse than "slaughter.") In other words, it is better to kill than to be persecuted.

The Koran was the holy scripture of Islam, said to be inspired by God Himself, and was regarded as the codified "will of Allah." It assumed its finished form sometime between 644 and 655 A.D., as a medium-sized book divided into 14 chapters, known as "suras." Compiled from oral and written records of the revelations, thoughts, and teachings of Muhammed, collected shortly after his death in 632 A.D., the Koran became the source of all Islamic teaching and law, addressing subjects as diverse as social justice, economics, politics, criminal codes, religious tolerance, jurisprudence, and civil law. Themes emphasized in the book are Allah's mercy to mankind, mankind's ingratitude and misuses of Allah's gifts, evidences of God's creative powers in nature, the bliss of paradise after death (where every Muslim male will supposedly be given thirteen virgin girls to be his personal servants), the dead being reborn, the Day of Judgment, punishment of followers who go astray including the horror of hell, and the missions of former prophets—including Christian apostles. It is clear that Muhammed's teachings were heavily influenced by Judaism and Christianity, as there emerged uncanny similarities between the three religions: there is only one true God; there is a hell and a heaven; every human being must account for all his or her earthly deeds. A number of Judaeo-Christian tales are found in the Koran, such as the stories of Noah's Ark and Aaron's rod. Even the story of Creation in the Koran is strikingly similar to the older Christian account, with mankind's expulsion from the Garden of Eden a consequence of eating forbidden fruit.

One peculiar feature of the Koran, which would have a profound effect on the religion and its followers, is that each verse begins with the phrase, "Allah has said. . . ." Originally intended to emphasize Muhammed's passive role as a mere recorder of Allah's will, this phrasing, along with the short time in which the book was written and codified, would cause the Koran to become something of an inflexible, immutable document. The repeated categorical declaration of its divine origin left little room for debate, elaboration, or adaption of its doctrines to changing circumstances in the world. Its inflexible nature and presumed infallibility would become an essential part of Moslem tradition, which in turn would exert a powerful influence on Moslem societies, particularly those of the Arabs, who have remained far more tradition-bound than any other people in the Middle East, Asia, or Europe.

After the death of Muhammed, from a wound to the head received in battle in June of 632 at the age of 61 or 62, there was a brief period of rebellion among some of the Arab tribes, but a series of short, sharp "Wars of Apostasy"—literally punitive campaigns—soon brought them to an end, and Islam dominated every aspect of daily life in Arabia.

This was not a bad circumstance, for it resulted in a sense of unity and identity that the Arabs had previously never known. Although originally designed to foster a religious community and to overcome the different factions and jealousies of 7th-century Arab tribalism, a system of theology and law gradually evolved. Initially there were no sacraments, formal rituals, or priesthood in Islam, but in time the offices of the *imam*, who lead prayers in mosques, and the *mullah*, who teach the word of Allah, came into being. A distinctive Islamic civilization was created, with *kathis* and *shariah* courts administering Islamic law, while rituals were introduced, such as the washing of hands and face, prayer five times a day (in the company of a congregation within a mosque whenever possible), alms-giving, fasting during the month of Ramadan, recital of Islamic creed to reinforce a believer's faith, and a pilgrimage to Mecca. While never producing the sort of political, ethnic, or national cohesion that the Western concept of the nation-state would eventually provide in Europe, Islam did imbue the Arabs with a sense of belonging to something larger than merely their tribe or locality, and provided the foundation for a culture that they had previously never known. It would prove to be an astonishingly powerful influence.

A core Islamic doctrine, which shaped the course Islam would follow throughout its history, declared that there were two states of existence in the world: those who followed Islam, both people and nations, were said to be in a place of peace, while those lands and peoples outside the faith were said to be in the place of war. It was the duty, then, of the faithful to bring those places of warfare into the peace of Islam. In the late 20th and early 21st centuries it has become fashionable among Moslem theologians–along with some Christian philosophers—in Western nations to explain away the terms "peace" and "war" as having only a spiritual, interpretive meaning, rather than a temporal, literal one. However, during the first thirteen hundred years of Islamic history, the Moslem faithful took those doctrines very literally. Any nation or people who did not openly embrace Islam was regarded as hostile to the faith and ripe for conversion.

The 7th and 8th centuries saw a furious expansion of Islam, as a series of holy wars carried the faith beyond Arabia and into the rest of the Middle East, then to Persia, North Africa, Spain, and India. Eventually Islam would spread as far as Indonesia and the Philippines. Yet, curiously, for the first four hundred years of its existence, Islam remained essentially a pure religion, untainted by the ambitions and excesses of temporal rulers and politics; *jihad*, for all its violence, was used solely as a means of expanding the faith, not as a method of aggrandizing a realm. It was as if the leaders of Islam found a way to allow their religion to shape their politics rather than the other way around. Yet when politics and religion meet, one or the other must give way, and that would happen when Islam ran headlong into the other great religious force in Europe and Asia Minor--Christianity.

The first collision came when Arab Moslems surged out of Arabia and ran headlong into the Byzantine Empire in 636. The last remnant of the Roman Empire, ruled as a separate entity since 395 A.D. , the Byzantine Empire at the time covered much of present day Turkey, Armenia, Jordan, Syria, Israel, and Egypt, and was nominally Christian, while all other religions were officially forbidden. By Islamic interpretation, such proscription constituted persecution, leaving Byzantium outside of Islam's "realm of peace" and thus ripe for conquest.

The Byzantines had just concluded a long and costly war with the Persians, who themselves were exhausted and soon fell to advancing Islamic armies. The Byzantine Empire, however, would prove more difficult for the Moslems to overwhelm—even in her weakened state Byzantium was strong. Only a combination of unrelenting pressure applied by the Moslems coupled with disorder and discord within the Empire allowed the Arabs to gradually conquer most of the Byzantine lands, a process which took almost four hundred years.

But the great clash between the Moslem world and the Christian world which would permanently shape their perceptions of each other took place over a span of two centuries in the form of a series of military campaigns, led by the European nobility and sponsored by the Church, in the region of the Middle East known as the Levant—modern-day Israel, Palestine, Lebanon, Jordan, Syria, and Iraq. Driven at first by purely religious motives, these campaigns gradually evolved into a series of political wars whereby European kingdoms and principalities, as well as the Papacy, sought to extend their temporal power into the Middle East. The two centuries of conflict left deep and lasting scars on the collective mind and soul of Islam, forever confirming the idea that the two faiths were inimically hostile, and that Moslems and Christians were fated to live in conflict. Those campaigns became known to history as the Crusades.

The origin of the Crusades lay in the two critical events of the 11th-century Church: the Great Schism between the eastern and western churches (the result of a mutual excommunication by the Pope and Patriarch); and the collapse of what remained of the Byzantine Empire at the hands of Turks in 1071. In 1072, the Eastern Roman Emperor, who now ruled little more than Constantinople, the Bosporus and the Dardanelles, appealed to the Papacy in Rome for military assistance against the Saracens—the name given by medieval Europeans to the

Arabs, and by extension to Moslems in general, whether they were Arabs, Moors, or Seljuk Turks—in return for an assurance that he would effect a reunion between the eastern and western churches. Not much came of the original appeal, but when it was renewed a few years later, Pope Urban II announced his plan for an armed pilgrimage to the Levant, exhorting the church leaders to "Rid the sanctuary of God of unbelievers, expel the thieves, and lead back the faithful." *"Dieu le volt!"* (God wills it!) became the rallying cry of thousands of clergymen and nobles across Europe as preparations began for what would become the First Crusade.

Before they could set out for Constantinople, however, a number of the lower-ranking clergy, notably an itinerant monk of particular eloquence who styled himself Peter the Hermit, took Urban's call to the common people, gathering some fifteen thousand followers in less than two years and setting out for the Holy Land. Resembling an undisciplined rabble more than an army, this mob reached Constantinople in August 1096, where the Emperor Alexius saw them across the Bosporus and into Turkey. Poorly armed and lacking leadership, they were ambushed by a Turkish army near Nicaea (modern Iznik), and slaughtered. Only a few thousand survived to return to Constantinople, those left behind alive being captured and sold into slavery.

Meanwhile, from late summer 1096 through the following May, masses of European chivalry gathered at Constantinople. As each force arrived the Emperor Alexius pressed their leaders to take an oath of fealty to him in order to guarantee that any former Byzantine territories they captured would be returned to him. This was a development of profound significance, for it began the process by which the emphasis of the Crusades would shift from being a Divinely inspired mission to become a means to various political ends. That this was the case was revealed the following June when the Crusaders attacked Nicaea. Following the accepted customs of war, the city yielded rather than face the prospect of a successful assault and sacking: the Turks made the point of surrendering to the Byzantines rather than the Crusaders, denying the Europeans the booty to which they would have been entitled.

The following month the Crusaders defeated a Saracen army under Killij Arsian at Dorylaeum, and began besieging the city of

Antioch. The city fell to treachery, but no sooner had the besiegers occupied it than they became the besieged, as a Turkish army marching to Antioch's relief took up the Crusader's former positions outside the city walls. Starvation and disease weakened the Turks and Christians alike during the nearly year-long siege, but the Crusaders were able to mount a sally in early June 1098 and route the encircling Turks. Five months later, in November, the Christians began their march on the Crusade's stated objective, Jerusalem. After laying siege to the Holy City for six weeks, the Crusaders stormed the walls and Jerusalem was taken. In an orgy of bloodlust, nearly every man, woman, and child in the city was massacred, "purifying" the city in the blood of the "defeated infidels."

The fall of Jerusalem and the slaughter of its people was a fearsome shock to the Moslem faithful—here was an enemy as ruthless and determined as any army of Islam at its most furious. Equally apparent was that both sides, superficially at least, were driven by spiritual motives: each referred to the other as "infidels," each regarded itself as the defender of the "true faith" of the "one true God." Curiously, both claimed to worship the same God, yet each refused to acknowledge anything in common in their doctrines or beliefs. The possession of Jerusalem was a particular point of contention, as the city was sacred to both faiths: to the Crusaders it was the cradle of Christianity; to the Moslems, it was the site of Muhammed's ascension to heaven. It was a situation that left little room for compromise and none for tolerance.

A Moslem army marching up from Egypt to retake Jerusalem was defeated at Ascalon (modern Ashquelon in Israel) in August 1099, effectively bringing what came to be known as the First Crusade to a close. Following the capture of Jerusalem, the Crusaders established four states in the Levant: the Kingdom of Jerusalem; the County of Tripoli, on the Syrian coast; the Principality of Antioch, in the Orontes Valley; and the County of Edessa, in eastern Anatolia. Godfrey de Bouillon had been nominated by the Pope to be the King of Jerusalem, but Godfrey had no desire to be called the king of the city where Christ was killed, so instead he assumed the title of *Advocatus Sancti Sepulchri* (Defender of the Holy Sepulcher); however, his successors would be crowned Kings of Jerusalem.

The First Crusade was the only one that would accomplish the goals it set out to achieve–specifically, the taking of Jerusalem and other sites holy to Christendom from the Moslem "infidels." There was to be no peace between Islam and Christianity, however, as the Turks, Arabs, and Egyptians all strove for the next five decades to drive the Europeans from their newly acquired conquests. The first real success the Moslems had was at the siege of Edessa, which fell to them in 1144. Having not forgotten the treatment the populace of Jerusalem had received at the hands of the Crusaders, the Moslems slaughtered the Christians *en masse* as they stormed the city.

Responding to Edessa's recapture by the Turks, Pope Eugenius III proclaimed a Second Crusade in 1145, while the king of France, Louis VII, and the Holy Roman Emperor, Conrad III, announced that they would lead this new campaign. Through no direct fault of the two monarchs, the effort was doomed to failure, as a Moslem army ambushed the German force of some 30,000 men near Dorylaeum in Asia Minor in 1147. There were few survivors. As the French advanced toward Antioch, they were continuously harried by Saracen armies and suffered severe causalities; less than half of the original force reached Jerusalem in 1148.

Once there, the remaining Crusaders joined with King Baldwin III of Jerusalem to attack Damascus. After a siege of less than eight days the Crusaders withdrew, declaring that taking the city was impossible with the forces they had on hand. In truth, conflicting ambitions on the part of the French and Germans, personal rivalries between Louis and Conrad, and a failure to cooperate with the subjects of the Kingdom of Jerusalem had undermined the efforts of the crusade. It was becoming clearer with each passing season that the spiritual motives that had been the driving force of the First Crusade were mainly spent, and those of the Second had been little more than a religious veneer concealing the political ambitions of the French king and Holy Roman Emperor. The Kingdom of Jerusalem, the goal of the entire saga of the Crusades, had forty years to live.

It was shortly after the end of the Second Crusade that the greatest warrior in all of Islam's history appeared: Saladin. Born in 1138 of Kurdish parents in the city of Tikrit, in what is now Iraq, in 1152 he entered the service of the Syrian Sultan Nureddin as a junior officer.

By 1164 he was demonstrating remarkable leadership as well as considerable military skills in three campaigns against the Kingdom of Jerusalem, and was soon named second-in-command of the Syrian army under his uncle Shirkuh. Shirkuh became vizier of Egypt, but died just two months after his appointment, whereupon Saladin assumed his office.

He then spent the next two decades in a protracted political struggle as he consolidated his position as de facto ruler of Egypt, extended his power into Syria and northern Iraq, and skirmished with the Latin Kingdom of Jerusalem. By 1187 he felt strong enough to challenge the might of the Crusaders, and after a three-month campaign he defeated the army of the Kingdom of Jerusalem in a fierce battle at the Horns of Hattin, near Tiberias on the Jordan River. Among the spoils of the battle were the True Cross, the most sacred of the Crusaders' relics, and Guy, the King of Jerusalem, whom Saladin held for ransom. The remaining strongholds of the kingdom quickly fell to Saladin, and by the end of 1187, the only major city in the Levant remaining in Crusader hands was Tyre.

Responding to the fall of the Kingdom of Jerusalem, Pope Gregory VIII proclaimed the Third Crusade in October, 1187, to be led by the English King, Richard Coeur-de-Lion (the Lion-Hearted); the French King, Philip Augustus; and the Holy Roman Emperor, Frederick Barbarossa. Misfortune plagued the Germans once again, as Frederick drowned while crossing a river in Anatolia on his way to the Holy Land, and most of the German army then returned to their homes, having reached only as far as Antioch and never coming to battle with Saladin's Saracen armies.

Richard arrived in the Levant after Phillip, having first taken Cyprus to use as a secure base for his supplies. Together the two kings led their armies to the port city of Acre, on the Mediterranean coast, which was then under assault by the remnants of the army of Jerusalem, led by the now-ransomed King Guy. After a prolonged siege, with almost no food left in the city and the walls crumbling after repeated attacks by the Crusaders' engineers and miners, Acre surrendered in 1191, the city's inhabitants offering themselves up for ransom.

Saladin at first refused to pay the sum demanded by Richard and Phillip Augustus, hoping that exhaustion would set in on the Crusader

forces and compel them to allow the hostages to go free, but eventually he relented. However, payment was delayed, and soon the
Crusaders grew tired of waiting. Richard ordered more than 3,000
Moslem captives—men, women, and children—to be executed on a
hillside near the city of Ayyadieh. It was this one act more than any
other that cemented the lasting enmity between Islam and
Christendom, as Richard would be remembered as "The Butcher of
Ayyadieh" among Moslems. (For centuries Arab parents would silence
unruly children by hissing at them, "Hush! Or England will get you!")

Eventually Richard's and Saladin's armies met in at Jaffa in 1192,
and after a bitter, hard-fought battle, the Moslems withdrew in defeat.
The casualties on both sides were so severe that Richard lacked the
strength to recapture Jerusalem, while Saladin was unable to drive the
Crusaders into the sea. The two warriors, who had come to admire
and respect one another as kindred souls, concluded a treaty which
established fixed borders between the Latin lands and Moslem territories, and which allowed unarmed Christian pilgrims to visit
Jerusalem. A month later Richard departed the Levant forever.

Forty years would pass before another military expedition on the
scale of the first three Crusades was attempted. Meanwhile, the Fourth
Crusade, launched in 1204, was a fiasco, serving as little more than a
pretext for a mercenary army in the pay of Venice to sack and burn
Byzantium, the greatest Christian city in Asia Minor, crippling the city
as a financial rival to the Venentian lending houses. Though condemned by the Church in the strongest possible terms, the sack of
Byzantium left a Venetian puppet on the throne of the Eastern Empire
for the next sixty years.

The Holy Roman Emperor Frederick II vowed in 1215 to lead a
crusade, but repeated delays in his preparations and departure led to
his excommunication by the Pope in 1227.   Frederick finally set
out for the Levant in 1228, where his crusade was characterized by its
diplomacy rather than by its militancy. Having negotiated the recession of Jerusalem to Christian rule and a ten-year truce, Frederick was
crowned King of Jerusalem in 1229. Had subsequent Crusaders followed Frederick's example, the history of relations between Christians
and Moslems might have taken a very different turn, but because of
his excommunication his bloodless policies were received with little

regard among the European nobility, and so the religious slaughters would continue.

In the autumn of 1248, Louis IX of France, who would become known to history as Saint Louis, sailed to the island of Cyprus where he spent the winter preparing for an attack on Egypt that was launched in the spring. After capturing the port of Damietta, Louis' army moved on Cairo, but the Crusaders left their flanks unguarded, allowing the Egyptians to close in behind them as they advanced. By knocking down dikes and opening floodgates on reservoirs behind the French forces, the Egyptians created floods that isolated the crusading army on low ground. Disease soon ran rampant, forcing Louis to surrender, the only European monarch to be captured by the Moslems during the whole of the Crusades. When his ransom was paid, Louis went directly to Palestine, where he spent the next four years strengthening the defenses of the Kingdom of Jerusalem, finally returning to France in the spring of 1254.

Louis' efforts were for naught, however, as one by one, the remaining cities and castles of the Crusader states fell to the Saracens. Antioch surrendered in 1263, Tripoli in 1289. Acre, the last major Crusader stronghold, was taken in March 1291, as well as Tyre that May, and Haifa and Beirut in July. The Europeans had been driven from the Levant. Aside from a few castles and fortifications, and a handful of churches scattered across Asia Minor, little remained of two hundred years of bloodshed caused by the Crusades. However, the scars left on the minds and hearts of the Moslem faithful would prove to be enduring.

At the same time a distinct change came over the motivation driving Islam's expansion in the centuries that followed the Crusades. There was an unmistakable element of vendetta in the Moslem campaigns against the remnants of the Byzantine Empire over the following two centuries. Constantinople was seen as the staging point for every Crusader incursion into the Levant, while the Empire's continued official proscription of Islam seemed to be an openly defiant attitude, if not a direct challenge to the Moslem world. If that were so, it was a very foolish stance for the Byzantines to take, for Constantinople no longer possessed even a fraction of the power it once held. The sack of the city during the Fourth Crusade and the more than half a century of Latin rule weakened the Eastern Roman Empire such that it could no longer fend off the repeated incursions of the Turks, who, led by the Ottoman Sultan Mehmed, finally captured Constantinople in 1453, renaming it Istanbul.

Yet, by then it was no longer the imperative to holy war that fueled the Turks' efforts to take Constantinople, or that compelled the next two hundred years of struggle in the Balkans, from where the Ottoman Turks ultimately drove to the gates of Vienna. No longer did Islam embody a drive to conquest in order to spread the word of the Prophet and so turn all of the world to the rightful worship of Allah. The facade of *jihad* had been largely stripped away from Ottoman ambitions by then, and the wars in the Balkans were was as much a consequence of the desire for conquest and vengeance as it was a means of spreading the faith.

After decades of absorbing the incursions of warriors from the central Asian steppe, Islam had been coopted to serve as the religious camouflage for overt wars of territorial expansion. The purpose of the Islamic sword was no longer conversion but conquest: foreign lands were subjugated in the name of Allah, but for the greater glory of Empire. The Moslems had learned well the lessons of their Crusader teachers three centuries earlier, and were now empowered to teach new ones.

But the Sudan was a long way away from the Levant, and what news came to that arid land of the struggle between the two faiths were only rumors of wars. And yet, the two centuries of warfare between Christians and Moslems were bound to leave their mark, and that which was left on the Moslem world was an indelible impression of hostility toward Islam on the part of Christendom. For the common people of Islam what would resonate for the eight hundred years that followed the Crusades was not how the faith had become a tool of the politically ambitious, much as had happened to Christianity. Instead, what they would come to believe was that Christianity and all who tolerated it were forever outside of Islam's "realm of peace."

CHAPTER 2

THE COMING OF
THE MAHDI

The tales of the passing centuries have been replete with charismatic religious and political figures whose origins are lost in obscurity, shrouded in controversy, or otherwise deemed "mysterious." And fittingly enough it could not be otherwise for Muhammed Ahmed 'ibn Abdullah, known to the world as "the Mahdi"—"the Expected One." He would materialize unheralded out of the sand-blown desert of the Sudan, and like a meteor burn a scar across Africa, the Middle East, and Europe to sear Islam and Christendom alike, and then suddenly die within months of his greatest victory.

Unlike so many figures of the past, however, the obscurity of Muhammed Ahmed's origins were not fabrications deliberately contrived to enhance his mystique or add to his stature through tenuous claims of divine or royal descent. The cloudiness surrounding his early years stems from the region in which he was born and attained maturity. He was born sometime between 1840 and 1844, the latter date being the most widely accepted, although there is some debate over its accuracy within Arab and Moslem tradition.

Almost without doubt his birthplace was Dirar, an island just above the Third Cataract of the Nile River, off the Sudanese city of Dongola. It is widely accepted that his family was of mixed Arab and Nubian heritage, and that he was the son of a shipbuilder, although there is some sketchy evidence that there were some religious figures of note in his ancestry. His grandfather in particular was said to be a "shariff" known for his good works among the people of Dongola. Tradition held that his father was named Abdullah and his mother

Aamina. As early as the age of five he began to show a comprehension of the sometimes complex and subtle doctrines of Islam that was far beyond his years, and from then on his education began to focus on theological studies. By early manhood Ahmed was widely admired among the Moslem clergy of the southern Sudan for his piety and asceticism. He learned the Holy Koran in Khartoum and Kararie and later he studied *fiqh* under the patronage of Sheikh Muhammed Kheir, a northern Sudanese nobleman. Muhammed Ahmed mastered different aspects of Islamic studies and was known for his Sufi tendency among his mates. In 1861 he approached Sheik Muhammad Sheief, the leader of the Sammaniyya Sect of the Sufi, and requested to become one of his students to learn more on Sufism.

Sufism, while today regarded by many Moslems as being outside the realm of Islam, was at that time seen as the inner, esoteric, mystical dimension of Islam. In its simplest form, Sufi practice was quite simple: it was surrender to God (Allah), in love, embracing each moment of the soul's consciousness as a gift from or manifestation of God. It was, in short, a gentle philosophy, a far cry from the fiery brand of Islam Muhammed Ahmed would ultimately embrace. Muhammed had shown a great deal of devotion and dedication to his Sheikh and teacher as well as a great deal of faith which distinguished him from his colleagues. When Sheikh Muhammed realized Muhammed Ahmed's dedication and devotion he appointed him *shaykh* (teacher) and permitted him to give instruction on *Tariqa* and *Uhuud* (guidance to the spiritual path to God) to new followers wherever he happened to be.

Upon becoming a religious teacher, Ahmed married a remarkably charismatic presence to his gifts for scholarship and rhetoric, and he began advocating adherence to a branch of Islamic teaching known as Wahhabiism, a distillation of Islam to its most austere form, which discarded the formality and ceremony that had accumulated about Moslem worship over the centuries. The Wahhabi sect had actually begun as a reform movement in Islam, essentially a purification of the Sunni sect, originating in Arabia in the middle of the 18th century. First expounded by Muhammed ibn Abd al-Wahhab, a Moslem cleric born sometime around 1703 in the heart of the Arabian peninsula, who gave the movement its name, Wahhabiism taught that all rituals and religious trappings, the veneration of holy persons, and any form of ostentation in worship, as well as the accumulation of wealth and personal luxury—all of which had begun to overtake Islam by the middle of the 9th century—were false and must be abandoned by the truly faithful. As a result, Wahhabi mosques were simply constructed, built without minarets, and Wahhabi adherents were quite plain in their dress and did not smoke tobacco or hashish–a most unusual sacrifice among Arabs.

Al-Wahhab's austere teachings, delivered with considerable force and conviction, quickly became unpopular in the city of Medina where he made his home. The leading Moslem authorities in the city, who enjoyed their wealth, ostentation, and trappings of worship, soon drove him and his followers out of Medina and into the Nejd Desert in northeast Arabia. It was there that they were found by a tribe of nomadic Arabs, the Saud. Upon hearing Al-Wahhabi preach, the Saudi sheik became convinced that he had been given a holy mission to purge Islam of its corruption, and so declared *jihad*—holy war—and began the conquest of the neighboring tribes in the Arabian peninsula, sometime around 1763. Within a half-century the Wahhabis, having come to dominate the Saud tribe, ruled all Arabia except for the province of Yemen, from their newly-founded capital at Riyadh.

The power of the Wahhabi message to move and inspire ordinary Moslems became even clearer when the Ottoman sultan in Constantinople, who at least nominally ruled Arabia, repeatedly sent out expeditions to crush the Sauds and their tribal allies and vassals—who in turn repeatedly crushed the Ottoman forces. It wasn't until the sultan turned to his Egyptian viceroy, the great Muhammed Ali, that Ottoman supremacy was restored to the Arabian peninsula. By 1818 the Wahhabis were once more driven into the deserts, this time into both the Nejd and the Sahara. Wahhabi power experienced a brief resurgence in the 1820s and 1830s along the Arabian coast of the Persian Gulf, but afterward it began to decline until the Wahhabis lost control of Arabia in 1884.

But Wahhabism was far from dead, and in finding a disciple in Muhammed Ahmed, it would undergo yet another transformation, eventually becoming a political and military power that would threaten the religious and social structure of the entire Middle East, and in doing so leave a spiritual legacy that would endure for the next century. In a land as barren and daunting as the Sudan, the austerity of Wahhbiism had an inevitable appeal to Sudanese Moslems, and Ahmed's teachings quickly began to make a virtue of the Sudan's poverty while offering what appeared to be a way out of its suffering.

Ahmed began by teaching his Sudanese followers that they would never be free of misery and oppression unless they embraced a life of simplicity and piety. Applying action to his words, Ahmed took to living in a cave on the island of Abba, located on the Nile near the city of Berber. The sincerity of his teaching was borne out by the example he set: according to one tradition, when he first settled on Abba, Muhammed Ahmed began selling firewood in Khartoum, until he learned that one of his customers was using it to fuel a distillery. The Koran forbids the consumption of alcohol, and to Ahmed it was as much a transgression to aid in its production, however indirectly, as it was to drink it, so he immediately ceased supplying wood to Khartoum.

It was from his new home on Abba that Ahmed began to openly proclaim how much he despised the venal Egyptian overlords who ruled the Sudan on behalf of the Ottoman Turks, but who plundered the already impoverished country for their own aggrandizement. It was a grievance of long standing with Ahmed: when as a young man he learned that the food supplied to the students at the mosque where he was studying was provided by the Egyptian government, he never took another meal at that mosque. He felt profaned by it, believing as he did that it had been purchased with extorted tax money.

Though the Sudan had fallen under Egypt's sway several times in the past millennia, the present domination of the land by the Egyptians dated from 1821, when the Ottoman Viceroy in Cairo, Muhammed Ali, sent his armies down the Nile to subjugate the Sudanese. Ali's rule over Egypt had begun when the French evacuated the country in 1805, and by many standards Ali was a progressive, enlightened ruler. Abolishing the feudal aristocracy, he produced a program of reform and modernization that left Egypt virtually autonomous within the Ottoman Empire by the fourth decade of the 19th century. Farmers were forced to abandon methods that dated back to Pharaonic times as agriculture was modernized and diversified into cotton, sugar, and tobacco, while farm machinery, seeds, and fertilizers were introduced, yielding enormous increases in crop production. Ali also brought industry to Egypt, in the form of textile mills and factories for munitions production.

The latter proved to be significant, for Ali—once characterized by English political philosopher Jeremy Bentham as the Peter the Great of the Moslem world—had designs for conquest running through his mind, and so set about expanding, reorganizing, and reequipping his army. The first target for the revitalized Egyptian forces was the Sudan, which Muhammed Ali invaded in 1821, bringing an end to the four centuries of Funj rule.

From the moment the first Egyptian troops crossed the border into the Sudan, it was clear that Ali had no intention of bringing the same sort of reform and progress to the Sudan that he had introduced to Egypt. The Egyptian occupation was neither gentle nor enlightened, and Ali had no desire to make the Sudan an integral part of Egypt, preferring to keep it a subject, or vassal, state, ripe for periodic plundering. In 1823, when Ali's son Ismail was killed by a local chief from Shendi, his death was avenged by Ali's son-in-law, Defterdar, who in reprisal massacred thirty thousand civilians in Kordofan. Utterly cowed by such ruthlessness, the Sudanese meekly accepted the Ottoman and Egyptian colonizers, who set up a central government in Khartoum, from whence corruption, exploitation, and the slave trade flourished.

Muhammed Ahmed scorned the Egyptian overlords for their weakness and corruption, and was equally derisive of the Ottoman Turks for allowing their nominal vassals to continue their oppression of the Sudan. Nor did scorn stop there: when British and French influence began to grow in Egypt after the Suez Canal was opened in 1869, Ahmed declared that the Christians' luxurious lifestyles, love of money, and failure to embrace the true faith of Islam made them as morally corrupt as the Egyptians or Turks. In their anger and frustration, the Sudanese people were more than receptive to Ahmed's teachings.

Yet despite his railings, and the popularity with which they were received, if he had been an ordinary man, Ahmed might have been forgotten by history, just one more of a countless number of provincial holy men of various doctrinal shades and sectarian colors who have ranted against established powers and traditions for whatever obscure reasons motivated them. But Ahmed was not an ordinary man. By the time he reached manhood, the remarkable charisma that he would come to use in charming so many of his followers began to appear.

Certainly he was an attractive figure physically. Father Joseph Ohrwalder, an Austrian missionary to the Sudan who would one day spend seven years as Ahmed's prisoner, wrote of him, "His outward appearance was strangely fascinating, he was a man of strong constitution, very dark complexion, and his face always wore a pleasant smile. He had singularly white teeth, and between the two middle ones was a vee-shaped space, which in the Sudan is considered a sign that the owner will be lucky. His mode of conversation, too, had by training become exceptionally pleasant and sweet." To the end of his life, Father Ohrwalder, himself a man of considerable courage and conviction, who would suffer near-starvation and considerable physical abuse as the Mahdi's captive, remained fascinated by Muhammed Ahmed as both a man and a religious leader.

It was while he was in his self-imposed semi-exile along the shores of the Nile from 1874 to 1879 that Muhammed Ahmed came to consider the idea that he had personally been chosen by Allah to lead a holy war with the purpose of first liberating the Sudan, then sweeping the entire realm of Islam clean of corrupting Western ways and washing their influences from the faithful. At the same time such cleansing would facilitate the further spread of the "pure" Islamic faith. It was not a mere delusion that overwhelmed him, then swept him away on his holy crusade: during the time he spent living on the island of Abbas he traveled widely up and down the coast and along the Sudanese Nile, teaching his doctrine of austere piety, exhorting the Islamic faithful to follow the "path of God Almighty."

His travels took him as far as Dongola in the north, along the banks of the Blue Nile region, to Kordofan in the western reaches of Sudan, and Sennar in the east. While it can be honestly said that Ahmed was wandering the Sudan as a sort of itinerant holy man, serving the poorest of the Sudanese as a healer and scribe, the overly-romantic misconception that in return those he aided filled his begging bowl with food does him a disservice, for it downplays the position held in the Sudan by learned Islamic clerics: he was neither a beggar nor poverty-stricken. Everywhere he went he made disciples among people who heard him teach, many of whom made their way to Abba Island, where he would give them further instruction, eventually sending them back out into the countryside to carry his message of piety and simplicity.

Wherever his wanderings took him, Muhammed Ahmed found that the Sudanese people's discontent with the rule of the Ottomans and Egyptians mirrored his own, and in their desire to break their bondage they began to look for the appearance of "the Mahdi" to save them. So great was their desire for the guidance of this "Expected One" that whenever a teacher appeared possessing great knowledge, dedication, and devotion to Islam they would readily believe him to be the Mahdi, though no one had yet proclaimed themselves to be him. Ahmed himself began to preach of a "mahdi" who would first cast out the infidels and heretics from the Sudan, then purge all Islam of its excesses and venality, returning it to the path of true righteousness.

In the theology of Islam, the "Mahdi" is a savior figure, a pre-messianic messenger, sent to prepare the world for the appearance of the actual messiah, who will bring justice to the earth, restore true religion, and usher in a short golden age before the end of the world. Yet it is no small point to note that any doctrine concerning the figure of the Mahdi or his mission cannot be found anywhere in the Koran, and there is little among reliable *hadiths* (the sacred teachings of the Prophet Muhammed's successors) about such a personage either. The idea of the Mahdi seems to have evolved during the first two or three centuries of Islamic history. Many scholars have suggested—in particular regarding the Shi'ite doctrines of the Mahdi—that a clear inspiration for the Mahdi comes from Christianity and its ideas of a judgment day in the hands of a religious renewer.

In 19th-century Sudan the conflict between Shi'ite and Sunni Islam, which assumed vital geopolitical importance elsewhere in the Middle East, was not a major factor to devout Muslims such as Muhammed Ahmed. In fact, it can be seen that Ahmed, who rose as much from the Sufi tradition as Sunni, was able to borrow, if unconsciously, Shi'ite concepts of what it meant to be the "Mahdi." In Sunni Islam, which included the Sudan, a "mahdi" is simply a particularly enlightened teacher, while the "Mahdi" of Shi'ite Islam has a real eschatological importance, and is in the future an essential figure for Islam as well as the world. At this point an understanding of the schism within Islam is important to understand, not only for a perspective on Muhammed Ahmed's rise to power but as it increasingly affects the West at its current flashpoint in Iraq.

Thirty years after the death of the Prophet Muhammed, Islam was plunged into a civil war which eventually produced the three major sects of the faith. Uthmann, the third Caliph, or successor to Muhammed, was killed by mutineers in Mecca in 656 AD, and within months open warfare erupted across Arabia as three distinct groups emerged from the ranks of Islam's faithful, each fighting for power within the faith. It has been suggested that the Caliph's assassination was simply a pretext for the struggle, which pitted the Muslims of modern-day Iraq and Egypt, who resented the power of the third Caliph and his governors, against rival factions of the mercantile aristocracy in the rest of the Middle East. Whatever the actual motives for the killing, it precipitated a bloody conflict—part civil war, part religious conflict—and left a divide within Islam. The war ended with the establishment of a new dynasty of Caliphs, who called themselves Sunnis, who ruled from Damascus. In reaction to them there emerged two other factions: the Shi'ites and the Kharijites.

The Sunnis held themselves as the true followers of the *sunna* ("practice" or "way") of the prophet Muhammed, from whence they derive their name. Sunnis also maintained that individuals and congregations within the Islamic community (the *ummah*) could not possess their own spiritual autonomy but must always be guided. To this end the Sunnis were willing to recognize the authority of the Caliphs, who maintained rule by law and persuasion, and by force if necessary. The Sunnis became the largest division of Islam, establishing themselves in positions of dominance throughout most of the Middle East and Asia.

Of the two smaller factions created from this schism, the Shi'ites and the Kharijites, the latter eventually became a small and obscure fragment of the Moslem world. The Shi'ites, however, remained a minority of sufficient size—roughly a fifth of the faithful—and influence to remain a power within Islam. The fact that the former Persian

Empire—today's Iran—went into the Shi'ite fold lent the schism political and ethnic importance. Much as the conflict between Catholics
and Protestants in Northern Ireland had less to do with religous theology than with the ability of Great Britain to hold sovereignty over
Ireland, so did the Persian dominance of Shi'ite Islam present a political challenge to Sunni Arabs.

The fundamental dispute between the Shi'ites and Sunnis is that
the Shi'ites believed that the only legitimate leadership of Islam rested
in the lineage of Muhammed, specifically through his cousin and son-
in-law, Ali. Consequently they did not recognize the legitimacy of the
Caliphate when it passed to Abu Bakr and his successors, after Ali had
been killed in battle near Karbala, Iraq. Instead the Shi'ites regard the
twelve descendants of Ali as Imams, or spiritual successors of the
Prophet. The name "Shi'ite" came from the Arabic phrase "shi'at
Ali," which literally means the followers of Ali. The Sunnis in turn
refused to accept that Ali was the designated successor to Muhammed.
Because within the validity of the succession to Muhammed rests the
legitimacy of all the laws, teachings, and instructions given by those
who have held the office of the Caliphate, it was—and remains—a
major issue to Moslems.

Because the Shi'ites are a minority—and not a particularly popular one—within Islam, they have often been subject to varying degrees
of persecution at the hands of their fellow Moslems. Because of the
persistence and sometimes severity of the persecution, Shi'ite theology
has made the suffering of Shi'ites at the hands of Sunni and infidel
alike an essential doctrine of their belief. Shi'ite theologians teach that
because the Sunni know they are wrong in their belief that the Caliphs
were the true successors to the Prophet, and the infidels know they are
condemned to perdition by their refusal to embrace the true faith,
both feel the need to bring suffering to the Shi'ite faithful in order to
assuage their guilty consciences. So deeply did this sense of persecution
become ingrained in Shi'ite dogma that no amount of reassurance to
the contrary by either Sunni Moslems or Christians could convince
them otherwise.

It is an attitude and belief that has persisted into the 21st century,
though on an ever-shifting playing field. On the one hand, in today's
Iraq, for example, the West can see the battlelines drawn starkly

between Shi'ite and Sunni areas; on the other hand, the war against Israel waged by the Shi'ite group Hezbollah ("Party of God") in Lebanon in 2006 forged a common front, after initial resistance, across both major Islamic groups. Though the difference between Shi'ite and Sunni Islam is profound, the West would do best not to overestimate the division, just as any invaders of Christendom—past or present—would be advised not to misjudge the degree of theological or political separation between Catholics and Protestants.

Into this somewhat volatile mix of beliefs stepped the theological figure of the Mahdi. Because the doctrine of the Mahdi was not found in the Koran, the Sunni, who recognized the authority of the Caliphs, embraced the tradition of "mahdis" as enlightened teachers, and imbued them with much less credence and authority than did the Shi'ites. To the Shi'ite Moslems, the Mahdi was the "hidden Imam," the ultimate true successor to the Prophet Muhammed. To them, the Mahdi would carry greater authority than any of the Caliphs, second only to that of the Prophet himself.

The Shi'ite tradition held that the Mahdi would appear during the last days of the world, and precede the second coming of Jesus, who Moslems believed to be the Messiah. The Mahdi and Jesus were two distinct individuals, who would work together to fight the evils of the world and effect justice on Earth. The Mahdi would first come to Mecca, then rule from Damascus, preparing the world for the return of Jesus. He would confront and reveal the false Messiah, known as Dajjal, but not defeat him: that was to be done by Jesus, who would overthrow and destroy the pretender. Once Dajjal was defeated, Jesus and the Mahdi would live out their lives on Earth. Some teachings even maintain that Jesus would marry and have a family, eventually dying a natural death. There is an old Moslem tradition that claims a grave has long been excavated for him next to Muhammad's in the Masjid al-Nabawi in Medina.

There was even considerable detail about the Mahdi's exact appearance, in order that he would be properly identified and to eliminate the chance for a false claimant to usurp the title. It was believed that the Prophet Muhammad had actually foretold the coming of the Mahdi, having said that the Mahdi's father would bear the name Abdullah (as did the father of the Prophet), while his mother's name would be Aamina, (the same as the Prophet's mother). He would be born in "medina"—the word as used literally means a township, not the city in Arabia—and he would be forty years of age when he was revealed to be the Mahdi. A sign that would indicate his appearance would be twin eclipses of the sun and moon in the month of Ramadan just prior to his appearance. The Mahdi would be tall and smooth-complexioned, facially resembling the Prophet Muhammad. He would speak with a slight stutter, and at times strike his thigh as a means of breaking the stutter. Finally, there would be a v-shaped gap between his upper front teeth, a sign of good luck and favor from Allah among Arabs.

As to his character, Ali ibn Abi Talib, the fourth Caliph, said that the Prophet Muhammed declared of the one who would become known as the Madhi, "Even if only a day remains for the Day of Judgment to come, yet Allah will surely send a man from my family who will fill this world with such justice and fairness, just as it initially was filled with oppression." One striking detail that emerges from the accumulated teaching and doctrine regarding the Mahdi is the remarkable similarity between the Mahdi and the Christian figure of John the Baptist. In 19th-century Sudan, which was unaffected by the broader conflict between Shi'ite and Sunni Islam, Sufism, aspects of Shi'ism, and Sunnism, including its stern Wahhabi offshoot, were all available to earnest students of the greater faith.

Although Muhammed Ahmed was careful at first to avoid making any claim to being the Mahdi, such was the strength of his message and the power of his personality that many Sudanese came to believe of their own volition that he actually was the Expected One. A murmur of resentment toward their Egyptian conquerors had been running through the Sudanese for nearly four decades, but they lacked a leader to give focus to their unhappiness. Dismayed not only by the bleak condition of Islam in the Sudan under the self-proclaimed shaykhs who were little more than tools of the Egyptian government, but also by the suffering of his countrymen directly at the hands of the Egyptian officials, Ahmed began to see himself as sent by Allah to purge Islam of its evils and to return it to the purity of the faith of Mohammed the Prophet. His teachings began to take on end-of-the-world overtones as he gradually came to view himself as the rightful leader of Islam, the successor to the Prophet Muhammed, the great presiding figure of the end of time.

While it may have been that at first Muhammad Ahmed found himself being carried along by a tide of quasi-nationalist and anti-foreign, as well as religious, feelings, his upbringing and religious training unquestionably made him susceptible to being seduced by such sentiments. Certainly he gave in to the feelings expressed by the majority of the Sudanese he saw every day—the wishes and desires of the people in their expectation of the imminence of the Mahdi. Yet there is little if any evidence that Ahmed had consciously aspired to become more than a great imam and mullah.

Though passionate about his faith and in its proclamation, there seemed to be little of the fanatic or militant about him. Undoubtedly there was a strong streak of mysticism in his character, as quite early in his youth he made it clear to his father that he had no desire to follow into the family trade of boat-building, preferring instead to continue and expand his studies in Islam. That mysticism took him into the realm of Sufism, the most esoteric and ethereal branch of Islam, then brought him into a form of semi-exile on the island of Abba, from whence he journeyed across the Sudan, preaching, teaching, and healing where he could, feeling that in every step of the way his life was being divinely guided by Allah.

At the same time it would be foolish to suggest that Muhammed Ahmed was unaware of the unique combination of gifts he possessed. He had a sharply analytical mind capable of quite subtle thought, an uncanny ability to understand the motives, desires, and greeds of any man brought before him—along with the personal charisma that allowed him to manipulate those motives and desires to his own ends if he chose—and a commanding physical presence and persuasive speaking voice which could dominate, even overwhelm, the masses to whom he spoke. He was handsome, intelligent, articulate, and charming—a combination of characteristics that have proven throughout history to hold the potential for great danger, especially when possessed by any would-be demagogue.

Yet it is no small step from inspired and inspiring religious leader to divinely appointed visionary; it is a step that countless imams, mullahs, ministers, pastors, and priests of every religion, denomination

and sect never come close to taking. But something deep within
Muhammed Ahmed compelled him to cross that invisible divide that
separated him from being simply a spiritual guide for his people to
assuming the mantle of a God-anointed, semi-divine figure of prophe-
cy who would lead his people to a victory pre-ordained by Allah
Himself.

Undeniably, there were numerous similarities between Ahmed and
the prophetic description of the Mahdi. His place of birth, the names
of his parents, his physical appearance, the slight stutter, even the gap
in his teeth, all tallied exactly with the prophecies told of the Mahdi.
Yet there were differences—when Muhammed Ahmed chose to proclaim himself the Mahdi, for example, he was probably only thirty-
seven years old, three years short of the prophesied age. But despite
such inconsistencies, Ahmed believed—or chose to believe—that he
truly was "the Expected One."

So it was that in 1879—the exact date is maddeningly uncertain,
for as always there were few records kept by Ahmed or his followers—
he proclaimed himself the true Mahdi. Disciples began gathering on
the island of Abba, dedicating themselves to him and the cause he
espoused—which before long Ahmed began to make inseparable—
and were prepared to sacrifice their lives for him. Because of their
scarcity the records are unclear exactly what shape the opening of the
Mahdi's rebellion took, although it seems that in the beginning Ahmed
was exhorting his followers to a form of passive resistance to the
Egyptian authorities. This soon escalated into outright defiance, as the
Sudanese finally discovered a release for the great wellhead of anger
they had accumulated over a half-century of suffering and oppression.

"Suffering and oppression" is a convenient catchphrase that is
often too easily tossed about, as if the words themselves have meaning
without a context; frequently the phrase is used by political activists
to describe some real or imagined impugning of civil or political rights
and ideals by an authoritarian government. Unarguably the Sudanese
were subjected to the severest social oppression, even by the standards
of the mid-19th century. They had no civil liberties, no civil rights, no
habeas corpus. The law was whatever the local Egyptian magistrate
decided is was at any given moment; people could be imprisoned
indefinitely without ever being charged, simply on the whim of a gov-

ernment official. Flogging and torture were part of every day's routine in Egyptian-run prisons.

But there is still a vast difference between the "suffering and oppression" experienced by those who are at the mercy of a capricious legal and political system, and the suffering and oppression known by those to whom the words represent starvation and ruin for themselves and their families because of the rapacity of their rulers. In the Sudan in 1879, the suffering was physical and brutal, and so was the oppression—the country was literally falling apart.

What little infrastructure once existed was crumbling, as Egyptian officials lined their pockets with the money intended to build roads, dig wells, and construct public buildings. Taxation was confiscatory in the literal sense, as the levies were extracted in kind as well as in cash, and often farmers were compelled to turn over as much as three-quarters of their crops to their Egyptian overlords, usually at gun- or sword-point.

The slave trade, which involved some fifteen thousand Arab Moslems in the Sudan, had grown to unprecedented proportions. By the beginning of the 1870s some fifty thousand slaves were being brought out of the Sudan each year, sold in the markets of Khartoum in the north and on the island of Zanzibar just off the Red Sea coast in the south. The slave traders were so powerful that in some places they had become a law unto themselves. One trader known as Agad, for example, was awarded a contract by the Egyptian government which made him virtually autonomous over an area of 90,000 square miles in central and western Sudan. He was even permitted to raise and maintain a small private army. The Sudanese had become so demoralized that by 1875, Khartoum, once a thriving city of thirty thousand people and the Egyptians' administrative capitol in the Sudan, had shrunk to half that size. There had been a brief respite in the late 1870s, when a British soldier of fortune, General Charles Gordon, had been appointed governor over the northern half of the Sudan by the Egyptian Khedive Ismail, and Khartoum's population swelled once more, rising at one point to nearly a hundred thousand inhabitants. But when Gordon resigned his post in 1879 after a quarrel with Ismail over the Khedive's spendthrift ways, the chaos that followed his departure was worse than it had ever been.

Cairo's refusal to ease its economic stranglehold on the Sudan and thus its sensitivity to the Mahdi's rising rebellion was due to the absurd level of mismanagement to which Egypt's own economic affairs had fallen. Muhammed Ali's successors, while never quite as ruthless as he, shared little of his intelligence but all of his love of extravagance. In the thirty years following Ali's death, they managed to plunge what had been a dynamic Egyptian economy into recession and deep debt.

Muhammed Ali had hoped that his dedication to the development of Egypt—building factories, railways, and canals, and bringing in European architects and technicians to create a modern state—would continue under his grandson, Abbas. Instead, Abbas abandoned Ali's system of protective tarriffs, opening Egypt to free trade—and consequent exploitation by European business enterprises—while at the same time closing schools and factories, effectively halting the momentum toward industrial development and economic self-sufficiency Muhammed Ali had set in motion. Said Pasha, Abbas' son and successor, tried to reverse the backward slide, developing Egypt's infrastructure of roads, railroads, and canals, and most importantly brokering a deal with the French engineer Ferdinand de Lesseps, who wanted to build a canal between the Mediterranean and the Red Sea at Suez.

The Suez Canal was completed in 1869, by which time Said's son Ismail had become the Ottoman viceroy, bearing the new title "Khedive." Ismail was ambitious, both personally and for his country. Under his rule old factories were reopened and new ones built; telegraph and postal systems were established; canals and bridges were constructed; and the cotton industry thrived, particularly during the years of the American Civil War. But with expansion came a price: modernizing Egypt created a huge national debt, and when the bottom fell out of the cotton market in 1865 with the end of the American war, an economic crisis overtook the country.

Had Khedive Ismail been able to curb his own expensive habits, he and Egypt might have weathered the storm together, but Ismail had the regrettable habit of regarding the national treasury as his personal bank account. No one would have questioned the wisdom of spending the money building railroads and irrigation canals, but Ismail, determined to become as thoroughly Westernized as possible, also chose to spend it on an opera house and theater in Cairo, on gifts of a steam yacht and diamond studded diner plate to the Sultan in Constantinople (who in return issued a *firman*, a rescript or decree, granting virtually autocratic powers to Ismail), as well as a half-dozen new palaces, a huge collection of French furniture, artwork, jewels, and an enormous household entourage of slaves and harem girls. He traveled extensively (being received by Queen Victoria in 1867) and put on extravagant entertainments for royalty visiting one or another of his Cairo palaces. It all came at a price, however, for just as Ismail's spending reached its peak, the bottom fell out of the cotton market and Egypt's national debt soared from a quite reasonable £3,000,000 to an incredible £100,000,000 in less than five years.

When Ismail defaulted on a series of loan payments, foreign bankers and businesses that carried Egypt's (and Ismail's) debt began making threatening noises about seizing Ismail's assets and foreclosing on the Suez Canal. Rather than retrench and curb his spending, Ismail saw as one solution to his economic dilemma an escalation in the ongoing rapine of the Sudan. Determined to squeeze every last piastre out of that hapless land, Ismail had no tolerance for peasants who refused to pay their taxes, no matter how exorbitant, and authorized his troops to use force to extract payment. It was a mistake that would cost him his throne and Egypt her sovereignty. By 1879, Ismail would be forced to abdicate, while the influence of the Europeans, and in particular that of the British, would grow until Egypt became little more than a client state, and her new Khedive, Tewfik, a puppet of the European interests.

In contrast to the rather pathetic figures of Ismail and Tewfik, it was in these years that the Mahdi was at his best: his physique was still tall, sleek, and strong, and his features were still sharply handsome, as yet unmarred by a corpulence brought on by a life of unrestrained license and sensuality. Further, his character was still untarnished by the corruption that victory would bring, his faith still pure and honest, untouched by the megalomania which would later engulf it. There was still the strident ring of a genuinely righteous anger in his exhortations, as he urged his followers to act in the name of Islam for the good of Islam, without the unholy marriage of personal ambition and faith that was yet to come. His message was still filled with exhortations to shun the vices of envy, pride, and neglecting daily prayers. His followers, he stressed, should aspire to the six virtues of humility, charity, meekness of spirit, endurance, moderation in eating and drinking, and venerating the holy men of Islam. It was an admirable message, delivered by a still-admirable messenger.

His followers gave themselves over to his service with a readiness that went beyond devotion. In the words of Alan Moorehead, "They never . . . questioned his authority, they thought him semi-devine, and from the most powerful Emir to the humblest water-carrier they were ready to die for him."

The Egyptian authorities, in both the Sudan and Cairo, certainly had no idea of the whirlwind that was about to sweep over them. The first attempt to counter the Mahdi's influence was laughable for its comic-opera quality: in early 1881, a delegation of government officials went up the Nile to Abba Island in an attempt to persuade the Mahdi to temper his rhetoric and cease his agitation of the Sudanese. The delegation simply vanished in the Sudanese wastes. At last becoming alarmed at the rising threat posed by Muhammed Ahmed and his growing band of disciples, Cairo chose to resort to force to impose silence on the Mahdi.

That August, Abu Saoud, then the governor of Sudan safely ensconced in Khartoum, received instructions from Cairo to put an end to the annoying holy man on Abba Island who was creating so much trouble for the Egyptian overseers and tax-collectors. Badly underestimating the forces arraying against him, as well as the devotion of the Mahdi's followers to their leader, he sent a column of two hundred soldiers up the Nile to Abba, with orders to arrest or eliminate the Mahdi.

Armed only with clubs and rocks, swords and spears—and a fanatical belief in their leader and his teachings—the Mahdi's disciples ambushed Saoud's soldiers and literally butchered them. Immediately after their victory, the Mahdi and his faithful, now between ten and twelve thousand strong with their motley armament augmented by the captured muskets of the annihilated Egyptian column, left Abba Island and headed for Mt. Jebel Gedir, in the depths of Kordofan, intent upon retaking the Sudan in the name of Islam.

It was a ragtag force, impressive due to its sheer size rather than from any organizational strength or tactical abilities. Still, the Mahdi would prove to have considerable natural skills in logistics and in moving masses of his followers over long distances. When, in December 1881, a second column of some fourteen hundred Egyptian soldiers met with the same fate as the first, he rapidly began gaining an aura of invincibility. Each victory, however small or large, brought in hundreds of new followers, while adding new weapons to the army's arsenal and swelling its coffers with money, jewelry, and personal valuables looted from the bodies of the slain.

What had seemed for so long to be a smoldering rebellion against Egyptian authority now flared up into open revolt throughout the Sudan. For reasons that were beyond the Mahdi's control but from which he would benefit, the uprising was no longer just a "situation" but an all-out crisis for Cairo. When the Mahdi finally faced Cairo's next attempt to bring him to bay, it would be no small column of soldiers he would encounter—it would be an army.

CHAPTER 3

REVOLT IN THE DESERT

When the Mahdi declared himself and his followers in open revolt against the Egyptians in mid-1881, rebellion in the Sudan had already begun, but his proclamation of *jihad*, or holy war, against the "Turks" made him the rallying point for tremendous additional unrest that had been threatening to boil over for more than a decade. In the process he gave the energy aroused from discontent a purpose and a direction. Perhaps even more significantly, by proclaiming *jihad*, the Mahdi provided Sudanese defiance with a moral legitimacy, a spiritual underpinning that would not only sustain it but even increase its fury.

His proclamation was powerful, sweeping, and strident: "Verily these Turks thought that theirs was the kingdom and the command of Allah's apostles and of His prophets and of him who commanded them to imitate them. They judged by other than Allah's revelation and altered the Shari'a of Our Lord Muhammed, the Apostle of Allah, and insulted the Faith of Allah and placed poll-tax (*al-jizya*) on your necks together with the rest of the Muslims. . . . Verily the Turks used to drag away your men and imprison them in fetters and take captive your women and your children and slay unrighteously the soul under God's protection." He then went on to issue his call to arms: "I am the Mahdi, the Successor of the Prophet of Allah. Cease to pay taxes to the infidel Turks and let everyone who finds a Turk kill him, for the Turks are infidels."

At the same time, he added yet another aspect to his proclamations, one that would be a cornerstone of militant Islam for generations to come: xenophobia and a hatred of Christians. Because Great

Britain, and to a lesser degree France, had become entangled in Egyptian politics, and were perceived as the real strength propping up a weak and venal Egyptian Khedive, they–and by extension all Christians–were added to the Mahdi's growing list of those who had, either directly or simply by reason of their existence, defiled the faith and thus were cursed as "infidels."

Prior to the construction of the Suez Canal, Great Britain had little interest in Egypt, regarding it essentially as one more province of the Ottoman Empire. But because of the canal's strategic importance in maintaining Britain's sea lanes to her Far Eastern empire, in particular India, indifference to Egypt was not a position the British government could any longer maintain. By 1878 Her Majesty's Government was inextricably drawn into the quagmire of Egyptian affairs by the continuing financial folly of the Khedive Ismail, which finally bankrupted the Cairo government in 1878. Control of Egypt's finances was given over to an Anglo-French debt commission, which was also saddled with the responsibility for settling the Khedive's debts. The commission forced Ismail to liquidate all his holdings in the Suez Canal Company, and at the urging of Prime Minister Benjamin Disraeli, Great Britain bought all of the outstanding shares, which in one deft stroke gave the British a controlling interest in the Canal. It was a decision at once shrewd and fraught with peril: regardless of whatever legal niceties may have existed, the cold, hard political reality of the situation was that whichever nation controlled the Canal controlled Egypt. By 1879, when the British and French persuaded the Sultan of the Ottoman Empire to depose the impecunious Ismail and replace him with his son, Mohammed Tewfik, the notion of Egyptian sovereignty was quickly becoming a rather transparent fiction.

Control of the Canal allowed Britain unhindered exercise of her seapower, which was vital to maintaining her economic, political, and military positions abroad, but it also meant that Britain's policies toward both Egypt and the Sudan would for the next three-quarters of a century be determined by the need to protect the Suez Canal and the lifelines to the eastern marches of the Empire which passed through it. With the Khedive and his government perceived as little more than clients of the British and French, it was a situation that did not sit well with many Egyptians, particularly the Egyptian ruling class. These people resented European administration of what had been their responsibilities–in particular the Europeans' far more even-handed taxation, which of course eliminated much of the graft on which the Egyptian nobles had built their fortunes.

But of more importance than the resentment of the nobles was the anger of the common people, who clung to their dreams of an independent Egypt, or at the least of an Egypt ruled by a Khedive who was not perceived to be a Christian puppet. While the mass of Egypt's populace was composed of barely literate peasants, each of them was conscious in some way of the greatness of Egypt's past, and took pride in the knowledge, however imperfect, they possessed of Egypt's role as one of the earliest and most enduring of mankind's civilizations. That such a proud and ancient people should be ruled, however indirectly, by foreigners whose ancestors were still huddling in caves when Egyptians were building Luxor, Abu-Simbel, Memphis, and the Pyramids was a spiritual burden that weighed heavily on the Egyptian soul. As the Europeans' influence increased and became more open and obvious, so did the resentment felt by the Egyptians. By 1882, it had reached a fever pitch, and an open revolt broke out within the Egyptian army.

The army was under the control of the Under-Secretary of War, Lieutenant-Colonel Ahmet Arabi. There had been rumblings of discontent among the officers and other ranks alike, and soon talk of open rebellion, toppling Tewfik and replacing him with someone who would defy the "Christians"—as the Europeans were called—or even throw them out of the country entirely, was heard in the streets of Cairo. In May 1882, the Royal Navy, in the form of eight battleships and eleven cruisers, steamed into Alexandria Harbor as a show of support for Tewfik. It was an ill-chosen gesture, for it seemed to confirm the viewpoint of those who felt that the new Khedive sat on his vice-regal throne only at the sufferance of the Europeans. Throughout May and June, chaos overtook Alexandria and Cairo, resulting in the massacre of several Europeans. By now the Egyptian army, openly led by Lt.-Col. Arabi, was in full revolt against Tewfik, the British, and the French, refusing all orders to disperse or disband, and seizing several key fortifications overlooking Alexandria Harbor, from which they threatened to shell the British ships anchored in the bay.

On July 3, 1882, the European population of Alexandria was evacuated to the waiting fleet, and an ultimatum was issued to Arabi's followers: surrender Alexandria's forts to the British, or the Royal Navy would shell the city. When the Egyptians failed to respond, the battleships and cruisers opened fire at 7:00 AM on July 11. It was little more of a gunnery exercise for the British, and an exercise in futility for the Egyptians, as the bombardment began systematically demolishing the harbor forts. The Egyptians at first put up a brave return fire, but they had no guns heavy enough to seriously damage the British battleships, and by midmorning the last Egyptian battery had been silenced.

The next day, after setting fire to the city, Arabi's men withdrew from Alexandria, heading southward to Kasr-el-Dowar, and the British landed marines and sailors to secure the city. Within three days the British had established control over Alexandria, and after the Sultan refused to send his own troops to restore order in what was ostensibly his own domain, an expeditionary force was sent to crush Arabi's rebel forces. On August 25, 1882, 25,000 troops under the command of Lieutenant-General Sir Garnet Wolseley landed at Alexandria. After a brilliant series of feints, diversionary attacks, and raids, Wolseley concentrated his force on Kassassin and was ready to attack the rebels in their fortifications at Tel-el-Kebir in early September. Choosing to avoid fighting in the brutal heat of the day, he launched a surprise night attack against Arabi's position, throwing some 17,000 British soldiers and marines with 60 pieces of artillery against an entrenched Egyptian force estimated at as many as 30,000 regular infantry supported by 75 guns.

It was all over in less than an hour. A division of Scottish Highlanders attacked first, charging the Egyptians' first line and taking it at bayonet point. Other British regiments came up in support and soon the entire Egyptian army was routed, with British cavalry in hot pursuit. Meanwhile, some fifty miles southwest of Tel-el-Kebir, Cairo fell to a cavalry assault, some 10,000 Egyptian regulars surrendering without firing a shot. It was the end of Colonel Arabi's brief revolt. He surrendered to the British the following day and was exiled to Turkey. Great Britain's position as the arbiter of Egyptian affairs was seemingly more secure than ever, and the puppet status of the

Khedive was revealed for the world to see once and for all.

Whether it was by a quirk of fate or by some grand design–though no firm evidence of the latter has ever surfaced–the revolt in Cairo and Alexandria coincided with the rising of most of the population of Sudan in support of the Mahdi and his followers. The Egyptian government's position had already been badly weakened by a series of profound misjudgments made by Khedive Ismail before he was deposed, in an attempt to maintain some semblance of order in the increasingly unruly province. Soon it would get worse.

In the west of the Sudan, a region called the Bahr-el-Ghazal had been overrun by Arab slave traders. While they paid lip-service to their loyalty to the Khedive, the were in point of fact free agents, terrorizing the region and reducing the populace to a state of abject misery. Just as the slaver Agad had set himself up with a government charter that granted him near-autocratic power over almost 100,000 square miles of territory, another slaver, Zobeir Pasha, had carved out an even greater realm for himself at the expense of the Sudanese as well as the Egyptians. The Khedive, who in 1874 had sent out a column of troops from Khartoum to either arrest Zobeir or extract a promise of subservience from him, was horrified to learn that Zobeir's forces had defeated them, and had in turn invaded the independent province of Darfur. Zobeir claimed that he had annexed the province in the name of Khedive Ismail, and assumed the title of Governor-General. When Cairo refused to recognize his claim, he went to the Egyptian capital to press his case, and was immediately detained by the Egyptian government. But Zobeir continued to rule over his petty princedom through his son, Sulieman, who was, if anything, more ruthless and oppressive than his father.

The chaos that gradually overtook the Sudan in the 1870s led to a succession of minor interventions by the British, who mainly pressed various soldiers and officials onto the Egyptian government as replacements for corrupt or inept Egyptian officials in an effort to restore order. In 1878 a singular British officer, Major-General Charles Gordon, was appointed governor of Khartoum and given a mandate to suppress the slavers after fresh uprisings in Darfur and Kordofan. Gordon, acting swiftly and aggressively, broke up several companies of slave-hunters in both provinces. At the same time, Sulieman Zobeir, acting on the instructions of his father in Cairo, had broken out into open revolt against the Egyptians, in the same province as his father, the Bahr-el-Ghazal. Gordon entrusted Romolo Gessi, an Italian explorer and soldier of fortune who was possessed of remarkable courage and competence, with the task of crushing Sulieman. After a grueling campaign across some of the Sudan's most forbidding terrain, Sulieman was cornered and captured by Gessi. When Sulieman refused to renounce the slave trade, Gessi ordered his execution.

But the best that Gordon and his lieutenants could do were hardly more than straws in the wind, for what little order existed in the Sudan was fast crumbling. In one of his last acts of folly, Ismail quarreled with Gordon over questions of authority and pay, and Gordon resigned in disgust. When he left the Sudan he was succeeded at Khartoum by Raouf Pasha, already known for his venality and corruption, who happily revived most of the old abuses of the Egyptian administration, including the slave trade.

The disarray left by Colonel Arabi's revolt understandably distracted both Egyptian and British attention from the growing chaos to the south in the Sudan. When an Egyptian column of some fourteen hundred soldiers was massacred by the Mahdi's followers in 1881, Cairo began to take the revolt seriously, and sent a column of troops up the Nile from Khartoum to hunt the Mahdi down and restore Egyptian control over the Sudan.

By the autumn of 1881, after the defeat of the Khedive's punitive expedition to Abba, Muhammed Ahmed became even more open and confident in his proclamation of his divine calling. At times, the confidence spilled over into arrogance, as when he declared, "Cease to pay taxes to the infidel Turks and let everyone who finds a Turk kill him, for the Turks are infidels." Because the Egyptians were so closely identified with their Ottoman rulers, to the Mahdi and his followers, the word "Turk" had come to denote any enemy, regardless of nationality or faith. It was becoming more and more evident that any vestiges of the tolerance and compassion of the Sufi beliefs the Mahdi once embraced were rapidly vanishing from the his teachings, while the sense of persecution embraced by the Shi'ites was rapidly merging with the austerity of the Wahhabi, in the process forming a dangerous paranoia.

After each military success of the Mahdi and his followers, now known as the Ansar (the name also taken by the followers of Muhammed), his ranks and prestige grew, particularly among the Baggara, the nomadic Arabs of the western Sudan who most especially resented the Egyptians. In Muhammed Ahmed the Baggara found a leader who could be used to shake off Egyptian rule, and so their allegiance to him was quickly cemented. It was further assured when he took wives among the daughters of the Baggara sheikhs, and later decreed Abdullah, a sheikh of the Taaisha tribe, as his chief Khalifah. What the Baggara did not perceive was their usefulness to the Mahdi: their numbers alone gave him a power and authority that was unchallengeable by any other would-be leader in the Sudan, and made him sufficiently strong to openly defy the Egyptian government. The Baggara were to be the primary instrument of the Mahdi's *jihad*.

Followers numbering in the tens of thousands had flocked to his banner; the Mahdi proclaimed a *jihad* throughout the Sudan, and began to wage war on those he declared to be infidels. The Mahdi was now regarded by his followers as the only true leader of the faithful, the successor to the Prophet, and blessed with divine authority to spread Islam throughout the whole world.

Chillingly, though, for those who still cherished the belief that the Mahdi was devoted to purifying Islam, there were signs that he had begun to drift from what he had once held as a truly divine mission. In what he would have regarded as an act of blasphemy only a few short years earlier, the Mahdi altered the recitation of the *shahada*, the Moslem creed, adding the coda "and Muhammad Ahmad is the Mahdi of God and the representative of His Prophet" to the time-honored (and powerful) recitation of "There is no God but Allah and Muhammed is His Prophet."

Zakat, that is, almsgiving, was no longer an act of voluntary charity, but rather became a tax paid to the *Mahdyyah*. The *hajj*, or pilgrimage to Mecca, a holy obligation of all Moslems ordained by Muhammed himself, was replaced by service in the Mahid's *jihad*. The Mahdi also began modifying Islam's five pillars of faith in such a way that they came to support his dogma that loyalty to him was essential to true faithfulness. When a few courageous souls dared question him about these actions, the Mahdi justified his actions by declaring that he was acting on instructions from Allah that had come to him in visions.

The Mahdi carefully cultivated his followers' enthusiasm, making them feel they were an essential part of his plan to sweep aside the "Turks" and Christians. He began by styling his followers *dervishes*, from an Arab word originally meaning "doorway" (to the spiritual realm) but which came to mean a religious mendicant. They were thus identified as "the faithful." To further proclaim his followers' status, Muhammed Ahmed encouraged them to wear a patched *jibba*, a loose-fitting robe of indifferent cloth and quality, as their "uniform." The poverty implied by the jibba proclaimed the purity of their Islamic faith. Later he commanded the faithful to call themselves *ansar*, "helpers," referring to their coming role in the fulfillment of his personal ambition.

At the same time, Muhammed Ahmed was not unmindful of the duties required of him by Moslem doctrine and traditions as the true Mahdi. In a move as politically shrewd as it was religiously correct, Ahmed, in accordance with the tradition which required the Mahdi to have four deputies, proclaimed Abdullah el Taashi, a Baggara tribesman of somewhat dubious provinance, Ali wad Helu, a sheikh of the Degheim and Kenana Arabs, and Mahommed esh Sherif, the Mahdi's own son-in-law, as *khalifas*. Curiously, the fourth khalifaship, when offered to Sheikh es Senussi, was declined. Though he gave no reason for his refusal, it may well be that el Senussi saw even deeper than did Ahmed, and realized to how great a tragedy the *Mahdyyah* would lead.

For the "*Mahdyyah*" was what Muhammed Ahmed was now openly proclaiming—the coming of the kingdom of the Mahdi. By making them his *khalifas*, Ahmed bound the futures and fortunes of Abdullah, Ali wad Helu, and Mahommed esh Sherif so closely to his own that it was inevitable they would rise or fall together. Therefore it became a matter of some urgency for the three *khalifas* that the Mahdi be maintained, then enhanced, by any means they could manage. By announcing the *Mahdyyah*, Ahmed provided his revolt with the stamp of religious legitimacy that his followers lacked the sophistication to challenge, let alone refute. In doing so Ahmed established the pattern for generations of militant Moslems to come: the assertion of divine authority for acts of violence carried out against infidels.

Armed with swords, spears, and a ragtag collection of farm implements hastily modified into weapons, the Mahdi's army, now swelled to more than fifty thousand strong, systematically laid siege to the Egyptian garrison towns in Kordofan. The provincial capitol, El Obeid, held out for nearly six months in the last half of 1882. Starvation finally accomplished what the Mahdi's followers couldn't–by January 17, 1883, the defenders were too weak to resist a determined assault and the rebels overran the city in an hour. Gruesome scenes followed hard on the heels of the city's fall. Women and children were hacked to death, others raped and carried off to be sold to the Arab slavers; Egyptian officers and men were brutally executed, with a handful of surviving soldiers press-ganged into the Mahdi's forces. Despite the injunction once given by the Prophet Muhammed himself that Moslems should never kill or wage war on fellow Moslems, El Obeid was swept by an orgy of quasi-legitimized murder, as the Mahdi's disciples offered their victims the choice of renouncing whatever religion they followed and embracing the cause of the Mahdi. Those who refused were killed on the spot.

For more than a year there had been seemingly endless but indecisive skirmishing between Egyptian forces sent to hunt down the Mahdi and his motley army of those he deemed "the faithful." It was in February 1883, when word of the fall of El Obeid reached Cairo, that Khedive Tewfik decided to attack the Mahdi with what he regarded as overwhelming force, to retake the Sudan from these religious fanatics who dared flaunt Egyptian rule. The Khedive turned to Col. William Hicks, a British officer who had formerly served with the Indian Army, giving him command of an Egyptian expeditionary force numbering seven thousand troops of very indifferent quality, most of them the sweepings of Egyptian jails, along with a number of cavalry squadrons and some artillery. With this force Hicks was expected to work a miracle.

The expedition was the brainchild of the Khedive's government, acting against the advice of its British political and military advisers. The Khedive was warned not to think of attempting the reconquest of the Sudan, but instead to make every effort to evacuate the Egyptian troops and civilians living in that increasingly chaotic country, in particular the garrisons at Khartoum and Sennar. Instead Tewfik chose to act aggressively, hunting the Mahdi down in the Sudan rather than waiting for him to come to Egypt. A column of six hundred infantry was dispatched to Berber to keep the road clear from there to Khartoum, while the mass of the Egyptian Army was ordered to concentrate at fortified positions around Aswan for the defense of upper Egypt and the Valley of the Nile, preparatory to swinging over onto the offensive in support of Hicks.

Despite the misgivings of his government, Colonel Hicks, who was given the rank of Major General in the Egyptian army, and a number of other British officers who were retired or on leave, placed themselves at the Khedive's disposal, which he readily accepted. It was not an unusual state of affairs in the British Empire of the 19th century, as there were now more British officers than there were billets for them in the British Army, so foreign service was regarded as an ideal way to gain campaign experience and perhaps actually see some combat.

William Hicks was born in 1830, and entered the Bombay Army, the private Army of the British Bombay Company, in 1849. A few years later, in 1854, he married Sophia Dixon, and together they had four children. Hicks served through the course of the Indian Mutiny, and when the private armies of the Bombay Company and the East India Company were incorporated into the newly formed Indian Army following the Mutiny, he transferred his commission to it. He was mentioned in dispatches—a recognition of notable service for which there is no appropriate medal—for his conduct at the action of Sitka Chaut in 1859, and two years later he was promoted captain. During the Abyssinian expedition of 1867–68 he was again mentioned in dispatches and made a major. He retired in 1880 with the honorary rank of colonel and returned to England, but found he missed army life, and after the Arabi Revolt in 1882 he offered his services to the Khedive Tewfik, who gladly took him on, awarding him the Egyptian title "pasha."

Hicks was in most ways a typical British officer of the late Victorian Era. Not outstandingly brilliant nor possessing any great tactical or strategic gifts, he was a brave and competent, if unexceptional, soldier—disciplined, steady, moderately intelligent, not given over to much imagination. It was his misfortune to be given a command that would have taxed the genius of a Wellington, for the Egyptian force given him by the Khedive, was, to use the words of the Iron Duke, "an infamous army." Numbering some eight thousand fighting men, many of them were recruited from the *fellahin* (soldiers) of Col. Arabi's disbanded regiments, sent up the Nile in chains from Cairo. The presence of several hundred common criminals, the sweepings of the Cairo jails, among their ranks did nothing to improve the army's quality or its morale. Still, Hicks was determined to do his best with what little he had.

Hicks' staff was composed entirely of English officers who mustered considerable campaigning experience among them. They included Lieutenant-Colonel the Hon. John Colborne, formerly a major of the 11th Infantry Regiment and the scion of a distinguished military family; Lieutenant-Colonel Coetlogou of the 70th Infantry; Major Martin, who had served in a cavalry unit in South Africa; Major Farquhar of the Grenadier Guards; Captain Forestier Walker, late Lieutenant of the "Buffs" or East Kent Regiment; Captain Massey, late Lieutenant of the Duke of Cambridge's Own (Middlesex Regiment); Surgeon Major Rosenberg, Major Warner, Captain W Page Phillips and Mr. E.B. Evans, Intelligence Department. The cavalry was under the command of Major Martin; the artillery, armed only with light Nordenfeldt guns rather than heavier field-guns, was commanded by Captain Forestier Walker. Two German officers, one of them a Major Seckendorf, accompanied Hicks' staff as observers.

It was early in 1883 when Hicks, as a Major General in the Egyptian Army, went to Khartoum as chief of the staff of the army there, then commanded by Suliman Niazi Pasha. Hicks' own force followed a few weeks later and made camp at Omdurman, where he drilled and trained them as best he could for a month. On April 29, near the fort of Kawa on the Nile, Hicks led five thousand of his men against an equal force of the Mahdi's dervishes who were advancing on Sennar, defeated them, and then cleared the country between Sennar and Khartoum of the enemy. It was, Hicks hoped, a good omen, a success from which his men could build their confidence, both in themselves and in him.

At the same time, though, within Khartoum, the victory at Kawa resulted in the dismissal of Suliman Niazi, who because of his lack of success against the Mahdi's army was seen in Cairo as being ineffectual. No sooner was he relieved, his pride piqued and his sources of graft removed, than Niazi immediately began intriguing against Hicks with the Egyptian officials at Khartoum. In disgust, Hicks tendered his resignation to Tewfik in July. Rather than accepting it, Tewfik responded with a set of written instructions directing Hicks to lead his troops, now styled an "expeditionary force," into Kordofan to crush the Mahdi once and for all.

Hicks, who was not a stupid man, was well aware that his force was thoroughly inadequate for the proposed expedition, and in a telegram sent to Cairo on August 5, made this clear to the Khedive, stating his opinion that it would be best to wait for the situation in Kordofan to settle before attempting any further advance into the Sudan. The Egyptian ministers, however, did not believe that the Mahdi's strength was nearly as great as it actually was, and pressed their instructions on the reluctant general.

The expedition started from Khartoum on the 9th of September, 1883. It was made up of seven thousand infantry, a thousand cavalry, and two batteries of artillery, with nearly two thousand camp followers in its train. There were a total of thirteen Europeans with the column, most of them British officers on some form of official leave. On September 20 the force left the Nile at Duem and struck inland toward Bara, across the almost waterless wastes of Kordofan, for El Obeid. It was at the outset of the campaign that Hicks made his only really irredeemable mistake—he trusted the native guides assigned to him, not knowing that they were feeding information about the column's route and strength to the Ansar. At the same time, per the Mahdi's instructions, they were following a deliberately circuitous route through the desert.

Hicks' courage and determination were never in question, but his ignorance of the Sudan was abysmal. Rather than following any formulated strategy, Hicks seemed content to merely chase the Mahdi and his disciples to and fro across the landscape, apparently in the vain hope of running Ahmed to earth or simply driving his followers to exhaustion. Instead it was his Egyptians who were worn down, marching seemingly endlessly onward in the unbearable desert heat, suffering cruelly from hunger and thirst as their supplies dwindled.

The morale of Hicks' force, brittle from the outset, was rapidly disintegrating as the column approached the city of El Obeid.

While from the outset Hicks had grave—and well-founded—doubts about the overall quality of his command, his task wasn't an impossible one. The Egyptian infantry was well-armed, each man carrying a .50 caliber M1867 Remington rifle, along with sixty rounds of ammunition, with a ready supply of extra ammunition carried on pack animals in the column, a lesson learned from the British Army's disastrous defeat at the hands of the Zulus at Isandhlwana some four years earlier. The Remington, when properly used, could be a devastating weapon, throwing a massive soft-nosed lead bullet a half-inch in diameter and nearly an inch long at a velocity of 1,100 feet per second out to ranges that exceeded a thousand yards. The destruction wrought by such a round was best summed up by Kipling, who wrote of one of the weapon's victims having "a round blue hole in his forehead, and the back blown out of his head." Seven thousand Remington rifles firing five to seven rounds a minute would presumably present any attacker with a near-impenetrable wall of fire.

But for such a mass of fire to be effective, an enemy had to be willing to give battle, and the Mahdi's forces refused to stand and fight, instead drawing Hicks and his column deeper into the arid waste west of the Sudan, where heat, flies, dust, thirst, hunger, and boredom gradually took their toll on the Egyptian troops. On November 5th (some sources say the 3rd) the Egyptian army followed its native guides into a cul-du-sac in a Saharan wadi at Kashgil, some thirty miles south of El Obeid. With little or no warning, Hicks' column found itself attacked on three sides by the Mahdi's army. Forming a square, Hick's Egyptians stood on the defensive all that day and two succeeding days.

It should have been a massacre—and in fact it was, but not of the Mahdi's army. The formation of the hollow square is a formidable tactic for infantry to use against native troops, especially those who are armed with antiquated weapons. The "square" is just that–an open square or rectangle formed by the infantry, who form four ranks with fixed bayonets; the first two ranks kneel and hold their muskets or rifles forward, bracing the butts on the ground, presenting a hedge of bayonet points to the charging enemy. The third and fourth ranks are free to fire on the attackers, either individually or in massed volleys.

Often field artillery, Gatling guns, or Maxim machine guns were deployed at the corners, where they could rake the faces of the square as the enemy advanced. When properly employed, the square is devastating in its power: volleys of hundreds of rifles pouring into the ranks of an assaulting enemy, with rows of razor-sharp bayonets preventing the attacking troops from closing with the men firing into them. A properly commanded square can shred the enemy's ranks in a matter of minutes.

The keys to the success of the square were firepower and discipline, and, not surprisingly, when employed by British infantry the hollow square was nigh-on impregnable: at the battles of Ulundi and Gindgindlovhu in the Zulu War of 1879, the previously invincible Zulu impi, composed of thousands of the finest native warriors in the world, literally dissolved under the concentrated fire from faces of the British squares they were charging. Not a single Zulu warrior got closer than sixty yards to the British lines. Firepower, as with so many components of modern warfare, is essentially a British invention, and when the massed volleys for which British infantry was justly famous the world over was combined with the equally legendary steadiness of "Tommy Adkins," a battle's outcome was often preordained before the fighting even began.

But when employed by mediocre troops—and the soldiers given to William Hicks barely merited that level of quality—a square was another matter entirely. From the reign of the Pharaohs to the modern day, the average Egyptian peasant has at best made an indifferent soldier. Egypt has always been rightfully proud of its cultural heritage, while its warrior tradition has barely warranted notice. Discipline has never been a strength of any Egyptian army, and Hicks' force was no exception. That much of his infantry was composed of the leavings of various Egyptian jails and poorhouses only exacerbated the problem. Consequently, by the third day of the battle, despite the fact that Hicks' Egyptians had held firm against the Mahdi's forces for two whole days, their already feeble morale began to crumble, and with it the square which was their only hope of survival. Some troops tried to surrender to the attacking dervishes, others simply fled their positions, seeking the rather dubious shelter of the square's interior. In any case, during the third day the faces of the square began to give way, and in a mighty rush the Mahdi's forces surged forward and overwhelmed the defenders. Once the square began to waver, it was probably all over in less than an hour.

Over the months to come, fragments of news about the fate of Hicks' army drifted back to Egypt. Roughly a third of the Egyptian troops tried to surrender to the Mahdi, but most of them suffered the same fate as those Egyptian soldiers who were captured at the fall of El Obeid—most were executed outright, the remainder press-ganged into slavery. Those who stood their ground and fought died on the battlefield or in the orgy of slaughter that followed. Hicks was killed along with all of the other European officers; two or three of the European non-combatants are said to have been spared, taken prisoner and sent to Obeid, although none ever returned to Egypt.

One of the handful of survivors was General Hicks' cook, who later said that Hicks was the last officer to fall, run through by a spear wielded by the Khalifa Muhammed Sherif. Legend has it that Hicks defended himself ferociously, repeatedly emptying his revolver into the ranks of the advancing dervishes, and when he ran out of ammunition he kept his attackers at bay with his sword. In the end exhaustion caused him to let his guard down long enough for Muhammed Sherif to deliver his coup de grace. In what was meant to be a final humiliation for the defeated general, Hicks' head was cut off and presented as a trophy to the Mahdi.

The Mahdi's victory over Hicks was seen throughout the whole of the Sudan as a sign of Allah's blessing on his *jihad*. Who but one under the guidance of Allah, it was believed, could win such astonishing victories against the invaders? Now the Mahdi's army surged out of Kordofan, sweeping northward along the banks of the White Nile, threatening to cut off the remaining Egyptian garrisons in the Sudan, then pour through the Wadi Halfa into Egypt itself. What had been a serious situation for Tewfik and his government was now a crisis, as he feared another uprising among his own people.

The destruction of Hicks' army was also seen by the Mahdi himself as a sign of Allah's blessing. In an eerie foreshadowing of those who would follow in his footsteps more than a century later, the Mahdi dreamed of a world in which everyone in it would submit to the will of Allah and embrace Islam—if need be, at swordpoint. He proclaimed that after taking the Sudan he would conquer Egypt, then Mecca (which he promised to restore to its former glory), then Jerusalem; next would come Constantinople, and eventually Europe. The unfaithful of Islam, the infidels of Christendom, and the heathen and pagans of Asia would all bow before the scimitar of Islam, or else die by it.

And yet . . .

Few epigrams are as well known as Lord Acton's dictum that "Power tends to corrupt and absolute power corrupts absolutely." Rarely has the truth of Acton's perception been revealed as starkly as in the meteoric career of the Mahdi. The victory over Hicks' Egyptian army at Kashgil appears in retrospect to have been a turning point in the Mahdi's life, the moment which marked his departure from the path of a divinely guided mystic to instead follow the path of self-aggrandizement and glory. It is where the Mahdi ceased to be holy and began to become worldly. The beginnings of megalomania appeared, as he tightened the grip held by the concept of *Mahdyyah* (the Mahdi's Realm) on his followers.

Gone was the thoughtful, introspective scholar of the early days on the island of Abba; in his place was the religious dogmatic whose every pronouncement is inspired of Allah and infallible; gone was the righteous anger of the wandering cleric, desiring by example to simply return worship in Islam to its original humility, unencumbered by the trappings of wealth and pomp. In his place was a fiery evangelist determined to remake Islam in his own image. Gone was respect for the Koran, as in its place the word of the Mahdi became both civil and spiritual law. Surrounded by followers numbering in the tens of thousands and secure in his growing power, he turne his back completely on the gentle teachings of Sufism which had been so instrumental in shaping his early character. He now proscribed all Sufi orders, fearing the Sufi as potential rivals for power in the Sudan. Muhammed Ahmed no longer exhorted his followers; the Mahdi commanded them.

Yet the followers obeyed willingly, even gladly, for victory always generates its own enthusiasm, and the succession of victories achieved by the Mahdi's army grew ever more impressive. In Darfur province, in the extreme west of the Sudan, Rudolf Carl von Slatin, a young

Viennese officer in the service of the Khedive, struggled to maintain a grip on the province. He was completely cut off from supply or reinforcement after the fall of El Obeid, however, and finally surrendered to the Mahdi in December 1883. A similar struggle took place in Bahr-el-Gazal in the south, where the Egyptian garrisons, commanded by a former officer in the British merchant marine named Frank Lupton, were able to hold out until January 1884, when they were finally done in by hunger. Both Slatin and Lupton were made prisoners by the Mahdi, while their troops were mostly slaughtered out of hand.

Wholesale killing had become a routine feature of the Mahdi's regime. Placing the strictest possible interpretation on the Koran, he declared that all infidels who fell into the hands of his followers were to be given the choice of submitting to Islam or being immediately put to death. The Mahdi modified Islam's "Five Pillars"–faith in the Oneness of Allah and that Muhammed is His prophet; observing the daily prayers; care and almsgiving to the needy; self-purification through fasting; and the pilgrimage to Mecca—to support the dogma that loyalty to him was essential to true belief.

The strictures placed by the Mahdi over the daily life of his followers would find an uncanny echo a century and quarter later in the Taliban regime in Afghanistan, prior to its overthrow by the United States in 2001. His enforcement of Koranic law over those whom he ruled was harsh in the extreme. In a proclamation to the faithful after El Obeid, the Mahdi declared:

> Let all show penitence before Allah, and abandon all bad and forbidden habits, such as degrading acts of the flesh, the drinking of wine and smoking tobacco, lying, bearing false witness, disobedience to parents, brigandage, the non-restitution of goods to others, the clapping of hands, dancing, improper signs with the eyes, tears and lamentations at the bed of the dead, slanderous language, calumny, and the company of strange women. Clothe your women in a decent way, and let them be careful not to speak to unknown persons. All those who do not pay attention to these principles disobey God and His Prophet, and they shall be punished in accordance with the law.

Say your prayers at the prescribed hours.

Give the tenth part of your goods, handing it to our Prince, Sheikh Mansour [who the Mahdi had made governor of El Obeid] in order that he may forward it to the treasury of Islam.

Adore God, and hate not each other, but assist each other to do good.

Under the Mahdi's rule, "forbidden habits" came to include marriage feasts and celebrations of any kind, and singing or dancing for any reason. It became a deadly offense to read any books other than the Koran or the *hadiths*, or to wear anything but the humblest of clothing. In short, any behavior that could not be construed as advancing the cause of the Mahdi was officially proscribed. His enforcement of Koranic law over those whom he ruled was harsh in the extreme: the most frequent punishment for any of these transgressions was beheading or flogging to death; by comparison the penalty for stealing was mild—cutting off a hand or foot. It was a way of life more suited to the 7th century than to the 19th, and the two eras were about to collide before the full view of the world at a heretofore obscure city sitting at the confluence of the Blue and White Niles—Khartoum.

CHAPTER 4

THE CITY BETWEEN THE RIVERS

If a traveler determined to trek the length of the Nile in the early 1880s were to pause in his journey just a few miles below the confluence of the White and Blue Niles, and take to one of those fantastical balloons being popularized by Jules Verne in his writings in Paris in those same years, he would look down on a remarkable sight.

Looking first to the east he would see the rolling plain of the Nubian Desert, jagged and rocky, far different from the Sahara to the west. As he looked further east the traveler would see the plain turn to hills on the far side of the green belt of the Atbara River, eventually rising into the scrub- and scree-covered mountains of northern Abyssinia. Turning one hundred eighty degrees, looking west, the traveler would be confronted by the same vastness that defeated William Hicks: the northern reaches of Kordofan province and the empty waste that marks the eastern edge of the Sahara Desert. There is little there on which the eye can focus, simply endless vistas of rolling sand dunes, twisting wadis, and rocky outcroppings. This is the land of the Baggara, nomadic Arab tribes, who follow tracks and trails through the desert that only they can see, making their living in the slave trade.

It takes little imagination to understand how, by venturing into such a featureless plain of sand, Hicks came to his undoing, or to wonder why he chose to go there in the first place. To the north, the traveler would see the gently curving arc of the Nile gradually bending off to the northeast where it encounters the Sixth Cataract on its way to Berber, an important refueling stop for the picturesque paddlewheel steamers that ply the stretches of the Nile between the various cataracts which prevent the river from being navigable for its full length. If the balloon were high enough, the traveler could see the great S-shaped bend in the Nile where it winds its way around the Nubian Desert before crossing the border into Egypt at Wadi Halfa.

But it is what is below and to the south of the balloon that would command the traveler's full attention, for he would be looking down at a striking complex of towns and settlements, all of them centered around the city of Khartoum.

Khartoum was actually one of three sister cities built at the convergence of the Blue and White Niles: Omdurman to the northwest across the White Nile, North Khartoum to the north on the bank of the Blue Nile, and Khartoum itself on the south bank of the Blue Nile, not far from the triangle formed by the Blue and White Niles, a point known as the Mukran. A little farther up the Nile, in the middle of a large oasis, sat the town of Halfaya. A handful of small villages were scattered about the area, most notably Buri to the east of Khartoum, and Tuti and Khojaki in the plain above North Khartoum.

What gave the city of Khartoum its significance during the Mahdi's revolt was a basic fact of desert warfare. It was something learned by armies as far back in antiquity as the conquests of Alexander the Great and Scipio Africanus, and would be relearned by Britain's Desert Rats and Germany's Afrika Korps in the Second World War, and relearned by the United States and its allies in 1991 and 2003. Successful desert warfare has little to do with simply occupying territory; rather, it is a function of possessing certain key geographic features and strategic focal points.

Khartoum was exactly such a focal point, located at just such a geographic feature. Though there were numerous far-flung settlements and towns throughout the Sudan—through control of which a conqueror or occupier could gain at least a temporary dominance of the Sudan—they were all tied together in one fashion or another by the two Niles, the White and the Blue. Some were simply situated on one of the rivers, others were connected to them by caravan trails and trade routes; in the end, though, the two Niles were the determining factor. The two rivers, the White Nile in particular, were the living heart of the Sudan, and whoever controlled the Nile would eventually rule the land.

Khartoum was the great prize in any plan to conquer the Sudan because of its location at the confluence of the two rivers: an army holding the city could effectively deny the use of either river to anyone it desired, cutting off trade or travel at will. An army advancing down the Nile could not conquer the Sudan without taking the city of Khartoum. An army seeking to defend the country could not hope to succeed without holding the city.

Although that part of the Sudan had been intermittently inhabited since the neolithic times, Khartoum and her two sister cities had a relatively short history. Prior to 1821, the region lacked any strategic or commercial value, and was essentially deserted. But with the conquest of the Sudan by Muhammed Ali came the need for a central administrative center to regulate taxation and serve as a focus for the slave trade, and so out of this necessity the city of Khartoum was born. It was established as a purely military outpost at first, not far from the ruins of the last Nubian kingdom of Alwa a few miles to the east on the Blue Nile. Khartoum grew rapidly in size and prosperity between 1825 and 1860—in 1834 it was officially made the capital of the Sudan, and in the fashion of political centers everywhere, accumulated layers of bureaucrats and administrators, who in turn attracted fortune-seekers, opportunists, hangers-on, and the associated businesses and trades that accompany them.

By 1860, the population of the city had reached close to a hundred thousand, roughly a third of the inhabitants being Egyptian civil servants, merchants, and their families, along with the garrison. Sudanese merchants and craftsmen, along with a mass of servants and slaves, made up the rest. European explorers bound for central Africa, which was still a large blank spot on the world's maps, often made Khartoum the base for their expeditions. Khartoum was in a sense the last outpost of civilization sitting on the edge of a vast, wild emptiness.

More importantly, though, was the role that Khartoum played in the slave trade. Along with the island of Zanzibar, off the coast of Africa in the Indian Ocean, Khartoum dominated the African slave trade in the middle of the 19th century: slaver caravans traveling south of the Equator generally made their way to the coast, while those north of it descended on Khartoum. Just as they had exploited every other aspect of the Sudan, the Egyptian overlords who ruled the land were quick to take advantage of this lucrative trade, despite growing roars of outrage from the European powers. The infrequent European adventurer passing through Khartoum in the mid-19th century found the greed of the Egyptian officials astonishing, akin to organized pillage, as most of the "taxes"—extorted by force in cash or kind with equal facility—went into the pockets and coffers of the Egyptian over-lords.

It was the slave trade that first brought Khartoum to the attention of the outside world. In 1807 Great Britain had abolished slavery within the British Empire, and successive governments had dedicated themselves to eradicating the vile practice throughout the rest of the world, with most of the European powers agreeing to end slavery within their own territories by the middle of the 19th century. But the abolition of slavery by the Europeans did not eliminate the practice in Africa or the Middle East, and the slave trade in the Sudan flourished. With the expansion of French and British power and influence in Africa, it was inevitable that the Sudanese slavers would come to the attention of Paris and London. The intensity of anti-slavery sentiment in Great Britain in particular would play no small part in the policies Her Majesty's government would formulate for administering Egypt and responding to the question of what to do about the revolt in the Sudan.

One factor in the attitude of the Europeans—and especially that of the British public—toward the Mahdi and his followers that has often been overlooked or forgotten was a consequence of Islam's doctrines and teachings regarding slavery. The Koran explicitly guarantees Moslems the right to own slaves, either as spoils of war or purchased in a slave market. This is unsurprising, as the Prophet Muhammed was a slaveholder, owning dozens of men and women; in his later years, having become a wealthy man through the tithes of the faithful, he frequently bought and sold slaves at the market in Medina. Some of the misogyny inherent in Islam is evident in Muhammed's treatment of women taken captive in warfare: "Whenever Muhammed took a woman as a captive, if he imposed the veil on her, Moslems would say he took her as a wife, but if he left her unveiled they would say, 'He owned her as a slave'; that is, she became a property of his right hand."

As the teachings of Islam developed, it became an accepted doctrine that only children of slaves or non-Moslem prisoners of war could become slaves. Freeborn Moslems were never to be enslaved, although that was an injunction usually honored more in the breach than the observance. In the Sudan, permitting the taking of slaves as prizes in war eventually led to the concept of *jihad* being twisted into an awful perversion: Arabs regularly raided black tribes to the south—especially Coptic Christians—or even neighboring Moslem tribes for the sole purpose of taking captives to sell at Khartoum or Zanzibar, all in the name of "holy war." There was never an unequivocable denunciation of slavery within either the Shi'ite or Sunni factions.

While Islamic law—the *sharia*—laid down strict rules for the proper treatment of slaves, historically there were no fixed penalties for masters who abused their slaves, leaving them at the mercy of clerical "judges" who had no codified body of law to constrain them and who could be entirely capricious in applying justice. Slaves, of course, had no legal rights whatsoever, not even the right to appeal for judicial relief against abusive owners.

In a passage that reveals one of the darker sides of Islam, particularly how it institutionalized the inferior status of women, the Koran declares that a freeman should be killed only for another freeman, a slave for a slave, and a woman for a woman; it is startling to note both that women rank below slaves in importance, and that there is no female equivalent of "freeman." One *hadith* explicitly states that "a Moslem should not be killed for a non-Moslem, nor a freeman for a slave." Islamic teaching also permitted a Moslem slaveowner to enjoy the sexual services of his female slaves. (Women were not permitted to own property, hence they could never be slaveowners.)

Many of the African males taken as slaves were made eunuchs. While castration was against Islamic law, this was just one more minor legalistic obstacle to be overcome by the slavers, usually done by taking their captives outside Moslem territory where Islamic law was not considered binding to perform the mutilation. For African captives, nothing short of "castration level with the abdomen" would do, rather than simply removing the testicles, which was the common practice with Slavic and Greek captives. The reasoning behind this extreme violation of the slave's body is lost today, but whatever it was, it made

African males who were subjected to this brutality especially prized as harem guards.

By the time of the Mahdi's revolt, these details were known throughout the palaces, legislatures, salons, and pubs of Europe, and as European influence grew in Egypt so did pressure on the Egyptian government to bring an end to the slave trade in the Sudan. Under Ismail's rule that wasn't likely to happen, for much of the Khedive's fortune came from the payments made to him by the slave traders in exchange for almost complete immunity. When dealing with the Europeans the Khedive would pay lip service to ending the slave trade, but as usual he proved long on words and short on action.

It wasn't until the British and French took over financial control of the country and imposed a series of European governors for the provinces of Sudan on Ismail—and later on Tewfik—that any progress was made. Frank Lupton in Bahr-el-Gazal, Rudolf von Slatin in Darfur, and Romolo Gessi in Kordofan were ruthless in their pursuit and prosecution of the slavers; there was little mercy shown, most of the slavers being executed, the few exceptions being men like Zobeir Pasha or Agar Pasha, who had tremendous influence in Cairo. The most dedicated of these foreign governors was General Charles Gordon, who was first sent to the south of the Sudan, to the region known as Equatoria, then later moved to Khartoum when he became Governor-General of the Sudan. He was relentless in pursuing the slavers, and was so successful in his efforts that Khartoum, which had been falling into decay over the previous decade as the Sudanese in the region became demoralized by the depredations of the slavers and began resettling elsewhere, experienced a revival and recovered much of its lost prosperity.

But when Gordon left Khartoum in 1880 all of the excesses and abuses—as well as the slave trade—returned with his Egyptian successor. Although the slavers could no longer be as flagrant in their practices and their violations as in the past, and the Egyptian administrators in Cairo, now carefully watched by British overseers, could no longer be so blatant in their graft and corruption, it was still demoralizing to the Sudanese. It was a situation ripe for rebellion, and when the Mahdi's forces advanced out of Kordofan, the countryside around it rose up in sympathetic revolt—not because the Mahdi promised to

bring an end to the slave trade, but rather because he put the slavers on notice that he expected them to conduct their trade according to the laws of Islam. The slave traders, some who truly feared the Mahdi as a genuine holy figure of Islam, others who simply feared the size and power of his army, agreed to comply. This was a measure of protection that the people of the northern Sudan had not known for decades, and thousands of new followers flocked to his black and green banners.

At the same time, the people of Khartoum were faced with the threat of being cut off from the outside world, a prospect which held terrible import for the city's Egyptian population and garrison. Although they were nominally Moslems, the Mahdi had already declared that because they had not already embraced his cause, renounced their worldly ways, and adhered to Islam as he taught it to be practiced, they were regarded as infidels to be put to the sword without mercy. More than thirty thousand men, women, and children were threatened with a bloody execution if Khartoum fell to the Mahdi.

Such decrees were becoming part of the Mahdi's image and a means by which he held sway over his followers. By reminding them that he held the power of life or death over thousands, he bound those followers ever closer to him, lest they find themselves similarly proscribed in the future. To underscore his position as the Sudan's new ruler, Muhammed Ahmed set up his administrative capital in El Obeid. From there he began issuing summonses to all the various Arab tribes who had not yet joined his revolt, had new currency minted with his own name and image on them, and set about re-ordering the Sudanese way of life. He gave instructions that all newspapers were to be banned and all books except for the Koran, compilations of hadith, sharia legal texts, and books of Islamic theology be burned. He believed that such publications were the means through which corrupting "Western" ideas were introduced into the minds of the faithful. His social and religious "reforms" consisted of a series of proclamations which systematically forbade all of the customs and practices introduced by the "Turks" and in their place established the his own teachings, leading to the usual litany of instructions concerning ritual, prayers, moderation in food and clothing, and the behavior of women.

The status of women in Islam, as interpreted by the Mahdi, was little more than medieval. Even the average housewife in London or *hausfrau* in Berlin had more rights than did a woman in the Mahdi's Sudan. Concubinage was legal, and arranged marriages were the custom rather than the exception. Women were forbidden to own property, and possessed no economic or legal rights whatsoever. Girls were not permitted to go to school, but remained at home to learn the domestic skills necessary to make them suitable as wives. Adultery, which the Koran taught was a sinful act by men or women, was largely ignored if the offender was a man, while a woman accused of adultery would be put to death by stoning. A husband could divorce his wife without pretext and without notice, simply by giving her a writ of divorce, leaving the woman destitute and homeless; a woman was never permitted to divorce her husband.

As the Mahdi's army approached Khartoum, it became ever more clear that some sort of showdown was in the offing, either between the Mahdi and the Egyptians or, more likely, their British masters. Two men who would never set eyes on the city began to exert an influence over the events as they transpired, one of them in Cairo, one in London. They were Evelyn Baring, the British Agent for Egypt, and Prime Minister William Gladstone.

Evelyn Baring, who would eventually become the first Earl of Cromer, was one of those remarkable individuals with which the 19th century abounds: the wild rake who becomes the pillar of respectability. Born in Norfolk, England, in 1841, into a great British banking family, he was, by his own admission late in life, a high-spirited, even wild boy who received very little formal education. That was a circumstance that could be circumvented by families with the right connections, and in young Baring's case it didn't prevent him from obtaining a commission in the British Army at the age of eighteen. All the same, it could have stifled his career once he left the army, as might his hedonistic, spendthrift ways while he was still in uniform. As he later told it, the combination of the love of a good woman—his first wife, Ethel—and the example set by his fellow officers, most of whom were much better educated than he, caused Baring to transform himself into a sober, dedicated, and talented Colonial Office administrator.

Baring's childhood was not entirely wasted on play and pranks,

as it seems that somewhere he acquired a fair knowledge of and skill at international finance. It was this talent which led to him being named the British representative on the Egyptian Commission of Public Debt in 1877, at the age of thirty-six. His success there led to his appointment as finance minister to Lord Ripon, the new viceroy of India, in 1880, a post he would hold for three years. It was during this time that Baring became aware of Prime Minister William Gladstone's dedication to the entire concept of "reform," as Ripon had a complete agenda for India, endorsed by Gladstone, which he intended to carry out. Baring, in an unusually profound moment of insight, summed up Gladstone's entire attitude toward the Empire when he wrote to a friend, "I do not think that English statesmen . . . quite sufficiently recognize that the final cause of British rule in India is to teach the people to govern themselves."

When the opportunity came to return to Egypt in 1883, Baring took it with alacrity. Appointed as the British Agent for Egypt—in effect making him proconsul—he would come to regard the twenty years he would spend in Egypt as an exemplary demonstration of how a misgoverned country was rescued by a handful of dedicated men from the British Foreign Office, whose reforms brought order, justice, and prosperity to a chaotic country, and with some justification.

It's difficult to not see the ultimate results of British rule in Egypt as an example of what was best about the Empire, although there would be some quirks among those responsible for administering it. Baring, for example, developed a most peculiar attitude toward Egypt—he believed that there was no such thing as a "nation of Egypt," rather he saw it as a heterogeneous collection of wholly-Arab peasants and semi-European pashas, making up what he called the "dwellers of the Nile." It was an attitude that manifested itself in assorted ways, some trivial, others significant: Egyptian contemporaries would come to laud Baring for re-establishing Egypt's economy and introducing financial responsibility, while at the same time they would condemn him for a lack of educational opportunities and for denying them the right of self-governance. In particular, they took offense at his frequent comments about the rigidity and lack of sophistication in Islam. These were attitudes that seemed far removed from his earlier observation about India.

Whatever policies he put into practice, Baring did not have the authority to develop them himself. Instead he was expected to govern according to directives received from the Foreign Office, which in turn took its instructions from the Cabinet, which in its own turn essentially reflected the policies of the Prime Minister. In 1883, that meant the policies of William Gladstone.

William Ewart Gladstone was one of the towering figures of 19th-century British politics, and the dominant personality of the Liberal Party for almost thirty years. Deeply religious, always he combined his high sense of morals with a mastery of oratory and a genius for finance to produce some of the most far-reaching social legislation enacted by any parliamentary body in the world, ever-attempting to bring compassion to the face of the Empire. It could be said that in many ways he represented the best qualities of Victorian England.

Gladstone entered Parliament in 1833 as a Tory, curiously enough–he was the protégé of then-Prime Minister Sir Robert Peel, who made him Undersecretary for War and the Colonies. In successive Peel governments he moved to the Board of Trade, then to the Colonial Office. A split within the Tory ranks found him moving ever closer to the Liberals, and when named Chancellor of the Exchequer (the British equivalent of the United States' Secretary of the Treasury), he was vocal and eloquent in proposing and supporting free trade. Believing that it was a disgrace that less than one-fiftieth of Great Britain's working class was eligible to vote, he also adopted the cause of parliamentary reform.

His ascent to the position of Prime Minister was steady if not spectacular. He formed the first of his four governments in 1868, when his tenure would last for six years. It was a term of office memorable for the disestablishment of the Church of Ireland, a measure designed to pacify Irish Roman Catholics by reliving them of the necessity of paying tithes to support the Anglican church, as well as significant land reforms for Ireland meant to protect tenant farmers facing eviction by absentee landlords. The Emerald Isle would prove to be a recurring theme in Gladstone's career, and the question of Home Rule for Ireland would eventually bring the fall of his final government in 1894.

Gladtone was a reformer at heart: he utterly believed that the role of a nation's government was to do its utmost to improve the lives of its people. He would close his career proud of what he had achieved for Britain's middle and working classes. Among his reforms were the vote by secret ballot, a reorganization of Britain's civil courts, expansion of education, the introduction of competitive admission to the civil service, and abolition of the sale of commissions in the army.

Foreign policy, however, was his weakness, for he was not as interested in the great questions of imperialism and empire as was his Conservative rival, Benjamin Disraeli. Here Gladstone's conscience and morality was a handicap, for he was unable to adopt what he felt was a hypocritical pose by turning a blind eye to the excesses of other nations whenever it was convenient for Great Britain's imperial interests to do so. The year 1876 saw Gladstone publish a pamphlet, *Bulgarian Horrors and the Questions of the East*, attacking the Disraeli government for its indifference to the Turks' brutal repression of the Bulgarian rebellion, and his continued attacks on Disraeli's aggressively imperialist policies brought the Liberals back to power in 1880. During his second tenure as Prime Minister, Gladstone would be able to pass an even more effective Irish land act, along with two parliamentary reform bills which further extended the franchise and redistributed the seats in the House of Commons. But the overshadowing issue of Gladstone's second government, which would ultimately bring it down, was the fate of the city of Khartoum.

There was one essential element of Gladstone's personal and political convictions that would influence every decision he would or would not make in the coming crisis: he cordially detested imperialism. While "imperialism" has come to possess a near-obscene meaning in the late 20th and early 21st centuries, and with some just cause, in the last quarter of the 19th century it was an accepted—even expected—mode of conduct for Western European nations. More than any other issue, imperialism defined the differences that existed between the Liberal Party under the leadership of Gladstone, and the Conservative, or Tory, Party, led in the 1870s and 1880s by Benjamin Disraeli. Disraeli and the Tories gloried in empire, saw the expansion of Great Britain's dominion as a sort of British version of "manifest destiny," perhaps best expressed in the title of one of the more popular music hall ballads of the day: "We're Getting it by Degrees."

Unlike Disraeli, Gladstone saw no glory in empire for its own sake. While he understood that it was incumbent upon him to defend what Britain already possessed, and he was not prepared to abandon any of the Empire's sometimes far-flung marches, he felt no need to expand for expansion's sake. Gladstone's objections to imperialism were not found on moral grounds, but on financial: no matter how much a civilizing, stabilizing, and beneficial influence British rule might have on a region—and it would be wrong as well as unfair to maintain that British rule was never any of these things—it always cost money. That money, Gladstone felt, could be better spent at home in Britain, improving the lives of working men and women through better education and working conditions than in simply acquiring and holding distant patches of ground, often of quite dubious value.

To him, the Sudan was just such a place. Gladstone saw no reason for additional British conquests in Africa and wasn't all that keen on a large British presence in Egypt. He would have gone so far as to retire the garrison in Cairo had Baring been able to govern the country without it, though that wasn't possible. The extreme poverty of the Sudan meant that the cost of administering and garrisoning it would have made the Sudan a liability to Great Britain. Glory was an intangible that Gladstone could do without, as it was expensive in both lives and treasure, and he was determined to be sparing of both. So the Prime Minister figuratively drew the line at Wadi Halfa, where the Nile flows into Egypt, and declared that Britain's obligations ended there. If the Egyptian garrison and civilians in Khartoum were to be saved, it was the Egyptians' responsibility.

Baring agreed with Gladstone that it was unwise to commit British prestige or resources to the defense of Khartoum, though for not quite the same reasons. While Gladstone saw no reason for Great Britain to assume responsibility for the Sudan, Baring questioned the necessity for Egypt to continue to maintain it. He frankly admitted that he saw no reason for the Khedive to maintain his rule over the unhappy land to the south, so badly had it been mismanaged in the previous half-century. If Egypt were to defend itself, it should do so in the Valley of the Nile, at Wadi Halfa, not Khartoum. The defense of Khartoum, as Baring saw it, would serve no purpose save the defense of the Sudan, and that country was, for all intents and purposes, already lost.

Both Gladstone and Baring perceived a genuine threat in the Mahdi's rebellion, first to the Europeans living in Egypt, but more importantly for the Empire, to the Suez Canal. If the rebellion spread into Egypt and a genuine Islamic revolt took hold, the Europeans would be held hostage to the Moslems mobs, and would most likely be slaughtered out of hand, undeniably a tragedy of horrific proportions. But a closure of the canal was a possibility with frightening implications for the security of the Empire, for it would fundamentally alter the geopolitics of the day, with consequences as far away as Afghanistan, where Great Britain played a never-ending game of king-of-the-hill with Russia in defense of India, and in the Far East.

It was this threat that created an upheaval in Gladstone's Cabinet, denying him the opportunity to consign Khartoum and the Sudan to their fates. Everyone agreed that the Mahdi must be stopped; the question was where? Two of the most influential members of the Cabinet, Lord Hartington, the Minister for War, and Lord Granville, the Foreign Minister, strongly favored intervention in the Sudan. They felt that the farther from the Canal the rebellion was halted the better. Another part of their reasoning was the aftermath of the massacre of William Hicks' column the year before: because Hicks had been a British general, it was widely perceived in Africa and around the world that his command was composed of British troops, and that the Mahdi had handed Great Britain a galling defeat. For reasons of prestige alone, then as now no little consideration in international relations, Hartington and Granville argued in favor of a British expeditionary force being sent up the Nile to crush the Mahdi and his ragtag army once and for all. There was also a strong sentiment among the public in favor of such an action, and Gladstone knew he could ignore the voice of public opinion only so long without consequence.

It was at this point, in the first week of January 1884, that Gladstone, Hartington and Granville, in the manner of politicians throughout history, began formulating a political solution to what was essentially a military problem. No one in London wanted a war, although one was looming; no one wanted to spend the money required to whip the Egyptian Army into something resembling a disciplined fighting force. But the alternative would be to spend the money sending the British Army out to defend Egypt. No one wanted to commit Britain to the defense of the Sudan, yet they all wanted the Mahdi kept out of Egypt. Most of all, the government needed to appear to be doing something about the situation in the Sudan: to remain idle would be to ignore public opinion to such a degree that a reaction in the House of Commons might well bring Gladstone's government down. In order to accomplish these paradoxical goals Lord Granville came up with what seemed to be a workable solution. A senior British officer of sufficient prestige and well acquainted with northern Africa would be sent out to Khartoum. Though he would have no command authority, and carry no warrant from the government to do more than "report" on the situation there, it might well be possible for this officer to find a way to extricate the Egyptian garrison from Khartoum. It was even conceivable that once the Mahdi knew of the presence of the Crown's representative in the city, he would spare it, bypass it, or even bring his rebellion to a halt rather than risk rousing the ire of the British Empire.

As a solution to the problem it was elegant in its simplicity—and appalling in its stupidity. The Mahdi was not, as Granville and Hartington, and to a lesser extent Gladstone, seemed to believe, some desert vagabond with a rabble in trail who happened to get lucky against William Hicks' pathetic column of Egyptians. It completely escaped their grasp that what had occurred in the Sudan was a genuinely popular uprising, given focus and direction by the Mahdi's religious fervor, but one springing from decades of bitterness. It also fatally misunderstood the Mahdi, for despite the fact that he was ever more readily succumbing to the physical pleasures that his succession of victories had brought, as well as becoming more and more enamored of his seeming omnipotence and self-proclaimed semi-divinity, he still in his heart of hearts believed that he was chosen by Allah to lead this cleansing tide of *jihad* against the corruption that had perverted Islam. The Mahdi would not be turned aside by hollow threats or empty bluster—he was a man with a divine mission that would not be deflected one whit.

So, in their blind miscalculation, Granville and Hartington set about finding an officer who could carry out their impossible mission. It was a bitterly ironic twist that the officer they found—and as fate would have it, they did not have to look very far, for even as they conferred he was in London—was the one man in the whole of the Empire with sufficient courage, skill, and charisma who could have actually carried off their fantastical scheme. As it was, he would come closer to doing so than anyone could possibly have imagined. His name was Gordon.

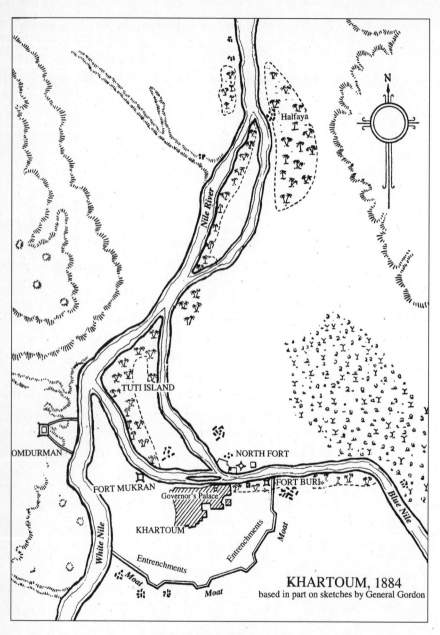

KHARTOUM, 1884
based in part on sketches by General Gordon

KHARTOUM IN 1884

CHAPTER 5

GORDON

 In the last half of the 19th century, a time when military eccentrics of the type that a later generation would describe as "mavericks" abounded, there were few as intriguing, fascinating, exasperating, or ultimately enigmatic as Major-General Charles George Gordon. Colorful is an inadequate adjective in describing this most unusual soldier: he could in turns be charming, imperious, baffling, flamboyant, tender, ruthless, impulsive, or calculating. He was, in short, the embodiment of a generation's ideal of the perfect British officer, the "very model of a modern Major-General." Prime Minister William Gladstone, rising in Parliament, would declare of him, "He is no common man. It is no exaggeration, in speaking of General Gordon, to say that he is a hero; it is no exaggeration to say that he is a Christian, and that in his dealings with Oriental peoples he has a genius—that he has a faculty of influence and command, brought about by moral means; for no man in this House hates the unnecessary resort to blood more than General Gordon; he has that faculty which produces effects among those wild Eastern races almost unintelligible to us Westerns."

 Gladstone's speech touched on two facets of Gordon's character that shone above all others: his remarkable talent as a leader of men, and his unswerving faith in his God. His courage was unquestionable; he would place himself at the head of his troops, marching to the sound of the guns, armed with nothing more than a walking stick and his own sense of invulnerability. When he fought his last battle, he is said to have dismissed a horde of his foes with a scornful wave of his hand, as if his sheer disdain would turn them aside. His religious convictions were unshakeable. He believed in a merciful, loving God and embraced the doctrines of the English evangelical church with the enthusiasm of a true disciple, and put them into practice decades before they became popular. In particular he gave financial support to charities, taking a particular interest in establishing schools for working-class children. He was also one of the earliest advocates of transition to native rule in the colonies of the British Empire. Together, these traits—at once strengths and flaws—would conspire to bring Gordon to his greatest triumphs, and ultimately spell his doom.

The path of Charles George Gordon's life that would bring him to Khartoum, and finally end there, began on 28 January 1833, at, appropriately enough, Woolwich Arsenal, where his father, General H.W. Gordon, Royal Artillery, was a staff officer. Charles was the fourth son in a family of eleven children, five boys and six girls; his education began at Taunton School, and continued at the Royal Military Academy, Woolwich, where he enrolled as a cadet in 1848. He had hoped to follow his father into the Royal Artillery, however disciplinary problems attributed to his fiery temper caused him to be put back on his course of study, and instead he graduated in 1852, to be commissioned on June 23 of that year as a second lieutenant in the Corps of Royal Engineers.

Rather than a setback, this development was to young Gordon's advantage: the Royal Engineers regarded themselves as the professional elite of the British army, and rightly so. They were posted all over the Empire, responsible for building fortifications, erecting bridges, constructing railways, quays for ships, designing buildings, and undertaking siege work. This proved to be an ideal environment for Gordon, who at Woolwich had shown himself to be hot-tempered, for the circumstances in which engineer officers were expected to work demanded that they be brave and impetuous.

Gordon followed his graduation from Woolwich with a course of instruction at the Royal Engineers Establishment, Chatham, and was promoted to lieutenant in 1854. That autumn he was given the task of assisting in the construction of the defenses of Milford Haven, a port on the English Channel, but he had hardly gotten his hands dirty before the Crimean War intervened and he was ordered on active service, arriving at Balaklava on January 1, 1855.

Gordon first saw action at the siege of Sebastopol when he was attached to one of the British columns which assaulted the main Russian position on June 18, and was present when the city was finally captured on September 8. He was immediately put in charge of the task of demolishing the Russian dockyard there, but when Russia and Great Britain were able to come to terms on a peace treaty a few months later, Gordon was ordered to join the international commission appointed to survey and set up the new boundary between Russia and Turkey in Bessarabia (now part of modern Rumania). He then went on to similar duties in the Caucasus and Asia Minor. It was an experience that would bear strange fruit many years later, for in the months he spent in northeastern Turkey, among the Armenian people, he had his first encounter with Middle Eastern culture, and was introduced to the doctrines and teachings of Islam.

It wasn't until the end of 1858 that Gordon was able to finally return to England, and his stay there was to be relatively brief. Immediately upon his arrival home he was promoted to the rank of captain and appointed an instructor at the Royal Engineers Establishment at Chatham in April 1859, but when war was declared on China in June 1860, Gordon was ordered to the Far East. He arrived at Tientsin in September, in time to join the column that would occupy Peking, and he would remain with the British occupation force in northern China until April 1862. That month the Taiping Rebellion broke out, and British troops, under the command of General Staveley, were ordered south to Shanghai to protect the European enclave there. Though virtually unknown in England at the time, Gordon's actions over the next two years would make his name a household word and a hero to the general population. It would also set him irrevocably on the road to Khartoum.

By the time he arrived in China, the shape and scope of Gordon's character was fully formed. Like most literate Victorians, Gordon was an inveterate writer and kept a diary in which he made almost daily entries, on some occasions multiple entries in the same day. These diaries allow succeeding generations a window into Gordon's heart, soul, and mind that would be denied them in their study of the Mahdi. Curiously, though not unexpectedly, there was much in common between Gordon and the Sudanese holy warrior. Both were equally

fearless, and each was a proven leader of men, possessing great charisma and powers of persuasion. Each man was highly intelligent, the
Mahdi being widely respected within a religious tradition long noted
for the quality of its scholarship. While his enforcement of Islamic law
may have seemed harsh to outsiders raised with Christian traditions,
the Mahdi's rule within his realm was noted for its even-handed, if
severe, impartiality, and the thoroughness with which it had been
thought out and promulgated. Although he made no pretensions to
scholastic accomplishments or academic achievements, Gordon was as
literate as Muhammed Ahmed, and his diary would one day prove
him to be a shrewd and insightful observer of humanity. And finally,
both were deeply and genuinely religious, each feeling called by and
bound to his God to accomplish some great mission on earth. In quiet,
introspective moments they even used similar terms to describe their
view of how their Divinities were employing them.

What the two men did not share was fanaticism in their sense of
mission. Unlike the Mahdi, Gordon never fell prey to messianic visions
of glory, and never felt called to cleanse the Sudan of what he regarded as pernicious influences. His suppression of the slave trade was an
act of common humanity, not a divine calling, while his determination
to stand at Khartoum was taken to avoid a wholesale slaughter, not to
defy and destroy some foresworn enemy or to overthrow a doctrine he
held to be false.

On the other hand, by the time Muhammed Ahmed's army had
invested Khartoum, Ahmed had imbued himself with the belief that he
was an Islamic messiah, destined to cleanse not only the Sudan of the
impurities brought to it by the Egyptians, the Turks, and the Christian
infidels, but to purge all of Islam from Western influences and restore
the lost piety of the true faith. How he distorted and twisted the *jihad*
to be his means of accomplishing his "mission" was an illustration of
how deeply his newfound power had corrupted him. Gordon's stand
at Khartoum was intended to be an act of mercy; the *jihad* proclaimed
by the Mahdi was not one that the Prophet Mohammed would have
recognized, nor was it one to which the Allah of the Koran would have
given His blessing.

This most fundamental of differences would manifest itself in a
myriad of ways in the months to come as Gordon and the Mahdi

fought their duel of wills before the city on the Nile. Ultimately Gordon's would prove to be the greater, though he would in the end be betrayed, not by his faith, but by his worldly resources—or lack of them. As for the Mahdi, it was becoming evident even as the siege of Khartoum began that his head was already turned by the power he wielded, and his piety overshadowed by worldly temptations.

Above everything else, Gordon was a genuinely religious man, devout in his belief in God and steadfast in his devotion to what he understood were fundamental Christian principles. His whole character sprang from that central core of belief: his devotion to duty, his sense of honor, and even his ability to recognize the potential for greatness in a mortal foe, as he would do with the Mahdi. At the center of that faith was his belief in his own insignificance and unworthiness in comparison to God: as an individual, he was nothing unless animated by Divine will, and whatever merit his lifework might one day be seen to possess would be in spite of his good intentions rather than because of them. As he put the case himself when writing of his victories in China, "I do nothing of this—I am a chisel which cuts the wood, the Carpenter directs it. If I lose my edge, He must sharpen me; if He puts me aside and takes another, it is His own good will. None are indispensable to Him." He developed this theme further when he embarked on his first mission to Khartoum: "I have an enormous province to look after, but it is a great blessing to me to know that God has undertaken the administration of it, and it is His work, and not mine. If I fail, it is His will; if I succeed, it is His work. Certainly, He has given me the joy of not regarding the honours of this world, and to value my union with Him above all things. May I be humbled to the dust and fail, so that He may glorify Himself. The greatness of my position only depresses me, and I cannot help wishing that the time had come when He will lay me aside and use some other worm to do His work."

It is also worth noting that there was an aspect to this faith that would have considerable influence on his decisions when he found himself besieged at Khartoum by the Mahdi's forces. The confidence he gained by his determination to carry out what he perceived to be God's will imbued him with a self-denying sense of duty, which in turn created an aura of fearlessness. If submission to the divine will would assure his own eternal happiness, then it followed that someone so faithful should have no fear of either consequences or death, particularly the latter, as a death in the line of duty would mean immediate transference to his eternal reward. To Gordon, doubt—about his mission, about the legitimacy of his Divine calling, about his interpretation of God's will—would be little short of blasphemous. Personal bravery, then, even to the point of foolhardiness, was the inevitable by-product of his faith. He would acknowledge this himself, in a phrase in one of his letters, where he says, "I am become what people call a great fatalist, viz., I trust God will pull me through every difficulty." Put another way, conduct that in other men would have been seen as culpable recklessness was in Gordon simply his faith put into action. Today it is a way of thinking, a moral compass, that is so rare as to be utterly remarkable, yet in Gordon's day his faith was notable only for how literally he carried it out, not that he possessed it.

Gordon's courage cannot be dismissed as merely exaggerated religious mysticism, however, for it proved to be highly contagious among those with whom he came into contact. In China, his example of dash and indifference to odds would inspire his soldiers with a fiery courage of their own, while at the same time spread a demoralizing influence among his enemies' forces such that they would be halfway toward collapse before they were even attacked. Nor was Gordon slow to exploit this advantage. Combining an innate tactical and strategic shrewdness with a keen appreciation of human frailty, he learned to strike quick and hard, and even whenever possible, to attempt to anticipate and thwart an enemy's plans, knowing that the weakened state of his opponents' morale would make their response slow and hesitant. His confidence in the inevitability of his victories assisted in making them possible.

Also characteristic of Gordon was his self-reliance. At first this may seem at odds with the belief of a man who felt that he was fully submissive to God's will, but it is in no way contradictory: having once decided on a course of action, no power on earth was able to deflect him from it, for hand-in-hand with his sense of divine purpose was the notion that if God chose him for a particular task, it was meant to be his alone to accomplish. Consequently he could not and would not rely on anyone else in order to achieve his purpose. Consistent with his self-reliance based on his perception of himself being the instrument of God's will was Gordon's sense of also being the instrument of God's justice—as opposed to being an instrument of judgment. That he appreciated the distinction and saw that his concept of God as a loving God required that mercy be exercised as well as chastisement was never clearer than the attitude he took toward the slave traders in the Sudan. "It is much for me to do to keep myself from cruel illegal acts towards the slave-dealers," he wrote, "yet I think I must not forget that God suffers it, and that one must keep to the law. I have done the best I can, and He is Governor-General."

Gordon was likewise sympathetic to those who suffered through no fault of their own, particularly those who were the victims of despotism and the capricious rule of tyrants. "Residence in these Oriental lands tends, after a time, to blunt one's susceptibilities of right and justice, and, therefore, the necessity for men to return at certain periods to their own countries to reimbibe the notions of the same. The varnish of civilized life is very thin, and only superficial. . . . Man does not know what he is capable of in circumstances of this sort; unless he has the lode star, he has no guide, no councillor in his walk." An essential element of his sympathetic nature was his capacity to admit to just how thin that varnish of civilized life truly was, or as a friend of some thirty years put it in a letter to the Times of London on February 20, 1884, "What in his mental constitution had struck me most was the manner—some people might even think the brutal manner—in which he sees through and cracks the crust of cant with which the world in general likes to envelop its doings."

Gordon was equally realistic about war. At one point he wrote, "People have little idea how little glorious war is; it is organized murder, pillage and cruelty, and it is seldom that the weight falls on the fighting men—it is on the women, children, and old people...." At the same time, he was an acknowledged master of battle. His stint in the Crimea had seen him primarily engaged in the tasks of an officer of engineers—building fortifications, constructing siege works, demolishing captured enemy positions—so it wasn't until he was sent to China in 1860 that he actually led troops in action. His opportunity came when the long-smoldering Taiping revolt flared into blazing insurrection in 1860.

The revolt, which in several notable ways would bear an uncanny resemblance to the Mahdi's uprising twenty years later, had begun in 1850 in China's Kwangsi province. Led by a sort of mystic, at once both political and religious, named Hung Sin Tsuan, the rebels swelled their ranks by playing on the lower class's feelings of oppression and exploitation by the Chinese nobility. Imperial troops sent to suppress the revolt were repeatedly defeated, and the revolt spread north through the provinces of Hunan and Hupeh, and down the valley of the Yangtze-kiang as far Nanking, which fell to the rebels in 1853. It was in Nanking that Hung assumed the title of Tien Wang, or Heavenly King, and before long his troops were conducting sporadic raids into neighboring territories. For the next five years a sort of semi-permanent state of war existed between the Imperial government of China and Tien's loyal followers, who styled themselves "Taipings," from "Taiping tien-quo"—the "Heavenly Kingdom of Great Peace," the name the insurgents gave to their movement.

It was a state of affairs that attracted little attention from the European powers then attempting to carve out various spheres of influence in China, at least until the Taipings began to advance eastward in 1858 to threaten the city of Shanghai, which had a large number of Europeans living there. A hastily raised force of Europeans and Filipinos was organized to defend the city, and it took up positions outside of Shanghai to block the Taiping advance. Placed under the command of an American, Frederick Townsend Ward, the motley force defended Shanghai for about two years, but by the time General Staveley's column arrived, the situation had become critical. Staveley decided to systematically clear the region in a thirty-mile radius around Shanghai. It was during this operation that Ward was killed, and his successor quarreled so violently with the Chinese authorities that Li Hung Chang, the governor of the Kiang-su province, requested that General Staveley appoint a British officer to take command of the ragtag contingent. Staveley selected Gordon, who had been attached to his staff as engineer officer, and who had been made a brevet-major in December 1862 for his previous services. It proved to be an inspired choice.

In March 1863 Gordon named his new command "The Ever Victorious Army," something of an exaggeration in light of its rather spotty history, and marched on Chansu, a town some forty miles northwest of Shanghai, which had been surrounded and cut off by the rebels. Breaking though the Taiping lines, he relieved the little garrison there, and won the confidence of his troops in the process. After reorganizing his small army, Gordon attacked Quinsan, another town near Shanghai, which he quickly took, though at the cost of heavy casualties. His troops' confidence was unshaken, however, and the capture of Quinsan was the beginning of a procession of conquest, for their reputation for steadiness under fire in front of Quinsan soon spread throughout the Taiping forces, which soon came to rightly fear the Ever Victorious Army.

The army soon had reason to fear Gordon as well, for as he marched through the country, driving the rebels out of one town after another, he imposed an iron discipline on his men. And when they challenged his discipline, he demonstrated a ruthlessness that cowed the fiercest among them. In an episode that showed for all to see the steel in Gordon's character, he decreed that the troops of the Ever Victorious Army would not be permitted to loot captured cities, a "privilege" that was granted the Imperial Chinese forces. Murmurings of mutiny sprang up almost immediately—some of the men openly rebelled against Gordon. He retaliated by having one of the mutineers brought before him and promptly shot the man dead. He then announced that he would shoot one of the mutineers an hour until the mutiny was over. Less than sixty minutes later the mutiny had ended.

The Ever Victorious Army's march of conquest continued until it reached the great city of Suchow. There it was joined by a column of Imperial Chinese soldiers, and the city was stormed on November 29, striking a crippling blow at Tien Wang's power. It was there that an incident occurred immediately after the city's fall which throws another intriguing light on Gordon, his concepts of morality and authority, and his capacity for compromising on smaller ethical issues without surrendering his honor or the integrity of his cause. When the city had been taken, a large number of rebel leaders, whose safety had been guaranteed by Gordon if they surrendered, were beheaded on the orders of Li Hung Chang. While not a harsh or unusual action according to Chinese standards of conduct, it was so contrary to Gordon's sense of honor that he withdrew his soldiers from Suchow and refused to take any further part in operations until February 1864. Eventually he came to the conclusion that ending the rebellion was of greater importance than his quarrel with Chinese sensibilities, and once more he began cooperating with Li; by mutual agreement no mention of the executions in Suchow was ever made. Gordon did get in the last word, though, after a fashion: he refused the decorations and rewards offered him by the Chinese emperor for the capture of Suchow.

In May 1864 the Ever Victorious Army advanced on Chanchufu, the Taipings' main position. When it fell at the end of the month, Gordon brought the army back to Quinsan and there disbanded it. A few weeks later Tien Wang committed suicide, the capture of Nanking by Imperial troops came shortly afterward, and the Taiping revolt had come to an end. It was due in no small part to the exploits of The Ever Victorious Army, which drew its inspiration and dash from Gordon. The Emperor was finally able to persuade him to accept both promotion and reward, appointing him Titu, the Chinese equivalent of a major-general, although Gordon did refuse the large sum of money that was offered to him.

His efforts did not go unnoticed by the British either: Gordon was promoted Lieutenant-Colonel of Engineers and made a Companion of the Bath. Now styled Sir Charles, he was often known behind his back by the affectionately familiar "Chinese" Gordon. Accompanying his promotion was an appointment to Gravesend as superintendent of the construction of forts defending the mouth of the Thames.

Physically, Gordon was not impressive, or at least should not have been so. Short of stature, he stood not more than five feet six inches tall, and he had a lithe, wiry build. His eyes were a very clear, calm gray, and his rather squared off jaw and brow were framed by a shock of reddish hair and a set of large sideburns, while he sported the typical "Sandhurst" moustache so popular among British officers of his day. What set Gordon apart was his presence, his manner of carrying himself that bespoke of great ability and self-confidence, and which allowed him to carry his authority easily and openly.

There was more occupying Gordon's time at Gravesend than just his construction work on the Thames forts. Just after his return, he received word that his father was dying. He hurried to Woolwich to be at his bedside and stayed with him until the elder Gordon died. Hard on the heels of his father's passing came news of the death of one of his brothers. Together, the two incidents had a deep and profound effect on Gordon's life. Heretofore he had paid lip service to his Christian faith, but when he returned to Gravesend, he resolved to put aside what he called "superficial religion" and put the faith he professed into action. Gordon's duties required his presence from 8:00 in the morning until 2:00 in the afternoon, after which he devoted himself to social work. If it were not so well documented his record would be difficult to believe. His house served at various times as a school, a hospital, an almshouse, and a church, according to need. He visited the sick and dying, gave money to the poor, and taught the street children in the local Ragged school. Calling them his "kings," the street boys were his special objects of attention and concern. He clothed them, fed them, nursed them when they were ill, and found them jobs, often writing letters of recommendation to ship owners and captains for one of his young men who was seeking a berth as a cabin boy aboard a merchant ship. He was the founder and one of the first benefactors of the Gravesend and Milton Mendicant Society, whose purpose was to aid itinerant workers who found themselves in dire straits.

For all of his genuine piety, though, Gordon never joined any church. He was equally comfortable in the company of a Church of England vicar, a Baptist pastor, a Presbyterian chaplain, a Methodist minister, or a Roman Catholic priest. He attended all of their churches at one time or another, and once remarked that, in his view, "the church is like the British Army, one army but many regiments." Gordon's devotion to social work in Gravesend became so complete that he excluded all other social contact, shunning the busy social life normally enjoyed by the commander of the Engineers in Gravesend. To him, though, it was no hardship for he fully believed that social work was his God-given duty.

It shouldn't be implied that he was a man without vices: there is still some considerable debate on just how heavily he drank—or didn't. Some accounts claim that he only drank rarely, while others have him consuming huge amounts of brandy. Certainly he had no taste for the wining, dining, and socializing that was characteristic of garrison life in so much of the British Army in the middle of the 19th century. He was also given over to severe, inexplicable bouts of melancholy, which sometimes lasted for days.

In the summer of 1872 Gordon was sent to inspect the British military cemeteries in the Crimea, and it was as he was passing through Constantinople on his return that he took the first steps down the road that would bring him to Khartoum to face the Mahdi. At a chance meeting with Nubar Pasha, then the prime minister of Egypt, Gordon was asked if would consider serving under the Khedive. While nothing was settled at the time, the following year he received a definite offer from the khedive to become governor of the Sudan. Once Her Majesty's government had given its consent to the appointment, he accepted, and made his way to Egypt early in 1874.

To fully understand the importance of Gordon's appointment by the Khedive, it is necessary to return again to Africa. By the beginning of the 1870s, when Egypt occupied most of the Sudan, the slave trade was still flourishing in the south of the country, in the region called Equatoria, despite the concerted efforts of the European nations to bring it to a halt. Particularly troublesome were the regions of the White Nile and Bahr-el-Ghazal. Captains John Speke and James Grant, who had come through Uganda and down the White Nile in 1863, as well as Sir Samuel Baker, who made the journey up the river as far as Albert Nyanza, returned to Europe with chilling tales of misery, disease, and death suffered by the victims of the slave hunters. Europeans, who had been swept by a fever of abolitionist sentiment in the middle of the century, were outraged, particularly the British, and in 1869 Khedive Ismail, bowing to both French and British pressure, sent a military expedition up the White Nile, with its objective the elimination of the slave trade in the Sudan.

Command of the expedition was given to Sir Samuel Baker, who encountered seemingly endless difficulties, and when his four-year term of service was up he had little to show for it, apart from the establishment of a handful of mud forts along the Nile. Exhausted and dispirited, Baker returned to Britain, never to set foot in Africa again. Gordon was to be Baker's successor, and it was hoped that he would be more successful. Gordon, for his part, was instructed to extend the line of forts begun by Baker as far south as Buganda, annex Buganda itself, and deploy a handful of specially designed gunboats on Lake Albert and Lake Victoria. If he also found the time to suppress the slave trade while doing all this, so much the better.

It was a post for which Gordon was ideally suited: incorruptible and indefatigable, he immediately immersed himself in his task. Arriving in Cairo on February 7, 1874, he spent two weeks assembling his staff—a mixed bag of Egyptians, Turks, and Britons, all of whom were chosen solely for their abilities rather than, as was typical of the time, their social skills and standing. One of Gordon's advisers was even a notorious slaver, Abu Soud. Gordon explained his presence by declaring that Soud would bring an invaluable knowledge of how and where the slave hunters operated, as a sort of "poacher-turned-game-keeper."

Leaving Cairo, Gordon set out for Khartoum, traveling down the Red Sea to the port of Suakin, then crossing over the Nubian Desert to the Nile, where he boarded a steamer at Berber, which then brought him to the Sudanese capital. It would be the route that he always regarded as the best way to reach Khartoum from Cairo, an observation that others would later ignore to their cost and his. After spending nine days in Khartoum, where he was received at a state dinner by the Governor-General of the Sudan, Ismail Pasha Ayoub, he boarded another steamer, which took him up the White Nile to Gondokoro, his new capital, where he arrived twenty-four days later.

Gordon would remain in Equatoria for two and a half years, not returning to Cairo until October 1876. It was thirty months of endless labor, with mixed results. He immediately set about restoring discipline among the Egyptian garrisons, many of which, feeling forgotten or abandoned by Cairo, had ceased to resemble military units. The line of forts and garrisons along the White Nile was extended, while the river and Lake Albert were extensively charted by Gordon and his staff. At the same time, displaying the same sort of humanity that had characterized his time at Gravesend, he devoted considerable energy to improving the conditions of the people in Equatoria, from introducing medicines to digging new wells to trying to establish a rudimentary education system.

Most surprising of all was his progress in suppressing the slave trade. Drawing on Abu Soud's knowledge of slaver ways and using his reorganized and re-equipped troops to patrol and raid the routes and locales frequented by the slavers, Gordon was able to put a severe crimp on the trade, although he was hampered to a large degree by the fact that Khartoum and the whole of the northern Sudan was under the rule of Ismail Pasha Ayoub, who had been in collusion with the slave traders and was profiting handsomely from it. As a consequence he offered little cooperation or support for Gordon's efforts, which eventually fell short of the goals he had envisioned.

It was a bitter blow, for a man as moralistic and religious as Gordon could not help but perceive bringing an end to the slave trade as something little short of a divine mission. Finally Gordon decided that he was wasting his time and energy, when on one hand Khedive Ismail was urging him to suppress the slave trade, while on the other he was taking no action to prevent Ayoub from exploiting it for his own personal gain.

In October 1876 Gordon arrived in Cairo on leave, and promptly informed Ismail that he would not be returning to Equatoria. The Khedive did not believe that Gordon was finished in Africa, but by the time Gordon reached London he had prepared a telegram to the British Consul-general in Cairo, asking him to inform the Khedive that on no terms would he be going back to Egypt. Ismail Pasha responded by saying that Gordon had promised to return, and that he was expected to keep his word. It was a shrewd move by Ismail, who knew his man, for Gordon took the keeping of a promise as a sacred duty; consequently he decided to return as far as Cairo, but he was quite determined that, unless Ismail appointed him Governor-General of the whole of the Sudan, he would go no further. Ismail at first demurred, but before long he acceded to Gordon's terms—Gordon was too good an administrator, a breed of person that the Khedive's government was sorely lacking.

Gordon's first challenge was to do what he could to redeem the sorry state of the political relationship between Egypt and Abyssinia, which revolved around a disputed territory in the Sudan. Both the Khedive and King John of Abyssinia claimed the district of Bogos, lying not far inland from Massawa, for their respective dominions, and the squabbling broke out into a full scale war in 1875. An Egyptian expedition that marched against Abyssinia was routed by King John near Gundet—it was the beginning of a pattern that Egyptian armies would follow for the next decade—and a second, larger expedition under Prince Hassan, Khedive Ismail's son, met a similar fate the following year at Gura. The Egyptians licked their wounds until March 1877, when Gordon made his way to Massawa to negotiate a settlement with King John. The Abyssinian monarch did not immediately reply, having felt after defeating two Egyptian field forces that he had little to fear on his northern frontier, and in fact he had gone south to make war on Menelek, king of Shoa. Gordon, sensing that the Abyssinian question could be put off for a few months, proceeded to Khartoum.

Once there he began restoring discipline among his native troops, ceaselessly drilling and training them, often working them to exhaustion. He would frequently set out from Khartoum on inspections, riding a camel and accompanied by an escort. The escort soon learned that Gordon was not content with the sedate walk to which they were accustomed, and which would often take up to twelve hours to reach their destination. He would get his camel up to a full gallop and would leave his escort behind, arriving some three hours after he set out. On his arrival he would then set about taking to task any poor soul found doing his job improperly; frequently he would sack them on the spot. He took the slavery issue head-on, by proposing a regulation making the registration of slaves compulsory, a move that would have ruined the slavers by placing them under government control, but his proposals were not approved by the Cairo government, for much the same reasons that Ismail Pasha Ayoub had thwarted Gordon just a few years earlier.

At the same time, an insurrection had broken out in Darfur, which required Gordon to take what troops he could spare from the Khartoum garrison to relieve the Egyptian forces trapped in the rebellious province. It wasn't long before he discovered two disturbing facts: the garrisons he was attempting to relieve were actually larger than the force with which he was marching, and second, that the rebel forces far outnumbered his little relieving army. Wisely choosing to rely on diplomacy rather than arms, he brazenly rode into the enemy camp to discuss the situation. Probably no one but Gordon would have attempted such a bold move, but given his conviction that he was an instrument of God's will, it was virtually inevitable for him. Gordon's curious mixture of quiet charm and martial flamboyance made for a powerful diplomatic presence. It would prove to be a shrewd move, as a large number of the insurgents joined his small army, while the rest retreated into the mountains to the south.

With the relief of the threatened garrisons accomplished, Gordon returned to the provinces of Berber and Dongola, to once again confront King John across the Abyssinian frontier. But once again there was to be no settlement of their differences, and Gordon returned to Khartoum in January 1878. A week later he was on the move again, returning to Cairo at the Khedive's summons, in order to assist a commission of inquiry into the country's finances and restore some semblance of order to Egypt's treasury after a decade of wastrel spending by Ismail, who seemed to regard the national treasury as his own personal pocket money. The Khedive at once appointed him president of the commission, with the understanding that the various Europeans in Cairo who were holding bonds on Ismail's debts would not be members of the commission. Gordon accepted the position on these terms, for he saw, as did Ismail, that such men would be less interested in restoring Egypt to solvency than merely getting their money out. Admittedly, such concern on the part of Ismail for Egypt's finances had a certain element of the absurd about it, since he was responsible for the debacle in the first place, but he did have the measure of those who were arrayed against him. The consuls-general of the various powers quickly objected to the make-up of the investigatory commission and appointed their own representatives to it instead. Ismail was powerless to prevent this, and the result was that he and all of his property were turned over to his creditors; the Sultan in Constantinople deposed him as Khedive less than a year later, putting Ismail's son Tewfik in his place.

One of the consequences of this episode would lead directly to the confrontation between Gordon and the Mahdi at Khartoum five years later. In order to satisfy Ismail's debt, his creditors liquidated his shares in the Suez Canal Company, which were bought by the British government, which in turn made Great Britain the company's largest shareholder. It was a sensible move from a strategic standpoint, as the need to protect the canal and the Red Sea route to India was of paramount importance to the Empire. However, when the Mahdi's revolt spread up the Nile to Khartoum in 1883, the debate over how genuine a threat he posed to the Suez Canal would paralyze Prime Minister

Gladstone's cabinet for several critical weeks before a decision to relieve Khartoum was finally reached.

After the curious interlude of the financial commission had come to a close, Gordon headed south once more, this time to the province of Harrar, south of Abyssinia. It had been poorly administered by Raouf Pasha, an appointee and crony of Ismail Pasha Ayoub, Gordon's predecessor. Raouf was dismissed out of hand and in his place Gordon named an Italian, Romolo Gessi, who then swept through the province like a reforming whirlwind. His story long lost and neglected, Gessi was one of colonial Africa's brightest lights. He shared Gordon's passion for crushing the slave trade, and in 1879 fought a major battle with the slavers and their retinues in the Bahr-el-Ghazal district, arresting and eventually executing their leader, Suleiman, the son of Zobeir, the greatest slaver of all. Coupled with Gordon's successes in Darfur, Gessi's triumph crippled the slavers and put an end to the trade, at least for the moment.

Shortly afterward, Gordon was called back to Cairo for an audience with the new Khedive, Tewfik, who requested of Gordon that he attempt to reopen negotiations with King John of Abyssinia and bring an end to the border conflict that had broken out again. While Gordon was able to secure an interview with the Abyssinian monarch and found him a fascinating man, he was unable to make any progress toward a peace treaty between Egypt and Abyssinia, as the king sought considerable concessions from Egypt, while the Khedive's instructions were clear that Gordon should concede nothing of worth. The affair ended with Gordon returning to Cairo to announce his resignation as Governor-General of the Sudan. He was physically and emotionally exhausted by nearly three years of non-stop work, during which he had ridden no fewer than 8,500 miles to and fro across the Sudan, earning himself another nickname, "The Camel Rider."

He returned to England where he quietly awaited his next assignment. He wrote articles and tracts for the Anti-Slavery Society, and consented to be interviewed by anyone seeking knowledge of the Sudan, but otherwise chose to avoid public attention. In March 1880 Gordon visited Brussels at the invitation of the Belgian monarch, King Leopold, who suggested that at some future date he take charge of the Congo Free State. Gordon said that he would consider the offer, and

while he was pondering it, a summons arrived for him in the form of
a telegram from the government of South Africa's Cape Colony, offering him the position of commandant of the Cape's local forces.
Gordon loved having the command of troops, but he declined the
appointment, as he felt that it was too fraught with political pitfalls.
The Marquess of Ripon, who had been named Viceroy of India in
May, asked Gordon to serve as his private secretary. This post lasted
for all of three days, for Gordon discovered that Lord Ripon had the
disconcerting habit of claiming to have read his official correspondence, when, in fact, he had not done so, and expected Gordon to
cover his ignorance for him. Ripon refused to accept his resignation,
and so Gordon accompanied him to India, but once there was able to
make his resignation stick.

Hardly had he done so when a telegram arrived from Sir Robert
Hart, Inspector-General of customs in China, inviting him to go to
Peking to help arbitrate a touchy situation between China and Russia.
He set out at once for Tientsin, where in July he was met by his old
colleague Li Hung Chang, and learned that the situation had deterio-
rated to the point where the risk of war with Russia was very real.
Gordon then rushed to Peking where he used all of his charm, wit, and
powers of persuasion and intimidation—which were considerable—to
influence the various representatives from Russia, China, and Great
Britain to favor a peaceful settlement. War was avoided, and Gordon
was able to return to England, where in April 1881 he exchanged positions with another officer of the Engineers who had been ordered to
Mauritius as Commanding Royal Engineer, but who for family reasons was unable to accept the appointment.

He remained in Mauritius until March of the following year,
when he was promoted to the rank of major-general, and was once
more contacted by the government of the Cape Colony. This time he
was asked to go to the Cape to consult with the government as regards
settling disputes with the native population of Basutoland. The
telegram was explicit in stating the gravity of the situation and the
importance of having someone of proved ability, firmness, and energy
to step in to resolve it. Gordon sailed at once for the Cape, where in a
meeting with senior government officials he was asked to not go to
Basutoland for political reasons, but to take the appointment of com-

mandant of the colonial forces at King Williams Town instead. Not certain as to why the government's position had changed so dramatically, he consented, and spent the next few months reorganizing the colonial forces in much the same way as he had his Egyptian troops in the Sudan. When Gordon was later requested to go to Basutoland to try to arrange a settlement with the chief Masupha, one of the most powerful of the Basuto leaders, he began to see the design behind the earlier political maneuverings: J.W. Sauer, a member of the Cape government, was conspiring with Lerethodi, another Basuto chief, to depose Masupha. Gordon was appalled. Not only did this place him in a position of grave danger, but it appeared like an act of treachery. He promptly advised Masupha not to have any further dealings with the Cape government until Lerethodi's forces were withdrawn and disbanded, and he further resigned his appointment. He considered that all the problems that the Cape Colony had been having with the Basuto people was due to poor and avaricious administration by the colonial government, a view that was vindicated a few years later when Basutoland was separated from Cape Colony and placed directly under the Imperial government.

Returning in disgust to England, and having no official position, Gordon chose to distance himself entirely from any form of government service, at least for a while, and decided to visit Palestine, where he remained for a year, spending his days immersed in the study of Biblical history and the antiquities of Jerusalem. In late 1883, King Leopold of Belgium reminded him of his earlier promise to take charge of the Congo Free State, and Gordon accepted the mission, returning to London to make the necessary preparations. But within a few days of his arrival the British government requested that he instead return immediately to the Sudan.

One of the consequences of Col. Arabi's abortive revolt in 1881 was a paralysis of the Egyptian government, just at the moment when the Mahdi's army began to pose a serious threat, not only to Egypt's suzerainity over the Sudan, but to southern Egypt itself. There was also a collective fear among the Egyptian, British, and French governments that the peasantry of Egypt, still quietly seething after the Arabi fiasco, might prove sympathetic to the message being proclaimed by the Mahdi a thousand miles to the south. This mysterious new figure, the Mahdi, preached an end to the institutionalized inferiority and exploitation of Moslems by Christian interlopers, and a purification of Islam, which he said had been maligned and demeaned by "Turk" and Christian influences alike.

In London, Prime Minister Gladstone was gravely worried. To him the Arabi revolt had seemed pregnant with the possibility of open warfare between Britain and France. The French had long coveted control of Egypt, had done so since the days of Napoleon Bonaparte, and had maintained an enduring tradition of participation—many Egyptians would have said "interference"—in Egypt's affairs. It had been French engineering expertise and French capital that had built the Suez Canal, and it now galled France to see Britain the master of it. To Gladstone, the chaos of Arabi's revolt seemed to offer the perfect pretext for France to seize Egypt for herself.

But for once Gladstone's political acumen failed him, for the French leadership, in a rare display of perception that would elude French politics for the next century and a quarter, understood that a threat to any European power in Egypt was a threat to all of them, and should the Egyptians force the British to leave their country, the French would soon follow. So while the British forces in Egypt crushed Colonel Arabi's rebellion without French assistance, they also did so without French hindrance.

Meanwhile, as British troops entered Cairo in September 1882, the situation in the Sudan was growing more serious every day. Gladstone was pressed by experts and authorities from all sides, most particularly by the British Consul-General in Cairo, Sir Evelyn Baring, probably the most knowledgeable man of Anglo-Egyptian affairs in either country, who warned that, having pacified Egypt, it was imperative to suppress the Mahdi's revolt in the Sudan at once. Had Gladstone listened, and then acted promptly, the rebellion could almost certainly have been crushed before it spread. Gladstone, however, his head and heart filled with anathema toward imperialism, could only see such action as another form of conquest. He wanted no part of further annexations or expansion. It was to be Great Britain's policy that the Sudan was Egypt's province, therefore if action was to be taken, it would be taken by the Khedive's government. The first result of that policy was the utter disaster of Hicks' expedition.

The massacre of that army at the Mahdi's hands proved to be an acute embarrassment for Gladstone, as the whole issue of what to do about the Sudan simply would not go away; and although the British government reversed its position on staying out of Egypt's affairs in the Sudan in December 1883, it only acted to declare that the Khedive must abandon the Sudan, or else leave Khartoum and the Egyptians garrisoned there to their fate. Abandonment, however, proved not only difficult to accomplish, involving thousands of Egyptian soldiers, civilians, and their families, but politically dangerous as well. Gordon's replacement as Governor-General, Abdel Kader Pasha, was asked to undertake the work, but he found it a task beyond his abilities. Sensing that he must do something to avoid a political uproar at home, Gladstone requested Gordon to go back to Khartoum to report on conditions there, believing that even the appearance of action would be better than nothing at all. It was an idea that proved highly popular in England, although Sir Evelyn Baring was at first opposed to Gordon's appointment.

It seems that Baring's objections were purely personal, for although he and Gordon got on very well, and each held the other's accomplishments in high esteem, they were very different in temperament and method. Where Baring was deliberate, methodical, and logical, Gordon was impulsive, rash, and intuitive. Both men were highly successful within their chosen professions, but their thinking and habits were so unalike that it's possible that the two men could never have understood each other. It was a situation that would bear bitter fruit in the months to come.

It was also at this point that both Gordon and Gladstone encountered a phenomenon which a century later would be all too familiar to leaders and officials striving to counter and suppress the radical extremists who were the spiritual descendents of the Mahdi. This was the newly found power of the press. William T. Stead, the editor of the influential *Pall Mall Gazette*, unexpectedly took the question of what was to be Britain's policy toward the Sudan out of the Cabinet's hands and thrust it firmly into the forefront of public consciousness. It was an intervention that would have decisive consequences for the fate of Khartoum, and he would continue to play a role in the drama that would unfold at the confluence of the two Niles. For that reason,

Stead himself, as well as his motives, deserves a closer look.

Stead was the first great modern journalist, characterized by Geoffrey Marcus as "half charlatan–half genius." Barbara Tuchman called him "a human torrent of enthusiasm for good causes. His energy was limitless, his optimism unending, his egotism gigantic." The *Pall Mall Gazette* was an unashamedly pro-Liberal daily, and in it, Stead launched crusades that garnered a readership for the Gazette so great and wide-ranging that at one time it even included the Prince of Wales. The scope of his campaigns included railing against life in Siberian labor camps, decrying Bulgarian atrocities in the Balkan wars, and denouncing slavery in the Congo. He espoused with equal passion the causes of baby adoption, housing for the poor, and public libraries. Stead became the center of a national scandal when he published an article titled "The Maiden Tribute of Modern Babylon," in which he described how for £5 he was able to purchase the services of a thirteen-year-old prostitute. The article resulted in Stead's arrest and conviction on a charge of abduction, for which he was compelled to serve a brief prison term, but the resultant public outcry over his sensational revelation resulted in his quick release and a subsequent act of Parliament that raised the age of consent from thirteen to sixteen.

He invented the modern "interview" and subjected men as diverse as Tsar Alexander III, Cecil Rhodes, Admiral John A. "Jackie" Fisher, and General William Booth of the Salvation Army to this particular form of legalized interrogation. He was a friend of men like Henry Edward Cardinal Manning and James Bryce, and even had lunch with the future king, Edward VII. His mission, as Stead saw it, was to champion all "oppressed races, ill-treated animals, underpaid typists, misunderstood women, persecuted parsons, vilified public men, would-be suicides, hot-gospellers of every sort and childless parents." Short, ruddy-complected, with piercing blue eyes and a reddish beard, habitually dressed in tweeds, Stead presented almost a caricature of the quintessential English eccentric. "He was very nearly a great man," the magazine *Truth* would later declare of him, "and certainly a most extraordinary one." To T.P. Connor, he was "a Peter the Hermit preaching the Crusades out of his time."

Understandably then, Stead was drawn to the situation in Khartoum as a moth to a flame: here was yet another great crusade, replete with righteous cause and moral stance, to enjoin. How dare the government of Mr. Gladstone stand by and allow the Mahdi to over-run Khartoum and leave the Europeans living there, as well as the Egyptian population, to a bloody fate, all in the name of anti-imperialism? To Stead, the Mahdi was another Zobeir, a rebel who should be crushed as quickly and ruthlessly as possible, for unless he was stopped in his tracks, he presented a real danger to Egypt, the Suez, and the whole of the Middle East. Gordon had already shown what he could do with Egyptian troops once he had licked them into shape, and it seemed only proper that he be given the chance to do it again, this time standing against the Mahdi. "Why not," he wrote in the *Gazette*, "send General Gordon with full powers to Khartoum to assume absolute control over the territory, to relieve the garrisons, and do what can be done to save what can be saved from the wreck of the Sudan?" He then turned to the example of James Brooke, who had been given a free hand in Sarawak, on Borneo's north coast some years earlier, in similar circumstances. Stead called his solution "Sarawaking the Sudan." The essential point is that when Stead ranted, people listened.

Gordon had his own opinions about what should be done, and it is illuminating to see how clearly he perceived the deeper danger the Mahdi represented, not only to British interests but to the Christian world in general. "The danger to be feared is not that the Mahdi will march northward through the Wadi Halfa; on the contrary, it is very improbable that he will ever go that far north. The danger is altogether of a different nature. It arises from the influence of the spectacle that a conquering Mohammedan power, established close to your frontier, will exercise upon the population which you govern. In all the cities in Egypt it will be felt that what the Mahdi has done they may do; and as he has driven out the intruder and the infidel, they may do the same. Nor is it only England that has to face this danger. The success of the Mahdi has already excited dangerous fermentation in Arabia and Syria. Placards have been posted in Damascus calling upon the population to arise and drive out the Turks. If the whole of the eastern Sudan is surrendered to the Mahdi, the Arab tribes on both sides of the Red Sea will take fire. In self defense the Turks are bound to do something to cope with so formidable a danger, for it is quite possible that if nothing is done the whole of the Eastern Question may be reopened by the triumph of the Mahdi."

In short, a "triumph by the Mahdi" could result in an open conflict between Britain, France, and Russia, as each nation would be confronted with open revolts in several parts of their respective empires, offering possible advantages to the others in moments of distraction or weakness. The Great Game would suddenly assume entirely new dimensions and take on new threats.

Suddenly the views of the "Imperialists" in Gladstone's Cabinet, particularly Lords Hartington and Granville, gained new stature, and the shift in public opinion in favor of some form of British intervention in the Sudan became so marked that Gladstone knew that whatever gesture he made—for he was unwilling to commit to more than a gesture—toward saving Khartoum and the Sudan had to contain some element that would convince everyone that it was more substantial than in truth it was. He knew that sending General Gordon would send such a message to his Cabinet and the public alike. All the while, however, Gladstone adamantly refused to send Gordon to the Sudan with plenipotentiary powers, which would allow him to act as military commander and governor. At this point Lord Granville thought that he had a compromise solution that would be both workable and politically palatable.

He proposed sending Gordon to Khartoum in order to provide accurate reports on conditions there, while at the same time his personal prestige might be sufficient to bring about a peaceful solution to the developing confrontation. It was a dreadful miscalculation, for it underestimated both Gordon and the Mahdi. Once in Khartoum, no matter what his official status, Gordon could not help but take over the reins of power—rather than "report" he would defend. For his part, the Mahdi was not another desert brigand to be bought off with gold and guns: his fanatical dedication to his cause, as well as that of his followers, stemmed not from greed but from conviction. A man who truly believes that he is doing God's work will not be swayed by talks of compromise and concession. Both Gordon and the Mahdi believed, in their own way, that they were meant for such a calling. Should they ever meet it would be the irresistible force against the immovable object. When they did meet, it was a clash of titans.

It was Sir Garnett Wolseley who first offered this compromise position to Gordon, doing so in the War Office in Whitehall on January 15. Gordon accepted the offer immediately, and the next day he was in Brussels, seeking an audience with King Leopold to secure a postponement of his Congo appointment. Two days later he was back in London, and at noon met with the Cabinet. Gordon's diary described what transpired.

> At noon he, Wolseley, came to me and took me to the Ministers. He went in and talked to the Ministers, and came back and said, "Her Majesty's Government want you to understand this. Government are determined to evacuate the Sudan, for they will not guarantee future government. You will go and do it?" I said: "Yes." He said, "Go in." I went in and saw them. They said: "Did Wolseley tell you our ideas?" I said: "Yes, he said 'You will not guarantee future government of Sudan, and you wish me to go and evacuate it.'" They said: "Yes," and it was over, and I left at 8 p.m. for Calais.

Gordon departed from Charing Cross Station, where Wolseley, Granville, and the Duke of Cambridge gathered to see him off. Accompanying him was Colonel J.D.H. Stuart, who had been assigned to serve as Gordon's second-in-command. Stuart, an officer of the 11th Hussars on detached duty, was later described as energetic and able, but he was also imbued with the typical British disdain for "natives," a characteristic that was a distinct counterpoint to Gordon's open affection for the people over whom he had been given authority. The relationship between the two men in the months ahead, while never strained, was to prove a fascinating study in contrasting conceptions of the idea of "duty."

A small incident occurred just before the train pulled out, touching in its humanity: Gordon discovered that he had prepared in such haste for his departure that he had only a few shillings on him, and Wolseley pressed all of his own spare cash, along with his pocket watch, on Gordon. The train departed precisely at 8:00 PM, and none of the men left standing on the platform would ever see Charles Gordon alive again.

The train deposited Gordon and Stuart at Southampton, where they caught the steamer S.S. *Tanjore*, which took them to Egypt, arriving at Port Said on January 24. On the journey Gordon had bombarded Stuart with a steady stream of ideas about how he would accomplish his mission. Zobeir was on his mind, and it occurred to him that the old former slaver might actually be in communication with the Mahdi. Zobeir was dangerous, then—it might be best if he were removed from Cairo, possibly to Cyprus. Would it be possible to administer the Sudan as Britain had ruled India, through a chain of Sudanese sheiks set up as petty rulers in the territory, all clients of the British? How was the evacuation to be accomplished—what transport was available, and how soon could more be obtained? At the same time, Khartoum couldn't simply be abandoned—some sort of government must be left behind when the Egyptians departed—what was that to be? Most pressing of all, how close were the Mahdi's forces to the city? All the way to Port Said, Gordon fretted and pondered. It was clear that he was already beginning to think beyond the restrictions of his orders, and giving serious thought to defending, rather than evacuating, Khartoum.

When the *Tanjore* docked at Port Said, a message was already waiting for Gordon, requesting that he come immediately to Cairo, where he was to meet with the Khedive. It was only a few hours' journey by rail, and he arrived at the Egyptian capital late that afternoon. Once there he first received further instructions from Sir Evelyn Baring, and the following day was formally appointed by Khedive Tewfik as Governor-General of the Sudan, with executive powers. His next meeting was little short of surreal, for he called upon no less than Zobeir, of whom he had been so suspicious on the passage to Port Said.

The motives behind Gordon's visit with Zobeir were little short of astonishing. After having wrestled with the question of what form the government left behind in Khartoum would take, Gordon had come to an astonishing conclusion: he would offer the governorship to Zobeir! It was such an unbelievable turn of events that Gordon did not even discuss it with Colonel Stuart beforehand. His motives made sense in a strangely logical way, although it was a situation that would have never been acceptable to the British public once word leaked out.

When Gordon broke the news to Baring, the Consul-General was aghast. Zobeir was Gordon's sworn enemy, and held him personally responsible for the death of his son, Suleiman, five years earlier. Moreover, his reputation as a slaver, no matter how frequent and fervent his claims that he had given up the trade for good, made him suspect, if not actually despised, in the eyes of most Britons. The meeting between Gordon and Zobeir was awkward—Baring later wrote of it: "The scene was dramatic and interesting. Both General Gordon and Zobeir Pasha were laboring under great excitement and spoke with vehemence." Zobeir pointedly refused to shake Gordon's hand, an indication of where the interview would go. It ended with Zobeir walking out, the question of his assuming the governorship officially left open, but in practical terms very much an impossibility.

It had not been that unrealistic an idea, although Gordon's basis for it was somewhat peculiar. Upon arriving in Cairo he had, quite by happenstance, encountered Zobeir on the street, and suddenly felt himself overtaken by what he described as "a mystical feeling that this man [Zobeir] could be trusted." Baring, supremely practical, had little time for Gordon's intuitions, saying, "I have no confidence in opinions based on mystical feelings," but he had to admit that there were few men with the knowledge and connections in the Sudan who could rival those of Zobeir, and that he had to all outward appearances indeed repented of his slaver's ways. Appointing Zobeir as governor of Khartoum was an idea that may well have worked, but it foundered on the man's grief over his dead son, which itself may have been an indication of how ambition and greed no longer ruled his soul.

In any event, Gordon's time in Cairo was nearly done. The morning after his meeting with Zobeir, Gordon had one last audience with Khedive Tewfik, who presented him with a letter of credit for £100,000, along with two *firmans* (vice-regal prescripts). The first confirmed Gordon's status as Governor-General of the Sudan; the other proclaimed Tewfik's determination to evacuate the country. It read in part: "We have decided to restore to the families of the kings of the Sudan their former independence." These were brave words masking what was in truth a defeat—Egypt did not possess the strength to stand up to the Mahdi.

Gordon and Stewart left Cairo the same day, traveling by steamer up the Nile to Khartoum, where they arrived on February 18. The waterfront was swarming with the citizens of Khartoum, who greeted Gordon with the welcome of a returning hero, tinged with a sense of relief that they had been somehow delivered from the threat of the Mahdi. Gordon did nothing to immediately disabuse them of that notion, knowing that an immediate display of any intention to withdraw from the city might result in a panic among the populace. He did set about the task of sending the women and children, along with the sick and wounded, back to Egypt, and about twenty-five hundred souls were safely removed before the Mahdi's forces closed around the city.

Time, however, was running out for Gordon if he was determined to actually accomplish the evacuation. Daily, more Sudanese tribes were going over to the Mahdi, while a totally unrelated revolt in the eastern Sudan raised a new threat to the city. Egyptian troops sent to put down this new insurrection in the vicinity of Suakin met with a series of defeats, and eventually a British force under the command of General Sir Gerald Graham was sent out, and handily routed the rebels in several hard-fought actions.

Gordon telegraphed Baring in Cairo, urging that General Graham and his forces be used to hold open the road from Suakin to Berber. It was a reasonable request and one that Baring and the British military authorities in Cairo strongly supported, but it was refused by the government in London. In April the garrison of Berber, seeing that there was no chance of relief, surrendered to the Mahdi, a hundred and fifty miles down the Nile from Khartoum. Gordon, the city, and the Sudan had been abandoned to their fate.

CHAPTER 6

THE SIEGE BEGINS

When Gordon arrived at Khartoum on February 18, 1884, the welcome was more than tumultuous: it was a hero's welcome, a latter-day Roman triumph. Thousands of civilians crowded the waterfront as the General's steamer docked, cheering themselves hoarse, almost delirious with joy. An honor guard from the garrison presented arms as Gordon stepped from the gangplank, and as he walked toward the Governor's Palace, he was crowded on all sides as the people reached out to touch him, as if to assure themselves he was real.

The British Consul in Khartoum, Frank Power, cabled Evelyn Baring in Cairo that afternoon: "Gordon arrived here this morning, and met with a wonderful demonstration of welcome on the part of the population. The state of affairs here, since it was heard that Gordon was coming, gives every promise of the speedy pacification of this portion of the Sudan. His speech to the people was received with the greatest enthusiasm."

For all of the political machinations of Gladstone, Granville and Hartington, sending Gordon to Khartoum was a masterstroke. He alone possessed the moral authority to be able to command not only the garrison but the civilian populace. The memory of his fair-minded and even-handed governorship was still strong, and the memory of the chaos and cruelty of the five years after his departure strengthened the citizens' affection. While his mission might have been nigh-hopeless--and London firmly believed it was, since sending Gordon to Khartoum was intended as nothing more than a political sop to public opinion in order to relieve popular pressure on Gladstone—if there was ever a right man in the right place at the right time, it was Gordon in Khartoum during this crisis.

Perceptive observers would have detected a note of hysteria in the city's welcome, and Gordon, even while basking in the adulation, was most perceptive. Even putting the best face on the circumstances, the future facing the garrison and population of Khartoum was bleak. Contact with the outside world was only maintained by river steamer and a single telegraph line running to the north. The loss of either one would be crippling, as critical news of developments in Cairo and London might be delayed or lost altogether; the loss of both would be devastating, as no word of the city's condition could get out, and no information regarding any relief efforts would be able to get in. If that happened, Gordon and Khartoum would be on their own.

The loss of the river passage already appeared to be inevitable. As his steamer made its way up the Nile, it became evident that the Mahdi's reach was spreading further and faster than Cairo believed possible. The situation changed almost daily, as Gordon had learned as he was passing up the Nile. His steamer had reached Korosko, just fifty miles from the Sudan border, without serious incident on February 1, but there were already straws in the wind. Before they had even passed Aswan, Gordon and Stewart had quarreled, the General accusing the Colonel, with some justification, of being Gladstone's spy, specifically assigned to Gordon to be sure that he didn't exceed his orders or authority. When Stewart would not deny Gordon's allegations, tensions ran high between the two men for a few days. Common sense gradually prevailed and they effected a reconciliation. Stewart would eventually become Gordon's most trusted confidant and an effective second-in-command.

A bit more disturbing was a petty dispute which sprang up between Gordon and the Emir Abdul-Shakur. Shakur, whose shiekdom was in Dongola province, was one of the chieftains on whose loyalty Gordon was counting. It would have been a significant blow to the Mahdi's prestige among the Sudanese had Shakur remained firm in his friendship with Gordon, as Dongola was the city where he was born. The exact nature of the two men's disagreement was never revealed, but it was enough to affront Shakur to the point where he left the steamer at Aswan and made his way overland to Dongola.

While he would not go over to the service of the Mahdi, he was never fully trusted by the British or the Egyptians again.

The arrival at Berber on February 11 was marked by more dramatic and ominous developments. The sheiks around Berber were wavering in their loyalty to Egypt–the Mahdi seemed to be a very real threat to them, and indeed some of his followers had already been making their way that far north. A firm declaration of Britain's support and Egypt's determination to stand against the revolt could have kept the sheiks out of the Mahdi's camp, but Gordon, still feeling bound by his instructions from Gladstone and the Khedive, could offer neither. Instead he publicly declared that his mission was to evacuate the Sudan, not fight the Mahdi. Then he took what for him was an extraordinary step: he announced that while he was in Khartoum he would do nothing to interfere with the slave trade. "Whoever has slaves," he said, "shall have full right to their services and full control over them. This proclamation is proof of my clemency toward you."

While shocking at first glance—Gordon's reputation in the Sudan had been made by the ferocity with which he had suppressed the slave trade—in truth it was an empty gesture. He had no authority to interfere with the trade, and he apparently thought that it might cause the vacillating sheiks to feel more favorably disposed to him and his mission. Unfortunately, he was wrong. The Arab tribal leaders around Berber now began to drift into the Mahdi's sway, as it became clear that neither Egypt nor Britain could offer them any protection from the Mahdi's wrath. Only a few months would pass before Berber would fall without a fight to the Mahdi's army.

By the time Gordon arrived at Khartoum on February 18, the countryside around the Sudanese capital was swarming with the Mahdi's vast army. No determined assault had yet been made on the city or against its outlying positions, although there was minor skirmishing almost daily. Still, everyone within Khartoum's walls knew the fate that Muhammed Ahmed had decreed for them, and understood the fanatical zeal with which his followers would carry it out if given the opportunity. A sense of almost palpable dread had begun to grip the city.

It is difficult if not impossible at this remove to understand the fear, the sheer terror, created by the Mahdi and his proclaimed goals in the Sudan and Egypt, and how grave the concern was becoming in the capitals of Europe. It was an experience completely outside the experience of any of the related parties. Western societies in the opening years of the 21st century have become so well acquainted with the violence intrinsic to Islamic extremism that while it still possesses the power to shock, it no longer seems unbelievable or unthinkable. Indeed, when considering what militant Islamic fundamentalists may attempt in their efforts to impose their will on an unwilling world, thinking the unthinkable has become the natural response.

The succession of slaughters at the hands of militant Moslems has become something familiar, almost a litany of death and destruction: the bomb attack on the World Trade Center in 1993, with its intent to kill tens of thousands; the loss of TWA Flight 800 that same year, where all two hundred and thirty aboard died; United States embassies in Kenya and Tanzania torn apart by bombs that same year with more than two hundred were killed; Egyptian Flight 990, its copilot repeatedly crying out "I am in Allah's hands!" as he sent the airliner into its death dive and killed the two hundred seventeen people aboard; the attack on the U.S.S. *Cole* in 1998; time bombs set by Al Qaeda aboard commuter trains across Spain in 2003, the resulting explosions shredding railroad cars and claiming one hundred ninety-two more lives; two hundred fifteen killed by explosions ripping through tourist resorts and hotels in Bali and Egypt in 2002 and 2004; the London subway bombings of July 2005 that killed fifty-three; and the ultimate horror, September 11, 2001. The willingness of Moslem fanatics to take innocent lives—even those of fellow Moslems, in utter defiance and disregard of the strictures of the Koran—without warning or provocation has translated into a terrible reality that has become part of the fabric of life in the 21st century.

But it had never been so before the Mahdi. Even the most dedicated Wahhabi disciple determined to bring "renewal" to Islam had never envisioned coercion on the scale of that conceived by Muhammed Ahmed. Just as terrifying for many of Egypt's ruling class—as well as mystifying for the British and French in Cairo, London, and Paris—was how truly genuine were the Mahdi's motives: his dedication to spreading his vision of Islam and coercing the world into embracing it was complete, total, and unequivocating. While he may have begun to succumb to the physical pleasures of power, the Mahdi never gave any indication that he had lost faith in his divine calling. To the end of his life he believed he was on a mission from Allah. Not for him was Islam merely a convenient smokescreen to hide his personal ambitions, nor was it a sop to his followers to appease their religious sensibilities while he used them for his own political ends. This was a dynamic, dangerous, militant Islam that Europe had not encountered in nearly a thousand years—arguably it never had, for it was an entirely new phenomenon, not only to the nations of the Western world, but within Islam itself. Not since the days of the Prophet himself had a holy man arisen within the Moslem world with such purity of vision and dedication of purpose. Never before had a Moslem leader appeared who possessed such utter ruthlessness, for there were no moderating influences on the Mahdi, none of the restraints that are inherent in political ambitions, none of the forbearance incumbent on one who seeks harmony and dialogue with his neighbors, for he had no neighbors: he knew only those who submitted to his authority and those who did not. If they did not they were enemies. There would be no compromise; instead, there was only his burning vision of Islam, pure and unsullied, which was his mission on earth to bring into being.

It was in this way that the Mahdi came to be the forebear, the archetype, of the militant Islamic fundamentalist who would come to plague the late 20th and early 21st centuries. Convinced of his divine appointment and the infallibility of his beliefs, he abandoned all tolerance and with it any chance of peaceful co-existence with anyone who disagreed with him. He eschewed any shadow of the idea that the "infidels" might be persuaded to embrace Islam by example, instead embracing coercion and the threat of death to make his converts and keep them in his sway. It was an attitude that modern militant Islam would come to embrace in totality.

At the same time, in many ways, as much as the Mahdi's sense of mission foreshadowed the fanaticism of militant Islam in the 21st century, the Mahdi also resembled the dictators of the 1930s and 1940s. Although atrocities were committed in the name of God rather than politics, they still took place–"necessity" was the justification, in the Madhi's case the necessity of retaining religious purity. He surrounded himself with sycophants and tolerated neither dissent nor discussion. He was at once petty and tyrannical, constantly interjecting himself into the daily lives of his followers, determined to so tightly control their actions so that they would be unable to entertain any independent thoughts or actions that could be interpreted as disloyal. Wavering in faith in and devotion to the Mahdi was a sure guarantee of a death sentence at the hands of one of his clerical courts.

Yet there was one distinct difference between the methods of the Mahdi and those who a century later would choose to style themselves his successors. The latter-day Islamic extremists rarely openly proclaim themselves before the world prior to their actions, nor do they strike openly, announcing their presence and their intent. Instead they choose stealth, cunning and deception, hiding within the social fabric of their target, using a single individual or a small group to accomplish their "mission." It is, to Western eyes and values, a cowardly way to act, but it is a way of war long honored among Arabs, who constitute the vast majority of Islamic terrorists. The tradition of warfare as a contest between two individuals, or between an individual and his collective enemy, has roots that run back into Arab antiquity that precede Islam; the fear and dread induced by the Hashishim, the secret society of the Assassins, endured for more than four centuries and still exerts a powerful influence on Arabic culture. In this way only did the Mahdi differ from those who would emulate him a century later: he was brazen not only in his defiance of his enemies, but in his open presence before them.

Yet for all the bluster among modern Islamic militants about the fear they will strike in their enemies' hearts and the holy retribution they will bring down upon the infidels they despise, what the Mahdi was accomplishing in the Sudanese desert in 1884 was the goal that has consistently eluded modern Islam's "terrorists"—spreading true terror. "Terror" is an easily declared objective, but attaining it is difficult to achieve. As both the Allies and the Axis powers learned in the Second World War, and the Palestinians and Israelis have discovered over the last half-century, tactics and strategies intended to produce terror often result instead in anger and an increased resolve to resist among those who are the targets of such attacks, especially when the would-be victims are able to rally around a strong, charismatic leader.

Gordon was just such a man, and for Khartoum his aura of leadership might well have provided the difference between victory and defeat.

His task, though difficult and, as it ultimately proved, impossible, was clearly defined. His instructions from Baring were specific: "You will bear in mind that the main end to be pursued is the evacuation of the Sudan." The Khedive's commission was similarly explicit: "The object. . . of your mission to the Sudan is to carry into execution the evacuation of those territories and to withdraw our troops, civil officials, and such of the inhabitants . . . as may wish to leave for Egypt. . . and after the evacuation to take the necessary steps for establishing an organised Government in the different provinces." Gordon admitted that he was under no misconception as to his role. While still aboard the *Tanjore* he composed a memorandum in which he fully agreed to the wisdom of the decision to evacuate Khartoum and what remained of the Sudan still in Egyptian hands. In fact he went even further, stating that attempting to retake the Sudan without reforming its governance in the process was a waste of time and effort: "No one who has ever lived in the Sudan can escape the reflection 'What a useless possession is this land!'. . . I must say that it would be an iniquity to conquer these peoples and then hand them back to the Egyptians without guarantees of future good government."

Yet once he arrived in Khartoum, his attitude changed dramatically. Whether by dint of his reception or his innate belief that his life was still being directed by God, the confidence the General felt in the power of his personal influence was renewed. Reviewing the situation, he saw himself confronted with a vast array of obstacles, some of them tremendous: he was confronting a popular rebellion led by a leader every bit as charismatic as himself, with staggering numbers of followers at his disposal. The relative handful of troops Gordon commanded were of questionable reliability; he was a foreigner in a land where foreigners were always objects of mistrust; the whole of the rebellion had assumed the fanatical character of Islam marching against the infidel—and Gordon was a Christian commanding Moslem troops. Only a man either supremely confident or supremely foolhardy could have believed he could succeed in accomplishing an evacuation, let alone reversing the Islamic tide that threatened to overwhelm the city. In Gordon's case it might well have been both.

The same day that he arrived in Khartoum, Gordon again broached the issue of Zobeir Pasha with Cairo. He still believed that the former slaver could be useful: Gordon was pragmatic enough to recognize that sooner or later the fact that he was a foreigner could undermine his authority; better to rule through a proxy like Zobeir than risk being undone by insubordination or mutiny. In a telegram to Sir Evelyn Baring on March 1, Gordon declared: "I tell you plainly, it is impossible to get Cairo employees out of Khartoum unless the Government helps in the way I told you. They refuse Zobeir...but it was the only chance." A week later he pressed the point again: "If you do not send Zobeir, you have no chance of getting the garrisons away." His deputy, Colonel Stewart, agreed, and so, strangely enough, did Baring. "I believe," said Sir Evelyn when passing Gordon's telegrams on to London, "that General Gordon is quite right when he says that Zobeir Pasha is the only possible man. Nubar is strongly in favor of him. Dr. Bohndorf, the African traveler, fully confirms what General Gordon says of the influence of Zobeir." It is a mystery exactly what caused Baring to change his mind about Zobeir—these years were not exactly the most illustrious of Baring's otherwise distinguished career, and his memoirs are perhaps understandably thin and reticent on the subject. In any event the British Agent, whose relationship with Gordon was becoming increasingly turbulent, which is not to say hostile, brought all of his influence to bear in support of Gordon's recommendation; even the Egyptian government concurred. The merit of the idea seemed confirmed when even Queen Victoria approved after being privately consulted. In Winston Churchill's memorable phrase, "The Pasha was vile, but indispensable."

Gladstone, however, would have none of it. The Cabinet adamantly refused to consider the proposal and hardly bothered to discuss it. Cairo was bluntly told that London would not permit the Egyptian government to send Zobeir to Khartoum. It's not known whether any attempt was made to genuinely determine the mood of the British public on this question, or if it was simply assumed that they would not accept an ex-slaver as the governor of the Sudan. Certainly Gordon's motives behind his suggestion were never made public. Inevitably, though, the reason given by London was simply that Zobeir's history as a slave-trader made him unacceptably suspect to Her Majesty's government, no matter how he might protest as to his reformation. From London's perspective, it was all the justification needed; from Cairo's perspective it seemed to further highlight the Cabinet's near-total failure to understand what was actually happening in the Sudan. The power and prestige of the name Zobeir Pasha was such that it was still one to be conjured with in the northern Sudan, and it was not inconceivable that even the Mahdi might have hesitated before advancing against him.

Gordon was flummoxed at London's reaction. To his journal he confided, "Had Zobeir Pasha been sent up when I asked for him, Berber would in all probability never have fallen, and one might have made a Sudan government in opposition to the Mahdi. We choose to refuse his coming up because of his antecedents in re slave trade; granted that we had reason, yet, as we take no precautions as to the future of these lands with respect to the slave trade, the above opposition seems absurd. I will not send up 'A' because he will do this, but I will leave the country to 'B,' who will do exactly the same!" Frustrated at the government's intractability, he summoned Frank Powers, who was not only the British Consul in Khartoum but also a correspondent for the London *Times*, to the Governor's Palace, and there laid out the whole story, which Powers promptly forwarded to his newspaper.

The uproar doomed any possibility of the British government reconsidering its position. The Anti-Slavery Society declared that naming Zobeir the new governor of Khartoum would be "a degradation for England and a scandal for Europe." Up and down the country, Gordon's popularity was temporarily eclipsed by the furor as Britons condemned the entire idea. When it became known that at one point Gladstone had actually considered following Gordon's advice–a notion which he soon dismissed–the Conservative Opposition in the House of Commons lost no time in using it as a new stick with which to flog the government. Zobeir's usefulness came to an abrupt, bitter end.

With the possibility of governing Khartoum and the northern Sudan through Zobeir eliminated, Gordon quickly realized that there was no hope of carrying out the instructions given to him by the Gladstone government—to evacuate the Egyptian garrison and civilians from the city. To do so meant abandoning the city and its Sudanese populace, the majority of whom had little or no sympathy for the Mahdist cause, to the Mahdi's vengeance. To Gordon that was a moral impossibility: he regarded his presence in the city as a sort of personal pledge that he would see that the garrison and civil servants were evacuated–in essence he felt that his honor was involved in their safety. From this point on, nothing would induce him to leave Khartoum unless the city was relieved.

Her Majesty's government, on the other hand, was just as determined to do nothing that might get Britain further involved in the middle of Africa, not even to save Khartoum and its inhabitants. Gladstone was adamant in his refusal to send troops to the city, a position to which he would stubbornly cling until the overwhelming tide of public opinion threatened to bring down his government. The trap that Hartington and Granville had cunningly laid for Gordon now sprang shut, but it would be some months before it dawned on the Cabinet that it had trapped them just as surely as Gordon.

For his part, even as he prepared to defend the city, Gordon was determined not to nurse a viper in his bosom, so one of his first acts after arriving was to order the gates of the city thrown open for six hours, so that anyone who wanted to leave, either because they sympathized with the Mahdi or because they feared his vengeance should the city fall, could depart in peace. Once the allotted time expired, the gates were shut, and henceforth would only be opened at Gordon's specific orders. Just what effect this act had on the defense of the city is debatable. Perhaps ten thousand of Khartoum's forty thousand inhabitants left under Gordon's amnesty, but it remains a mystery whether or not there remained a Mahdist "fifth column" within Khartoum. There were a handful of Mahdist sympathizers who stayed behind, whose treachery would ultimately cost Gordon dearly, but they were careful to not make themselves known. If nothing else, the incident demonstrated the essential charity which was a cornerstone of Gordon's character, and which contrasted so greatly with that of the Mahdi. Unlike Muhammed Ahmed, Gordon would not condemn a man to punishment simply because of his beliefs.

Gordon's arrival at Khartoum had caught the Mahdi by surprise. Alarmed, Muhammed Ahmed and his Khalifas at first were fearful that his appearance heralded a direct intervention by the British Empire. While never wavering in his conviction that he was fulfilling a divinely appointed mission, Muhammed Ahmed knew that facing the disciplined, veteran battalions of the British Army was a far different prospect than overrunning brigades of ill-trained and unwilling Egyptian conscripts. There were sufficient tribal leaders in the Mahdi's ranks who had fought the British in the past to be able to impress on Muhammed Ahmed the folly of seeking battle with British infantry. Muhammed Ahmed himself was perceptive enough to understand that while he might order his followers to repeatedly throw themselves at British squares, fully confident that they would obey, he knew that the consequent slaughter would be so great as to possibly undermine his authority, or cause sufficient numbers of his followers to waver in their loyalty so that the survival of the rebellion might be endangered.

Gordon's Berber proclamation that his mission was only to evacuate the city and not confront the Mahdists also gave them pause, although the Mahdi had doubts about its sincerity; but after some weeks had passed and no reinforcements made their way up the Nile, the Mahdi's forces began to move against Khartoum itself. Like water that finds a weak spot in the hull of a ship, and then proceeds to flow wherever it encounters no resistance, the Mahdi's army began to move past and around Khartoum, gradually cutting the city off from Egypt.

Simultaneously, Muhammed Ahmed's strategy was given a boost when a separate, spontaneous rebellion broke out in the eastern Sudan. In the last month of 1883, the Hadendoa tribe had risen in a revolt of their own against the oppression and misgovernment of the Egyptians. Led by the gifted Osman Digna, the Hadendoa surrounded the Egyptian garrisons at the towns of Tokar and Sinkat. The British government refused to take any action to save them, but the Egyptian government was not so willing to abandon them. Here geography played a role in Cairo's decision, for both towns were close to the Red Sea coastline, which gave the Egyptians an opportunity for a naval evacuation. The result was more comic-opera farce than military operation.

In February 1884, a mixed force of thirty-five hundred ill-trained and untried Egyptian and Sudanese infantry under the command of General Valentine Baker was landed at the port of Suakin and began marching inland to relieve Tokar. On February 5, near the mud-hut village of Teb, they were attacked by about a thousand of Osman Digna's Arabs. The resulting fight should have been no contest as the defenders so heavily outnumbered their attackers, yet the ghost of William Hicks seemed to hover over this Egyptian force as it wavered and then collapsed in the face of the Arabs' fanatical assault.

It's easy to hear the frustration in General Baker's voice when reading his official despatch to Baring, recounting how "The square being only threatened by a small force of the enemy . . . the Egyptian troops threw down their arms and ran . . . allowing themselves to be killed without the slightest resistance." The European officers in command of the Egyptian force desperately tried to rally their men for a determined stand, but failed as friendly troops began firing on each other in the confusion and panic. Managing to scrape together some twelve hundred men, most of them without their weapons, Baker withdrew to Suakin. More than twenty-two hundred, including ninety-six officers, had been killed, while the column's artillery, small arms, and ammunition fell into Osman Digna's hands.

Emboldened by their success and now armed with modern weapons, Digna's followers pressed home their attacks on Tokar and Sinkat. With a courage born of desperation the garrison of Sinkat, eight hundred strong, broke out of the city and attempted to fight its way east to Suakin. It was hopeless. Harried and harassed, the little column was destroyed before it got halfway to the coast. A few days later the garrison at Tokar surrendered, only to be slaughtered out of hand.

Inexplicably, for Khartoum was by far the greater prize, Gladstone's government chose to bestir itself at this moment to attempt to restore Egypt's position in the eastern Sudan. For reasons never made clear, the Cabinet concluded that the loss of the Tokar and Sinkat garrisons were a greater blow to British prestige than would be the loss of Khartoum. In retrospect it can only be concluded that, with Gordon already at Khartoum, the government felt it had to give the appearance of doing something in the Sudan. The proximity of the towns to the sea, moreover, not only awakened Britain's traditional strategy of controlling the sea lanes but made the process of projecting strength there easier. Consequently an expeditionary force of one cavalry regiment and two infantry brigades was sent to Suakin, under the command of General Sir Gerald Graham, with the express mission of retaking the two towns and avenging the slaughtered garrisons. This was utter folly to Gordon, who bluntly told Baring that his position at Khartoum would be still further compromised by this operation, sited as it was on one of his only two lines of retreat, the other of course being down the Nile.

The soldiers, their equipment, and mounts were rushed to Suakin with almost obscene haste, particularly when compared with the dawdling that would mark the effort to relieve Gordon six months later. On March 4, Graham's forces drew up for battle near Teb, on almost exactly the same ground where Brigadier Baker's Egyptians and Sudanese had been routed. This time when Osman Digna attacked, the European-led force systematically cut down over three thousand Hadendoa warriors as they charged the scarlet square, driving the rest from the field in disorder. Another action was fought at Tamai four weeks later, with the same result. For the loss of just over three hundred officers and other ranks, the British had killed nearly six thousand Sudanese, effectively gutting the rebel fighting force.

Though Osman Digna, a charismatic warrior who had sworn allegiance to the Mahdi, would remain in the field for years to come, the force of his rebellion had been brought to a swift end. It was a poignant demonstration of what might have happened had British troops accompanied Gordon to Khartoum. For all that, it accomplished little, for the rugged country of the eastern Sudan was of little strategic value in the struggle against the Mahdi, and no amount of British success there could do anything to succor the besieged populace at Khartoum.

Because the telegraph line between Khartoum and Cairo was still open, Gordon had some knowledge of these events. It can only be guessed how much he rued the waste of British strength in what was a secondary conflict, or imagined what he could have accomplished had those same British troops been at his disposal. While two brigades of infantry and a single cavalry regiment would not have been sufficient to confront and defeat the Mahdi's army in the open field, within the defensive perimeter of Khartoum they would have made Gordon's position impregnable.

The frustration Gordon must have felt was one that has been shared by military commanders around the world since time immemorial. Karl von Clausewitz rightly stated that "War is a continuation of national policy by non-political means." What is not immediately obvious in that pronouncement—and it is a fine distinction not readily appreciated by most civilians, and almost never by politicians—is that military and political objectives are rarely the same. It is a point starkly highlighted by Gladstone's choosing of the time and place to intervene in the Sudan: by pursuing a swift and easy victory, he gave the appearance of taking decisive action at a moment when public opinion was beginning to turn against him, while in fact it accomplished little save the loss of 315 British soldiers and several thousand Sudanese. The Mahdi was the far greater threat, yet the defeat of Osman Digna had no effect on the progress of the Islamic tide advancing down the Nile.

It would be a problem which in the opening decade of the 21st century would continue to plague the military and political leadership of those nations targeted by Islamic terrorists. Some national leaders, desperate to reassure their populations and create the impression that they were taking decisive action against Islamic terrorists, would seek easy victories and pursue confrontations where there was little risk of failure, although the results often had little if any effect on what would become known as "the war on terrorism." Others, hiding behind a smokescreen of moral posturing, would hypocritically proclaim their support for the efforts of those nations confronting Moslem fanatics, while being careful to ensure that such support consisted of little more than lip service.

Gladstone's primary excuse for refusing to aid Gordon was money—it would simply be too expensive, he maintained, to send a full-scale relief expedition up the Nile. Similarly, the question of expense would haunt those nations which a century and a quarter later were earnestly fighting terrorism, although the cost in this case would not be so much monetary as moral. It would take a good deal of courage and resolve to commit to destroying the infrastructure of international militant Islamic, in particular in those nations which sympathized with them, rooting the terrorists out of hiding and then running them to earth. As any infantryman can attest, the toughest battlefield job of all is, in the British phrase, "winkling the other fellow out of his hole."

From this perspective, Gladstone's decision to authorize General Graham's expedition was puerile, even craven. Graham carried out his task with admirable speed and tactical dexterity–there was nothing wrong with his execution of the mission. But it did nothing to solve the central problem threatening Egypt and, by extension, the security of the Suez Canal—that is, the Mahdi's rebellion. Osman Digna was able to lead the Hadendoa in revolt precisely because the Mahdi had diverted so much attention away from the eastern Sudan; if there had been no Mahdist army flooding northward toward Egypt, Digna would have never chanced leading his own uprising. Gladstone's decision was a classic example of treating a symptom while ignoring the disease. Worst of all, it left Gordon stranded in Khartoum, almost completely surrounded by an Arab army that numbered at least a hundred thousand.

Yet Gordon was not without assets. Of the roughly forty thousand people still in Khartoum, almost eight thousand were soldiers, all of them well armed and equipped. There were twelve pieces of artillery—Krupp guns, 9- and 16-pounders—which were as good or better than anything fielded by the Mahdi's army. There were two million rounds of rifle ammunition in the city's magazines, and the munitions factory in Khartoum continued to produce about forty thousand rounds a week, so ammunition was the least of Gordon's concerns. He estimated that the storehouses held enough food to feed the city for at least six months, and that he would be able to control the river between Khartoum and Omdurman with the nine small paddle-steamers that remained, each of them armed with light artillery pieces and primitive Nordenfeldt machine guns.

All in all it gave Gordon reason to be confident of holding the city until some sort of relief expedition could be mounted. Given the powerful influence of his personality on the city's populace, had Gordon been assured of the support of Cairo and London and that relief would eventually come, in all likelihood he could have held the city indefinitely. As it was, with nothing more than faith in the British public, so that their opinions would force Gladstone's hand and compel him to send a relief column to save Khartoum, Gordon expressed an amazing degree of confidence. In another man it might have been a manifestation of a streak of fatalism; in Gordon, it was a demonstration of his faith in God and his own abilities as an engineer. The latter factor was a huge advantage for Gordon, for it not only gave him the opportunity to exploit the city's geographic position, it also allowed him to devise weapons and tactics that an ordinary officer of infantry might never have conceived.

Here the geography of Khartoum and Gordon's engineering skills met in a happy union. Sitting in a triangle surrounded on two sides by rivers that could only be crossed by boat, Khartoum's only real vulnerability was the exposed landward approach to the south. Here Gordon began excavating a huge ditch, four miles long, from the Blue Nile to the White, in essence creating an immense moat and turning the city into an island. Knocking loopholes in houses and buildings along the waterfront, siting his artillery so that it could cover any water-borne approach, and setting up regular patrols of the rivers by his steamers, Gordon felt confident that the city was secure from that quarter. Blacksmiths throughout the city began manufacturing caltrops—multi-pronged iron spikes that resembled a child's jacks, but on a huge scale, some measuring six inches and more across. Scattered throughout the sand on the landward approach to the city, the caltrops could cripple any man, horse or camel unfortunate enough to step on one. Aim points were set up for each artillery piece, along with range tables, while primitive landmines, made of wooden boxes filled with gunpowder and set off by fuses, were carefully sited.

Hastily mustering his infantry as sappers, Gordon put them to work reinforcing the city side of the moat, setting up parapets, barbicans, ravelins, revetments, and ramparts. Some of the earthworks apparently thrown up were deceptive—swaths of dyed cotton were used to simulate new diggings while the real work went on elsewhere. *Chevaux-de-frise* made of sharpened wooden poles were lashed together and positioned on ground firm enough to carry cavalry. Even broken bottles and window glass were put to work, their shards littering the ground along likely lines of advance. While his troops worked, Gordon waited.

The Mahdi, suddenly growing cautious in the face of Gordon's experience and reputation, understood that the wisest strategy to pursue against Khartoum was to first systematically cut off and annihilate the city's outlying positions and garrisons, gradually eroding Gordon's strength and steadily restricting his room to maneuver. Gordon had strengthened the garrison in Omdurman, bringing it up to a total of five hundred infantry, while ensuring it was well stocked with ammunition. Another eight hundred troops were sent to the oasis at Halfaya, eight miles north of Khartoum. Smaller outposts were set up in Khojaki outside of North Khartoum on the opposite bank of the Nile and at Fort Mukran on the point where the two Niles converged.

The Mahdi made the opening move in what would become an intricate game of military chess. In the first week of March he ordered the daring march of four thousand Arabs to the Nile below the city, which cut off the eight hundred Egyptian troops at Halfaya, a village eight miles to the north. The effect of taking Halfaya would be twofold: first it would cut off the Nile passage as a source of supply or escape; second, it would further constrict Gordon's room to maneuver, adding to the psychological burden of the inhabitants of Khartoum, heightening their sense of encirclement. The Arabs quickly entrenched themselves along the Nile opposite Halfaya and around the perimeter of the oasis, and kept up a heavy rifle-fire on the garrison, cutting off its line of retreat. The Egyptian troops fought back with surprising resolve, but the sheer volume of the Arab fire took its toll and casualties began piling up by the score. The Arabs cut off three companies of the garrison who had gone out to cut wood, capturing eight of their boats, and killing a hundred and fifty men.

General Gordon, who hadn't yet resigned himself to a purely defensive posture, decided that the situation called for an aggressive action against the Arabs in order to rescue the garrison at Halfaya. He was nevertheless cautious about it, writing in his journal, "Our only justification for assuming the offensive is the extrication of the Halfaya garrison." While he was willing to move aggressively against the Mahdi for a purpose, he wasn't about to fight for the sake of prestige or mere bravado.

On March 13 a sortie of twelve hundred men put out from Khartoum on board two grain-barges towed by a pair of river steamers. The steamers were protected with rudimentary armor plate which rendered them fairly invulnerable to rifle fire, provided they stayed in mid-river, while the troops aboard the barges hunkered down below the gunwales when the Arabs began firing on the little convoy from the riverbanks. At the south end of the oasis, Gordon's troops quick-ly formed square and began a deliberate advance to Halfaya, where they linked up with the with the remaining five hundred men of the garrison. Together the forces began a disciplined and systematic with-drawal, supported by the fire of the guns of the two steamers. Losses were slight as the entire force made it safely back to Khartoum, bring-ing with them a large number of camels and horses.

Three days later, on March 16, Gordon decided to take Halfaya back from the Mahdi's army. Loading two thousand men into the same grain barges, he once more took them to the south end of the oasis, where they formed square and began advancing on the village. The Egyptians were grimly forcing the Mahdi's soldiers to retreat from the town, when Hassan Pasha and Seid Pasha, two of Gordon's Egyptian officers, inexplicably rode toward the Arabs and called for them to come back.

The Egyptian troops, believing that they were about to be betrayed by their own officers, suddenly broke and fled after firing a single volley. The Arabs pursuing the fleeing soldiers came to within a mile of Khartoum, along the way capturing two Egyptian guns along with their ammunition. Gordon, livid with anger and wrapped in despair, wrote in his journal: "Sixty horsemen defeated two thousand men." Worse, there were two hundred dead left behind. Six days later, the two pashas were tried by court-martial. When questioned as to their reasons for riding toward the Arab lines, they explained that they had been encouraging the Arabs to surrender rather than trying to betray their own troops. Gordon would have none of it, and both men were swiftly found guilty and shot. After this affair Gordon gave up any idea of taking further offensive action against the Mahdi.

But the summer heat meant that any large-scale actions by either side were out of the question. There were a few exceptions, particu-larly a very determined attack in mid-April upon one of the steamers coming up from Berber, at the Salboka Pass. In a running fight that lasted several hours, the Mahdi's soldiers were eventually driven off after suffering terrific casualties. The Egyptian soldiers fired off more than fifteen thousand rounds of Remington ammunition during the battle, and earned high praise from Gordon for their steadiness. It also demonstrated the relative invulnerability of the river steamers, as the Mahdi's artillery was too light and too antiquated to do much damage. Thus there was still a way out of the city should Gordon choose to take it.

Gordon, however, had no intention of going anywhere. Having assumed the role of defender of Khartoum, he was determined to see the siege through. At first he hoped that diplomacy might succeed, as no one had yet attempted to actually treat with the Mahdi. Soon the men began exchanging letters, in which Gordon offered to recognize Muhammed Ahmed as the ruler of Kordofan province, in exchange for a pledge not to advance against Egypt or further attack Khartoum. It was an empty concession, admittedly, for it merely confirmed the Mahdi's grip on what he already held, but it was a ploy Gordon was willing to try.

It was an offer the Mahdi promptly rejected. Despite his sudden caution in the face of Gordon's experience—somehow Muhammed Ahmed, who already knew of Gordon's reputation as an administrator, discerned that he was not facing another William Hicks in command of the city's garrison—his delusions of grandeur and sense of "holy mission" had grown to such a degree that compromise could not be part of his calculations. There was no one in his camp who dared disagree with him, and no one to offer dissenting counsel or suggest alternative courses of action. Once the Mahdi made a decision, it was to be carried out without question. Singleness of purpose, an admirable quality in a leader, had become rigidity of thinking. In some ways it was inevitable, for the inflexibility of the Mahdi's religious views were bound to sooner or later infect his other perspectives. If he was indeed divinely appointed to carry out this *jihad* to cleanse and spread Islam, why should he have to listen to the counsels and ideas of those who were not blessed by such a calling? It was a mind-set that would prove the undoing of the Mahdi—and at the same time lead to the death of Gordon.

The Mahdi did appreciate what Gordon had attempted with his diplomatic overture, and responded with one of his own the next day. On March 22, a handful of envoys advanced from the Mahdi's camp toward Khartoum under a banner of truce. Once admitted into the

city they were conducted to the Governor's Palace, situated close to
the riverfront, where they were shown in to Gordon. There they presented the Mahdi's reply to Gordon's offer of suzerainty over
Kordofan–"I am the Mahdi" was Muhammed Ahmed's reply, as if
that were answer enough, which in the circumstances it was–and then
in turn held out a cotton-wrapped bundle to the General. Gordon
took it, unwound the coverings, and found a tattered and patched
jibba, an invitation to him to become a Moslem convert and follower
of the Mahdi. Accompanying the jibba was a letter from the Mahdi
which read, "In the name of God! Herewith a suit of clothes, consist-
ing of a coat [the jibba], an overcoat, a turban, a cap, a girdle, and
beads. This is the clothing of those who have given up this world and
its vanities, and who look for the world to come, for everlasting happiness in Paradise. If you truly desire to come to God and seek to live
a godly life, you must at once wear this suit, and come out to accept
your everlasting good fortune." Dismayed that the Mahdi should so
underestimate him, Gordon dropped the bundle to the floor and
declared the audience over. He would not submit to the Mahdi, nor
would he surrender the city.

As curious as the exchange between the General and the Mahdi
might seem, it was not inconceivable. A strange duality would come
to exist between Gordon and Muhammed Ahmed: each recognized the
deep religious convictions of the other, both understood that they were
men of their word, and that within each man's interpretation of duty
also lay his definition of honor. While the Mahdi might carry his sense
of destiny to a higher level than Gordon—after all, the General felt
that whereas he was God's tool, he could be discarded by the Almighty
whenever He chose, while the Mahdi believed his calling was divine
and irrevocable—each felt a moral imperative to his efforts. Gordon
could have no more abandoned Khartoum than the Mahdi could have
chosen not to take it. The two men would conduct an intermittent correspondence for the next eight months, yet nowhere in their exchanges
does an element of vitriol or vituperation appear. Their letters are
polite, almost familiar, giving the impression of an exchange between
two men who could have been friends under different circumstances,
but who now were pledged to each other's destruction by each one's
sense of duty.

Though the Mahdi would make at least three more offers to allow Gordon to convert to Islam, and even as late as September he would be willing to allow Gordon to personally leave the city, there would never be any further talk of compromise or negotiations between the two men. It was pointless: the Mahdi would not be satisfied until all had submitted to him, either through conquest or conversion to Islam.

On April 27, General Gordon received a report that may have caused him to finally understand the true gravity of his situation. Valey Bey, the Egyptian governor at Mesalimeh, located halfway between Berber and Khartoum, surrendered to the Mahdi's followers. There they captured one of Gordon's nine armed steamers, along with seventy shiploads of provisions and two thousand rifles. The Mahdi's power was now reaching far beyond the city, threatening Berber and raising the specter of cutting off all communications with the outside world. It was not a reassuring situation. Gordon, seeing farther and with greater clarity than either Baring or Gladstone, understood the essential nature of the Mahdi's rebellion, and in doing so defined the key to answering the challenge of militant Islam one hundred twenty years later: the appearance of success gave it credibility, yet should it meet with a sudden reverse, or face strong and determined opposition, it would eventually falter and fail. Not all of the Mahdi's followers were religious zealots; success gave the Mahdi an authority which mere religion could not provide, but should he fail or be seriously checked, much of his army would waver and dissolve. In the end Gordon knew that for all of his religious fervor, Muhammed Ahmed was little more than a petty tyrant, and that, as the Duke of Wellington once observed of Bonaparte, "His career is like that of a cannonball—he must constantly move from one success to the next; should he rebound he is finished." It was with this thought in mind that Gordon wrote a prophetic warning to both Baring and Gladstone:

If Egypt is to be kept quiet the Mahdi must be smashed up. Mahdi is most unpopular, and with care and time could be smashed. Remember that once Khartoum belongs to Mahdi the task will be far more difficult; yet you will, for the safety of Egypt, execute it. If you decide on smashing Mahdi then send up another £100,000, and send 200 Indian troops to

Wadi Halfa, and send an officer up to Dongola under pretense to look out quarters for troops. . . . I repeat that evacuation is possible, but you will feel effect in Egypt, and will be forced to enter into a far more serious affair to guard Egypt. At present it would be comparatively easy to destroy Mahdi.

This would be one of the last direct communications the outside world would receive from Gordon, as on March 19, the telegraph line between Khartoum and Cairo was cut by the Mahdi's forces. Gordon was completely cut off from London and Cairo, and could only hope and guess at what was being done about the plight of Khartoum. The only contact the city would have with the outside world in the next ten months would be a handful of messages smuggled in and out. Only time would tell if the governments in London and Cairo would heed Gordon's warning.

CHAPTER 7

LONDON AND CAIRO

Although the tempo of life moved much more slowly in the Victorian Era than it does today, a contemporary observer looking back on the drama that unfolded in London and Cairo during the three-hundred and seventeen-day siege of Khartoum would find little surprising in the responses of the British and Egyptian officials who found themselves compelled to react to the crisis. The dreary pattern that would within a few decades become all too familiar to Western nations confronted by aggressive tyrants first played itself out in London and Cairo in 1883 and 1884: the denial of the existence of a crisis, the evasion of responsibility, the slow acquiescence to public opinion, and the inevitably ill-timed and ineptly-executed response.

What was genuinely perplexing and peculiar was Gladstone's perception of the Mahdi and the rebellion he led. From the beginning the British Prime Minister seemed determined to misunderstand the nature of the uprising in the Sudan. Judging from his public statements and debates in the House of Commons, he appeared to regard the underlying causes of the Sudanese revolt as social and racial–the consequence of Egyptian exploitation of the Sudan. The Mahdi he regarded as a national leader attempting to achieve national aspirations. Yet Gladstone repeatedly failed to comprehend that Muhammed Ahmed's ambitions were driven by religion rather than politics. While the resentment the Sudanese felt toward the Egyptians was intense and deep-rooted, they had no real sense of being a distinct "people," nor did they have any concept of the Sudan being a "nation" in the accepted Western sense. In point of fact, the Sudanese were not a distinct people, but rather two peoples, the Moslem Arabs in the north and the animist and Christian black Africans in the south. The Mahdi's rebellion embraced only the Sudan's Moslems; the black Africans were in his mind consigned to the fate of being an endless supply of raw material for the Arab slavers.

Gladstone only saw the Sudanese rising against their Egyptian overlords; what he failed to see was that the Mahdi had encouraged the rebellion and eventually hijacked it for his own ends. It was not the case where, in what was one of Winston Churchill's least perceptive political judgements, "Within their humble breasts the spirit of the Mahdi roused the fires of patriotism and religion." Perhaps it may be that Gladstone, for all his genuine devotion to Christianity, did not regard Islam seriously enough, or it may be that he could not recognize that a religion might be something for which men were not only willing to die, but for which they were also willing to kill. Perhaps he had become too much of a politician himself, and so could no longer view world events save through the prism of politics, thus could not see any other motives.

Whatever the causes for the Prime Minister's myopia, it led him to make one of the most disastrous pronouncements of his political life, declaring, when asked if the Mahdi's rebellion was a popular political uprising, "Yes, those people are struggling to be free, and they are rightly struggling to be free." This was followed later by other speeches where he told the House of Commons that a military expedition to the Sudan to relieve Khartoum would be "a war of conquest against a people struggling to be free," while in still yet another defense of his policy toward the Sudan he recommended "the leaving alone of a brave people to enjoy their freedom." This was absurdity, and Gladstone knew it: the concept of "freedom" was meaningless to the Mahdi, who openly condoned the institution of slavery and was doing nothing to curb the slave trade within the territory he controlled.

This was Gladstone at his worst, the petty politician. He was capable of better: once he had been a rising star among the Tories, only to emerge a convinced and convicted Liberal, a champion of democracy. In his second term as Prime Minister, he was, though he did not yet know it, at the peak of his power. He was the pre-eminent statesman of the world's pre-eminent power, adored by the common people and respected on both sides of the House. Yet there was a flaw in his character that would undo him in a few short months: something in his nature provoked reactions with those who supported as well as opposed him. Though his personal modesty would never have allowed him to bask in the applause, the admiration, the adulation which the people of Britain were willing to offer, there was an over-confidence, almost an arrogance about him when questioned on decisions of policy. This eventually stirred a distrust that would transform itself into unparalleled animosity. For there were two sides to Gladstone: one the very model of the Victorian gentleman—upright, virtuous, and deeply religious—who brought his belief in justice to the table of politics and there put them to work; the other a hypocrite, a demagogue, manipulative of men and events for the purposes of his own ambition. As the crisis on the Nile grew, the perception that the latter was the true measure of William Gladstone gradually overtook the British public, the House of Commons, and even his own Cabinet.

That transformation was due in no small part to the British press. The Sudan crisis was one of the first incidents to highlight the growing power of the press to shape public opinion and influence government policy. The first great "penny daily," the *Daily Telegraph*, which in the 1880s boasted the largest circulation in the world, had originally been a great supporter of Liberalism, a position which gradually eroded until ending with the Eastern crisis of 1876, when it appeared that the Russians were advancing on Constantinople.

Decrying Gladstone's attempts at conciliation as tantamount to selling out Britain's interests, it changed its allegiance for good and became thoroughly Conservative. Now the paper was one of Gladstone's most outspoken critics. William Stead too, kept up a steady pressure on the Prime Minister. While Stead's *Pall Mall Gazette* was usually staunch in its support for the Liberal Party and in particular for Gladstone, the paper had also been the first public forum to promote the idea of sending General Gordon to Khartoum. Finally, the London *Times* posted a powerful commentary on March 20, 1884, declaring, "The position of General Gordon, besieged at Khartoum, unfortunately remains exceedingly precarious. Yesterday we published the unwelcome report that he is now totally isolated. All communications have been cut. A month ago the British government was fully warned that it would become necessary to employ something more than moral force at Khartoum. The necessity is now becoming urgent, but the government has not yet ordered the commander of British and Egyptian forces in southern Egypt to march to Khartoum." A formidable array of influential dailies was beginning to question not just Gladstone's policies, but the motives behind them as well.

With some justification, Gladstone believed that Gordon's refusal to leave Khartoum was a subtle form of blackmailing him into sending the British Army into the Sudan, which he flatly refused to do. At one point, he wrote a memorandum to Granville, which read in part, "We ought to act in the Sudan only by peaceful means, except for the safety of Gordon and his party. If, in consequence of his being in danger, we have to act by military means, the object of our action ought to be to bring him away at once from Khartoum, and he ought to know that. If Gordon continues at Khartoum knowing that we cannot approve of supplying him with any forces for military expeditions, he should state to us the cause of his staying and his intentions."

Certainly the British newspapers never went to any particular pains to point out that Gordon was deliberately defying his orders to evacuate the city, precipitating the crisis and the accompanying public outcry. If Gordon had been abandoned, as some of the Government's critics were charging, he certainly was not forgotten. In January 1884 Stead had so skillfully presented sending Gordon to Khartoum as the solution to the Sudan crisis that it gradually became an accepted article of faith among the public–as well as many members of Parliament and even Queen Victoria herself–that it had been the government's plan all along, and that backing him with an expeditionary force was an inevitable consequence of that policy. The subtlety of the idea Gladstone, Hartington, and Granville had actually formulated—sending Gordon out with nothing more than his own moral authority to evacuate the Egyptian garrison and civilians from Khartoum—was too intricate for the general public to grasp.

As the spring passed and the military situation around Khartoum changed, it became clear that Gordon would be unable to evacuate the Egyptians, and the public perception of this development was that Gordon had been cut off and abandoned by the Government. Of course, Gladstone, through Evelyn Baring in Cairo, repeatedly informed Gordon that if he were unable to bring out the garrison and civilians, he was still expected to make good his own escape.

To this Gordon replied that he felt bound by his original orders, which came not only from the Cabinet in London but also from the Khedive in Cairo, and if he could not bring the Egyptians out with him, he wasn't leaving Khartoum at all. In his journal he confided his feelings after one such order to quit the city was received, emphasizing the key passages: "I declare POSITIVELY AND ONCE FOR ALL, THAT I WILL NOT LEAVE THE SUDAN UNTIL EVERY ONE WHO WANTS TO GO DOWN IS GIVEN THE CHANCE TO DO SO, unless a government is established which relieves me of the charge; therefore, if any emissary or letter comes up here ordering me to come down, I WILL NOT OBEY IT, BUT WILL STAY HERE AND FALL WITH THE TOWN, AND RUN ALL RISKS."

To the British public, it seemed that Gladstone's policy had failed, which was disappointing, but the apparent inactivity of Her Majesty's government in refusing to send troops to Gordon and relieve Khartoum also began to generate a sense of alarm. One of the first to give voice to the growing concern over the safety of Gordon and the fate of the city was Queen Victoria herself, who sent Lord Hartington a telegram on March 25 saying, "It is alarming. General Gordon is in danger; you are bound to try to save him... You have incurred a fearful responsibility." On May 5, there was a protest meeting at St. James's Hall in London; four days later a mass meeting that numbered in the thousands in Hyde Park; on May 11 there was a similar gathering in Manchester. In each case those attending were vocal in their demands that Gordon be rescued and the city relieved.

At the same time the subject of increasingly acrimonious debates in the House of Commons was the safety of Gordon, but underneath lay the realization that Gordon was determined to remain behind because of his inherent humanity. It was a curious motivation, for Gordon was not one of those colonial administrators who become so enamored of their charges that they gradually "went native." No matter where his assignments took him, Gordon remained thoroughly English. At the same time, his Christianity compelled him to carry out his duty not only with dedication but with compassion. He may not like the people over whom he was given governance, but he was responsible for them, therefore he would do his utmost for them. While by all accounts he liked the Sudanese and the Egyptians, they weren't by any means beloved by him. There are often passages in his journals, such as the remark, "These people are not worth any great sacrifice," which may not be flattering to Gordon as a man, but make it even clearer that he was driven by his sense of duty and responsibility. If those were concepts that the Cabinet could not understand, that was their problem, not his.

It had been on March 16, by coincidence the same day as Gordon's unhappy expedition to retake Halfaya, that Lord Randolph Churchill rose in the House of Commons and took Gladstone's government to task for sending General Gordon to Khartoum then denying him the resources needed to carry out his instructions. Accusing the government of vacillation, he questioned the "purposeless slaughter" in the Eastern Sudan occasioned by General Graham's action there the previous month, and demanded an explanation as to why an overland evacuation route from Suakin to Berber had not been opened by the troops under Graham's command.

Quoting a report from a British officer who had been in Khartoum just a month before Gordon's arrival, he sharply put the question to Gladstone: "Colonel Coetlogon has stated that Khartoum may be easily captured; we know that General Gordon is surrounded by hostile tribes and cut off from communications with Cairo and London; and under these circumstances the House has a right to ask her Majesty's Government whether they are going to do anything to relieve him. Are they going to remain indifferent to the fate of the one man on whom they have counted to extricate them from their dilemmas, to leave him to shift for himself, and not make a single effort on his behalf?"

No reply came from the government bench, and once raised, the issue of what to do about Gordon refused to go away. The government's alleged mismanagement of Egyptian–and by extension, Sudanese–affairs had long been a convenient hook on which the Conservatives hung their Parliamentary attacks on Gladstone and his Cabinet, but as the debate continued throughout the summer it became obvious that the issue was not merely one of partisan politics. (Lord Randolph already had a considerable reputation for baiting his opposites, but in this case he had struck a genuine chord of discontent in the House.) Throughout the summer, Ministers and Members were given leave to state their positions on what should be done about Gordon and Khartoum, and tensions rose with each passing day. On the occasions when Gladstone rose to speak for the government, he continued to fall back on his argument that the Mahdi's rebellion was nothing more than a popular uprising of the Sudanese to throw off the Egyptian yoke.

Yet that argument began to ring more and more hollow as stories of Arab atrocities committed against civilian populations began to make their way into the popular press. When Sir Michael Hicks-Beach, a Conservative MP, rose to speak on May 12, 1884, he was emphatic on this point: "I believe that the people of this country are determined that General Gordon shall be saved together with those who have trusted in him. If General Gordon had been supplied with materials of war earlier, he would have been enabled to stem at Khartoum the wave of religious fanaticism and anarchy led by the Madhi. It is our duty to complete the commitments which we made when General Gordon went out to the Sudan. Her Majesty's government must leave no stone unturned to avert from this country the intolerable stain which would be left upon her honor by any injury inflicted upon General Gordon."

In his reply, Gladstone stumbled badly, uttering one of his least perceptive political judgments and revealing to the entire House how poorly he understood what was actually happening in the Sudan. "The government, he said, "was and is pledged to shield General Gordon from danger. Should necessity arise, the government shall do this. The Right Honorable Gentleman Sir Michael Hicks-Beach has said, though, that it is the duty of England to keep the Mahdi's movement out of Egypt and to put it down in the Sudan, and it is this task which the gentleman desires to saddle upon England. That means the conquest of the Sudan. I put aside for the moment all questions of climate, of distance, of the enormous expenses, and all the frightful loss of life. There is something worse involved. It would be a war of conquest against a people struggling to be free."

Even among the government's supporters there was an undercurrent of dissatisfaction with how the Sudan question was being handled. Gladstone remained unmoved and unmoving. As autumn

approached and with it the end of the Session, the whole matter came
to a head when Sir Michael Hicks-Beach moved for a vote of censure
for the government. Gladstone's tenure as Prime Minister hung by the
thinnest of threads.

It's not at all difficult to imagine Gladstone's frustration with the
whole affair, and it may be that frustration holds the key to his actions
as well as his inaction when deciding what to do about Gordon and
Khartoum, for by now the two were inseparable. The cries to "Save
Gordon!" heard throughout the press, the public–even from the
Crown–had within them the imperative to save Khartoum as well, for
Gordon had made it clear that he would never leave the city unless its
security was assured. The entire Sudan situation–Gordon, Khartoum,
the Mahdi–should have been a sideshow in his conduct of the affairs
of the British Empire, yet here it was an issue upon which the fate of
his government hung.

Strong-minded and stubborn, the Prime Minister had met his
match in Gordon. He was accustomed to the exercise of power, and
the power at his fingertips was immense, far greater than that wielded
by comparable statesman today: he could send military or naval expeditions against foes, civilized or savage, in any corner of the world
with far fewer complications and less accountability than any of his
successors a century later. The governments of lesser nations literally
rose or fell as a consequence of decisions made by the Prime Minister
of Great Britain. When the British lion roared, it was deafening, and
the whole world stopped to listen.

At the same time, though Gladstone held the power, he refused to
be precipitate in its use. Like most men, Gladstone tried to do what
was right, or at least what he persuaded himself was right, and in this
case he could not find a justification in ordering an expedition into the
Sudan that was worth the expense in lives, in treasure, in prestige. It
was not that he feared the responsibility; rather he felt that greater
responsibilities lay elsewhere.

Gordon, for his part, believed with equal fervor that he was right.
It would be immoral as well as politically irresponsible to abandon
Khartoum and its people to the Mahdi. Already the momentum
behind the Mahdist rebellion was so great as a consequence of his
unbroken string of victories over the Egyptians that allowing

Khartoum to fall to the Arabs could carry the rebellion into Egypt, where the Egyptian peasants would almost certainly rise out of sympathy. The consequences for Great Britain would be unthinkable: the loss of the Suez Canal, the possibility of revolt throughout the Ottoman Empire, allowing Russia an opportunity to exploit the chaos and seize Constantinople—even the specter of a Moslem uprising in India. Those were the political consequences, as Gordon saw them, of allowing Khartoum to fall, and in truth none of them were at all improbable. As for the moral questions, given the fate which the Mahdi had already made unambiguously clear awaited the garrison and the populace, it would be an affront to the Christianity which both Gordon and Gladstone each held dear to allow such an atrocity to take place.

It would be wrong to assert, as Churchill once did, that "If Gordon was the better man, Gladstone was incomparably the greater." Both were good men; both were in their own way great. What was being decided in London was whether or not Gladstone's greatness would suffer a momentary lapse in the name of political expedience. Yet even while the answer to the question was taking shape, events were taking the decision out of Gladstone's hands. The debate ground on, the motion for censure would come and be voted upon, but should the Government survive, it would find its policy dictated not by Gladstone, but by the public will. When the vote came, the motion of censure was defeated by only twenty-eight votes—a distressingly narrow margin. Gladstone's government survived the confrontation, but he understood that it could not survive another.

In Cairo, Sir Evelyn Baring had been doing his best since early February to act as an intermediary between Gordon and Gladstone. For over a month, beginning with Gordon's arrival in Khartoum, he had been bombarded with a steady stream of telegrams from the Sudanese capital, as Gordon would conceive of new ideas for executing his instructions, sometimes as many as thirty a day. Some were contradictory, some were far-fetched, and some, like the idea of using Zobeir Pasha as a governor-by-proxy, had considerable merit. Baring dutifully sifted through them all, discarding the ones that were clearly unfeasible or had been overtaken by events, and sending those worth consideration on to London.

Ironically, though perhaps inevitably, Baring came to bear the brunt of Gordon's frustration and growing animosity as his repeated demands and pleas for intervention by British troops went unanswered. Somehow it never seemed to occur to the General that the source of his frustration was in fact Gladstone's blunt refusal to involve the Empire any further in the Sudan. One searches Gordon's journals in vain for some hint of criticism or some venting of rage at the "Grand Old Man" in London. It seems that on some level he believed that Gladstone was playing a deeper game, and wanted Gordon to stay in the Sudan as a pretext for intervention; while Gordon would appear to be forcing Gladstone's hand, the Prime Minister could maintain that he was still opposed to imperialist adventures, but that circumstances were compelling him to act. The real villains of the piece, as Gordon saw them, were Granville and Hartington, who had conceived of the whole Khartoum adventure in the first place.

At the same time, the caustic and sometimes searing remarks Gordon records about Baring make it clear that he regarded the British Consul-General as an accomplice to Hartington and Granville, and that Baring was doing his level best to thwart whatever constructive actions Gordon might want to take in the Sudan. The journals are filled with Gordon's laments about Baring's incomprehension of the circumstances at Khartoum and his interference in how Gordon was conducting his affairs. It was perhaps inevitable because Gordon was first, last, and always a soldier, while Baring was the embodiment of British diplomacy. Not for Gordon the prevarication, posturing, deception, and duplicity, the endless maneuvering within moral shades of grey, which were of necessity a diplomat's stock in trade. His conduct in China demonstrated that for Gordon the world was simply black and white. His was a Manicheanist Christian perspective: good vs. evil, right vs. wrong. To Gordon his confrontation with the Mahdi was simple if not simplistic in nature: the Mahdi was evil, Gordon was good. That was all he needed to know and believe, and it would be his guide throughout the eleven months of the siege.

Baring, however, had no such philosophical luxury. With the memory of the Arabi revolt, with young Egyptian men roaming the streets of Cairo calling on the Moslems to kill the Christians within the city, still fresh in his mind, Baring knew that a Mahdist triumph at Khartoum might well trigger another uprising in Egypt, and by appearing to have defeated one of Britain's most popular generals, the Mahdi's myth of invincibility would gain credence throughout the Middle East. Consequently, Baring continually forwarded London's requests, demands, and eventually pleas to Gordon to leave the city, even if it meant abandoning the garrison and populace. This galled Gordon, who began to suspect that it was only Baring who wanted him to leave, not realizing that Baring was passing on to London the best of Gordon's ideas for saving the city, as well as the frequent explanations of his reasons for staying there.

The relationship between Baring and Gordon had always been somewhat stiff. It would be wrong to say that they disliked each other; more correctly it should be said that they simply didn't understand each other. It was more than the broad differences in perspective and opinion that always exist between a soldier and a diplomat. It was also more than contrast between Gordon's deep-seated Christianity and Baring's more pragmatic, less clearly defined view of the world. It was the difference between a man of action and a man of patience. Gordon was all for "doing," for acting and reacting, for making things happen rather than letting them happen. Baring, of course, was cautious and measured, always preferring to let events play themselves out and work the consequences to Britain's advantage rather than try to shape them as they developed. Gordon received a sense of this when he first met Baring in 1877 in Cairo: remarking on their introduction and the apparent coolness that immediately sprang up between them, the General observed, "When oil mixes with water, we will mix together." It was unfortunate for Gordon that he probably never understood Baring well enough to realize that while Sir Evelyn was not a friend or an ally, he was at least sympathetic to Gordon's aims. The same could not be said for the man in London who had sent Gordon to Khartoum in the first place.

One of the unsolvable riddles of the fall of Khartoum is why Gordon never seemed to understand that Gladstone was playing politics with his life. Gordon, to all appearances, never considered that Gladstone would simply abandon him in the middle of the Sudan once he chose

to stay in Khartoum. It may have been that Gordon trusted to
Gladstone's Christianity, which he regarded in many ways as robust as
his own, and believed that Gladstone was prepared to stand up to the
Mahdi's rising tide of Islam. He may even have believed that Gladstone had sent him to Khartoum in order to give the government the
necessary causus belli in the Sudan. Whichever the truth may have
been, what is inescapable is Gordon's belief that defending the city was
his destiny. His Khartoum journals put this beyond a doubt. Save for
a humorous reference or two about the shape of Gladstone's collars
and his passion for chopping wood, Gordon's journals are empty of
any telling criticism of Gladstone. Lord Granville is rightly treated as
a nonentity, while Lord Hartington is rarely mentioned. Instead it is
on Baring in Cairo that Gordon vents his displeasure. It would prove
tragic, indeed fatal to Gordon, that the two men did not understand
each other better, for had they done so and worked in harmony, the
story of the months and years to come may well have turned out dif-
ferently.

Ironically, it was a man who Gordon had dismissed as ineffectual
who ultimately forced the Government to do exactly what Gordon
had hoped it would. Lord Hartington, the Secretary of State for War,
and one of the architects of the plan that had originally sent Gordon
to Khartoum, came to believe that not only was the fate of the government tied to the fate of the city, but so was national honor. He was
the first within the Cabinet to finally acknowledge the obligation the
government had assumed when it sent Gordon to Khartoum. He then
brought to bear all his considerable influence to compel Gladstone to
send a relief expedition up the Nile.

Lord Hartington's conscience was a powerful motivating force,
for no one in all of Great Britain had a reputation for greater probity
and depth of conscience than he. So scrupulously fair and honest was
the man that it was something of a national joke–an affectionate
one–that whenever there was a dispute over cards at Hartington's
club, the matter was never referred to the club's governing board, but
sent to Hartington for resolution. In public affairs, no less than in private, Lord Hartington's decisions carried extraordinary weight. To the
vast majority of Britain's common folk, Hartington was a man they
could trust. For all his patrician lineage—and Hartington, who was

An Ansar warrior. The patched jibba was symbolic of his service to
the Mahdi, while the obsolete Schneider rifle was typical of the
firearms carried by most of the Mahdi's followers.

Muhammed Ahmed ibn Abdullah, the Mahdi. While there are no known photographs of the Mahdi, this wood-cut is widely accepted as an accurate portrayal at about the time his rebellion in the Sudan began.

Gladstone and his Cabinet, 1880–1885. Seated at the far right is the Marquis of Hartington, the Minister of War; next to him is Lord Granville, the Foreign Secretary.

Major General Sir Charles Gordon, photographed in Cairo in 1884 before his departure for Khartoum, wearing the uniform of an Egyptian Major General.

Dervishes engaged in one of their ritual dances, the wide, sweeping movements of which gave rise to the term "Whirling Dervish."

Dervish Warriors. They wielded their leaf-bladed broadswords with awesome skill, and in battle they were absolutely fearless.

Colonel William Hicks, seated second from right, and his staff. An officer of only average ability, Hicks died along with the rest of the Egyptian column he led into the Sudan to suppress the Mahdi's rebellion in 1883.

General Sir Garnet Wolseley. Although he was a brilliant organizer he was an unimaginative strategist, and his cautious advance of the Relief Column doomed Gordon and the city of Khartoum.

The Governor's Palace, Gordon's residence, in Khartoum, viewed from the Nile sometime in the 1930s. It was from this rooftop that Gordon looked northward in vain for the British relief column.

The hulk of the Nile steamer *Bordein*, which carried some of Gordon's last messages to the outside world during the siege of Khartoum.

Major General Herbert Horatio Kitchener. As a Major he had served with the Relief Column in 1885. Eleven years later, he commanded the force which retook Khartoum and the Sudan.

The Mahdi's Tomb after the Battle of Omdurman. Stray British artillery shells damaged the dome during the battle, and Kitchener plundered the tomb when he occupied the city.

Gordon's Memorial. Originally erected in the city of Khartoum, it now stands outside the boys' school Gordon founded in Surrey.

destined to eventually become the 8th Duke of Devonshire, had aristocratic roots that ran back to the Norman Conquest—he was the embodiment of what an Englishman should be. In the fifty-one year-old Hartington, with his tall frame, thin bearded face and hawk-like nose, Britons saw those qualities which they liked to believe resided in all of them: a passion for fair play, integrity and impartiality, and above all common sense. Never self-seeking, nervous or excited, Hartington was imbued with an unshakeable sense of duty, yet at the same time seemed to lack both ambition and imagination. Twice he would be asked by his Sovereign to form a government and twice he would refuse. It is likely that he was too honest to be a good Prime Minister and he knew it. Churchill, somewhat condescendingly, would write of him, "He would never, in any circumstances, be either brilliant or subtle, or surprising, or impassioned, or profound," and therein lay the source of his strength and his influence: whatever Hartington said or did could be counted upon to be sensible and well thought-out.

One significant defect that Hartington had for certain was that he never did anything quickly. He moved slowly, thought slowly, and acted slowly. It was not that he was dense, but rather that he took the time to appreciate a thought or a deed completely before carrying it out. Some observers felt that this was an impediment to his career. Neither quick-witted like Disraeli nor fiery and powerful like Gladstone, Hartington was at a disadvantage in the cut and thrust of parliamentary debate. Yet while speed can sometimes permit a statesman to escape unhurt from the consequences of a misjudgment or irredeemable mistake, it was the deliberateness with which Lord Hartington reached his conclusions that often allowed him to avoid disasters and mistakes in the first place. For all of Gordon's dedication to saving Khartoum, Baring's integrity in carrying out his office, Gladstone's passionate anti-imperialism, and the Mahdi's fanaticism, the fate of the British General in the Sudanese capital would be decided by Lord Hartington.

The process by which this happened is easy to follow. By the middle of March 1884 Hartington had become convinced that he—along with the rest of the Cabinet—had to take responsibility for Gordon's appointment to Khartoum and the danger the General now faced.

Acknowledging that danger, his conscience would not allow him to sit idly by while Khartoum fell and Gordon died. This led him to turn the awesome power of that conscience on the Cabinet, until they too felt compelled to take action on the General's behalf. When it appeared that his colleagues were vacillating, Hartington pressed his case all the harder, until the whole of the Cabinet came to agree that a relief expedition had to be authorized. Now it was Gladstone's turn to feel the brunt of Hartington's moral authority.

Clinging to the shreds of his anti-imperialistic arguments and his claims that the Mahdi's revolt was a Sudanese struggle for freedom, Gladstone resisted, prevaricated, delayed, and postponed any decision; proposal met with counter-proposal, straightforward resolutions met with subtle and complex objections. It soon became clear to Hartington that what he was really facing was Gladstone's inability to recognize that he had made a mistake, first in sending Gordon to Khartoum, then in refusing him military support. The whole affair exposed Gladstone's most glaring political vulnerability: the old man could not admit to an error in judgment.

That left Lord Hartington with only one course—to threaten to resign as Secretary of State for War unless a relief expedition was sent. In a Cabinet meeting on July 31 he drove the Prime Minister into a corner, stating that, unless an expedition was sent, he would resign. It was, he said, "a question of personal honour and good faith, and I don't see how I can yield upon it."

Gladstone was left with no choice. Lord Hartington's position in the Liberal party was second only to his own; as the leader of the Whig aristocracy his influence with upper, middle and lower classes alike was immense. Because of the influence and wealth that came with his title, no one would ever suggest that his political decisions were motivated by anything other than his perception of duty. Gladstone knew that he faced no idle threat, and that the resignation of Lord Hartington would be enough to bring the Prime Minister's government down. Less than a week later, on August 5, the House of Commons was asked to vote the sum of £300,000 in order "to enable Her Majesty's Government to undertake operations for the relief of General Gordon, should they become necessary." The resolution passed overwhelmingly.

Even then Gladstone was trying to find a way to avoid carrying out the commitment he had just made. A proviso he inserted into the resolution gave him the authority to suspend expenditure of the money if the Prime Minister found reason to believe the relief expedition was unnecessary. Hartington would have none of it. When Lord Granville wrote him, "It is clear, I think, that Gordon has our messages, and does not choose to answer them," implying that Gordon was in fact safe and that the relief expedition was unnecessary, Hartington made it clear that his threat to resign still held good. Gladstone was outmaneuvered and knew it. On August 26th, General Sir Garnet Wolseley was appointed to command what became popularly known as the "Gordon Relief Expedition."

Regarded by many as the outstanding British general of the second half of the 19th century, Wolseley had, at some level, taken a hand in every campaign fought by the British Army from the Crimean War to the Boer War. A dedicated professional with a genius for organization and logistics, Wolseley was once called "Our Only General" by Prime Minister Disraeli—a phrase not calculated to endear Wolseley to his fellow senior officers. To soldiers and civilians alike he seemed to embody all the Victorian virtues: exceptional courage, personal integrity, diligence, and an unshakeable belief in the Empire. "All Sir Garnet" became a catchphrase, first within the Army, then among the public, for situations well in hand.

Already well acquainted with Egypt after having successfully put down the Arabi revolt in 1882, Wolseley saw himself as being given a task which could be easily and safely accomplished if undertaken with the deliberateness that was his hallmark, but which was dangerous and doubtful if attempted in haste. Originally the size of the relief force was envisioned by Gladstone as little more than a brigade of infantry, perhaps some three thousand strong. After reviewing the situation, and in particular the critical position at Khartoum, Wolseley concluded that such a force was woefully inadequate for the task at hand, and recommended that the single brigade be expanded into three. The result was an expedition of more than ten thousand men, from regiments to be selected from the whole army. Wolseley was not about to allow his force to be overwhelmed by sheer numbers of the Mahdi's army, a la William Hicks. Such was the public's perception of the "Gordon Relief Expedition" that Wolseley knew, whether he liked it or not, that the whole of his reputation was riding on its success. It's hardly remarkable then that he chose to be deliberate and careful rather than swift and reckless. A wild, glorious rush into Khartoum might well achieve an astonishing success–but it could just as easily result in a horrible disaster.

There was another element at play in Wolseley's developing campaign which had a significant effect on his planning. His orders, drawn up by Baring, were explicit in the latitude he was permitted, as well as in regard to the ultimate purpose of the expedition. "The primary object of the expedition up the Valley of the Nile is to bring away General Gordon and Colonel Stewart from Khartoum. When that object has been secured, no further offensive operations of any kind are to be undertaken." In other words, the entire purpose of the campaign would be to carry out Gordon's initial instructions—there was to be no "smashing" of the Mahdi or occupying the Sudan. Baring, though he believed that the Sudan was still Egypt's responsibility, was of a mind with Gladstone in wanting to keep British troops out of that country. His concern, however, was not avoiding another imperial adventure, but rather avoiding any circumstance which might damage Britain's position in Egypt. The outright defeat of a British army at the hands of the Mahdi, however unlikely, could fatally undermine Britain's authority in Cairo. It appeared as if Gladstone, thwarted in his effort to avoid sending troops at all, would achieve his goal after all—there would be no expansion of the British presence in Africa. As for the fate of the city and its inhabitants, Wolseley's orders gave no instructions: Khartoum would be left on its own.

Throughout August and September Wolseley assembled his forces, and the regiments he chose read like an honor roll of the British Army. Among them were three battalions of the Guards: the 1st battalions of the Grenadier Guards and the Coldstream Guards, and the 2nd of the Scots Guards. Line regiments were represented by battalions from the Royal Sussex Regiment, the South Staffordshire Regiment, the Royal Berkshire Regiment, and the West Kent Regiment (once carried on the Army List as the 50th Regiment of Foot, the West Kents were known as the "Black Half Hundred" from the facing color of their uniforms), and Princess Victoria's Regiment. Light infantry

units selected were the King's Royal Rifle Corps and the Duke of
Cornwall's Light Infantry. There were two Scottish regiments: the
Royal Highlanders (the world-famous "Black Watch") and the
Gordon Highlanders, as well as two Irish regiments: the Royal Irish
Fusiliers and the Connaught Rangers.

Squadrons from eight different cavalry regiments were added to
Wolseley's expedition, coming from the Life Guards, the Royal
Dragoon Guards, the 2nd, 4th, and 5th Dragoon Guards, the Scots
Greys, the 5th Lancers, and the 19th Royal Hussar Regiment. In support of the horse and infantry were six batteries of the Royal Artillery
and a detachment of Royal Marines. The total strength of what was
now known as the "Gordon Relief Expedition" came to 10,500 officers and other ranks. While the regimental lists were being assembled,
Wolseley made arrangements with the Thomas Cook Company to
provide supplies and transportation for the journey up the Nile once
the troops reached Egypt. Then, while his forces were gathering in
London and boarding transports at Portsmouth, he went to Cairo,
where he arrived on September 9, and began planning his campaign.
Wolseley, who so perfectly embodied the quintessential Victorian commanding officer that he was almost a caricature—indeed he was the
inspiration for William S. Gilbert's "very model of a modern Major-
General"—was probably the worst possible choice to command an
expedition that required dash, determination, and, above all, a willingness not to be bound by the conventional wisdom of past experiences. Methodical, single-minded, not lacking in imagination but only
in the will to use it, Wolseley didn't have a sufficient grasp of the
details of desert warfare to understand the need to move both swiftly
and decisively.

In a message borne to Wadi Halfa by a native runner, Gordon had
made very clear what those details were, and at the same time offered
what could have been a blueprint, not only for a relief expedition to
Khartoum, but for operations against irregular forces and guerillas in
wild, open country that would stand as perfectly valid for the next
century.

> I cannot too much impress on you that this expedition will not
> encounter any enemy worth the name in a European sense of

the word; the struggle is with the climate and the destitution of the country. It is one of time and patience, and of small parties of determined men, backed by native allies, which are got by policy and money. A heavy lumbering column, however strong, is nowhere in this land. Parties of forty or sixty men, swiftly moving about, will do more than any column. If you lose two or three, what of it—it is the chance of war. Native allies above all things, whatever the cost. It is the country of the irregular, not of the regular. If you must move in mass you will find no end of difficulties whereas , if you let detached parties dash out here and there, you will spread dismay in the Arab ranks. The time to attack is the dawn, or rather before it (this is stale news), but sixty men would put these Arabs to flight just before dawn, which one thousand would not accomplish in dark. I do hope you will not drag on that artillery: it can only produce a delay and do little good.

It's not clear whether Wolseley ever saw this communication from Gordon; if he did, he apparently ignored it. Of course, the idea of professional jealously cannot be entirely discounted either. Gordon was junior to Wolseley; therefore, according to the strict system of seniority that existed in the British Army at the time, it was presumptuous for Gordon to believe that he knew more about warfare of any kind than did Sir Garnet, and that any of Gordon's ideas, however wellintentioned, could be superior to the tactical and strategic thinking of any senior officer was pure balderdash. Unfortunately, Wolseley's career would demonstrate that he was capable of exactly this sort of pettiness.

Wolseley had always considered himself something of a military innovator and constantly sought to produce some new tactical twist to his campaigns, though most often his "innovations" were more novelty or nuisance than useful. There were two strategies open to him in his effort to relieve Khartoum, the first was to land his forces at Port Sudan on the Red Sea, just north of Suakin, and from there march southwest across the Sudan to Khartoum. Recommending this strategy was that it was the shortest distance to the city, little more than three hundred miles, while its disadvantage was that the terrain was rugged and might offer the Mahdi an opportunity to make a defensive stand before the relief column reached the city. The other course of action, which Wolseley eventually chose, was a long, laborious trek up the Nile from Wadi Halfa. The distance was almost four times as great as from Suakin, but it offered the advantage of a secure line of supply and communications, namely the Nile itself.

Wolseley chose to draw on his experience in the Red River Campaign of 1870, fought in the upper reaches of Canada, adopting the same methods for moving his troops and supplies. The men, guns, and horses would be carried in a "river column" of specially constructed whaleboats drawn by a flotilla of shallow-draft Nile steamers, deploying where and when the enemy was encountered. While Wolseley was planning the advance, one of his officers was anxiously pressing to be allowed to take command of a "flying column" of camel-mounted troops which, once the relief force reached Korti, at the bottom of the great loop the Nile takes before it passes into Egypt, would dash across the intervening two hundred miles to the besieged city. Once there it would offer whatever support it could or bring out Gordon and the garrison, whichever course of action seemed best.

That officer was Major Herbert Horatio Kitchener, who was destined to become one of Britain's greatest soldiers, but who at this time was only beginning to make a reputation for himself as a particularly energetic and courageous officer. Chafing at Wolseley's refusal to sanction the "flying column," Kitchener eventually secured his commanding officer's permission to depart Cairo well in advance of the main column, which left the Egyptian capital on September 27. Kitchener's mission was to reach Debba, not far from Korti, where he hoped to set up an outpost where runners could make their way into and out of Khartoum with messages and intelligence.

It was more than just a daring endeavor—Kitchener was literally staking his life on the plan. Tall (he stood six feet, two inches) with piercing blue eyes that looked out from an exceptionally handsome face, Kitchener looked every inch the professional soldier. A dedicated officer, intelligent and insightful, and a gifted amateur archeologist, Kitchener spoke fluent French, Arabic, and some Turkish, and would run incredible risks in the months ahead to get messages to and from Gordon. Venturing deep into Arab territory, closely disguised as one of the Ansar—though one glimpse of his blue eyes would have given him away—Kitchener carried a bottle of poison with him at all times lest he fall alive into Arab hands. His exploits in the Sudan would eventually make his career in the Army, as well as turn his name into a household word in Great Britain, but none of that mattered to Kitchener: he was probably the most duty-bound officer to serve in the British Army since Wellington.

As for his request for a "flying column," Wolseley declined to consider it, worried that if the flying column were to encounter the Mahdi's army, the sheer numbers of the Ansar might overwhelm it before the rest of the expeditionary force could be brought up in support. It was perfectly sound thinking according to conventional military wisdom. Only time would reveal whether Kitchener's daring or Wolseley's prudence was the proper course to save Gordon and Khartoum.

CHAPTER 8

THE DUEL

In Khartoum Gordon had no knowledge of the drama that was unfolding in London as Gladstone was slowly being coerced into sending troops to the Sudan. When the telegraph was cut on February 13, all direct contact with the outside world was lost; the nearest telegraph terminal was now in Berber, and while the occasional message could get through when a river steamer chose to fight its way up or down the Nile, regular communication with the outside world had ceased. Messages that could be smuggled into or out of the city by native runners passing through the Madhi's lines would be almost the only means of news to and from the city, and those would be infrequent and fragmentary. The fate of Khartoum and its inhabitants now rested on the outcome of a duel of wills and wiles between Gordon and the Mahdi.

The siege of Khartoum would last for 317 days. It was a curious affair at first, almost more of a blockade than a siege. Each side had its own unique weaknesses which the other sought to exploit. The Mahdi had an enormous advantage in numbers, and was quite willing to be patient, hoping to starve Gordon out. His army was deeply deficient in firepower, however: the antiquated artillery it had captured from the Hicks column and in taking El Obeid were no match for the modern 9- and 16-pounder Krupp guns in Khartoum. Unable to bring his own guns close enough to bear effectively on the city's walls without exposing them to devastating counter-battery fire, the Mahdi had to content himself with keeping up a harassing fire from the Ansar's small arms.

141

Gordon had the advantage of being on the defensive, which was much less physically taxing than offensive actions. He was sitting behind secure walls and fortifications, with plenty of ammunition and an apparently sufficient store of food. Gordon's greatest weakness was lack of communications—he was sure that a relief expedition would be mounted, but could never be quite certain, nor know exactly when. There was also the disadvantage of being forced to remain inside a slowly shrinking perimeter. While his losses in men and material might be slight, the sense of feeling trapped was a psychological burden that would gradually come to wear on the garrison and the people of Khartoum.

As his masses closed in around the city, the Madhi issued a long and elaborate proclamation to the inhabitants of Khartoum. In it he asserted both his divine calling and the invincibility of his army, blessed as it was by Allah in the performance of *jihad*. He called upon the people of Khartoum to surrender and accept the mercy of Allah and his messenger, the Madhi.

Gordon, making his disdain blatantly obvious, had the proclamation read to the populace within Khartoum, then asked for an answer. The clamor to stand against the Mahdi's army was deafening. In a telling moment, one of Khartoum's most revered and learned sheiks declared that Muhammed Ahmed was a false Madhi. God would defend the city, he said, if the people put their trust in General Gordon. At the General's request, the sheikh drafted a reply to the Mahdi's decree, couched in theological terms, which rejected outright his call to surrender. The letter pointed out, with ecclesiastical precision, that Muhammed Ahmed had not fulfilled all the words of the ancient prophets. At his appearance, had the Euphrates dried up and revealed a hill of gold? Had contradiction and difference ceased upon the earth? Even more telling, did not the faithful know that the true Mahdi was born in the year of the prophet 255, from which it surely followed that he must be now 1,046 years old? And was it not clear to all men that this pretender was not a tenth of that age? It's not recorded how Muhammed Ahmed received these challenges to his divine authority, but from the moment his call to surrender was rejected, it was clear to everyone that the siege of Khartoum would end only when the city fell or the Mahdi's army was driven back into the desert.

The duel between Gordon and the Madhi for the fate of the city had begun.

For his part, Gordon was confident that he could hold out almost indefinitely—or at least as long as the city's morale could endure. The city walls were strong and well made, and more than proof against the Mahdist artillery; the least of Gordon's worries was a breach at any point. Ammunition for his guns and the troops' rifles was never a problem, and the food supplies seemed to be more than adequate for a siege of at least a few months. For as long as he could, Gordon staged raids on the Ansar camps, stealing whatever cattle and grain could be carried off, to help augment the supplies in the city. Sometimes Gordon would lead these raids himself, having never lost the taste for personal action. These raids also had the benefit of helping boost the morale of the garrison and the city, both by keeping the soldiers busy and giving the impression that the city and its defenders weren't completely helpless in the face of the Mahdi's threat.

But as the weeks passed, the grip held by the Mahdi's forces surrounding the city grew tighter, and the garrison grew correspondingly weaker. Omdurman continued to hold out, while the nine small river steamers under Gordon's command were able to keep its garrison reasonably well supplied. They also were able to keep up a steady skirmishing fire along both Niles whenever the Mahdi's troops were careless enough to expose themselves. In turn, the Ansar, the Mahdi's followers, forced their way into the village of Hadji Ali, on the north side of the Nile, and from there could bring a sporadic rifle fire down on the city, in particular on the Governor's Palace. Time and again Gordon's batteries of 16-pounders would bombard the houses where the Arab snipers hid, driving them off briefly, but always they returned, and as the weeks passed the volume and intensity of their rifle fire increased. But the crucial factor was food. El Obeid had fallen not because it had been overrun but because the garrison had been starved into submission; the situation confronting Khartoum was essentially the same.

Muhammed Ahmed made no determined attempt to take the city by storm until August. His experience with El Obeid and the other small towns and cities of the Sudan had shown him that starvation was his best ally. When no British troops followed Gordon into Khartoum in the months after the General's arrival, the Mahdi took it as a sign that the British government had well and truly abandoned the city to its fate, so there was no urgency to the task of taking it. Better to starve Gordon and the garrison into surrender than risk losing too many of the faithful to Gordon's guns and mines.

That was a lesson that the Ansar had learned fairly early. Gordon was not another William Hicks, nor was he a typical Egyptian officer, appointed more for his family connections than his competence. Gordon's moat between the rivers, his caltrops and mines, his carefully sighted guns, had all caused varying degrees of consternation and casualties to the Mahdi's army when they first approached the city. The Nile itself was Gordon's valuable ally: as the summer progressed and the river rose, the moat guarding the southern approach to the city became far too deep to ford, while Gordon's guns and mines had turned the open stretches around the moat into a killing ground. The Mahdi knew this, and knew that the handful of steamers Gordon kept on patrol in the Blue and White Niles were sufficient to drive off any attempt to cross the rivers by boat. The only watercraft the Mahdi had available were lightly constructed *dhows* and *feluccas*, shallow draft, single-masted sailboats built from wood. They were the types of boats that the Madhi had grown up watching his father build, and he well knew that a single hit from one of Khartoum's Krupp cannon would blow such craft to splinters.

At the same time, while the Mahdi's followers seemed to be "mere rag-tag and bob-tail" to Gordon, more rabble in arms than army, he lacked the strength to go out and meet them in open battle. While his estimate that "five hundred brave men" could have driven off the Mahdi's army was clearly wishful thinking, he knew too well after the Halfaya debacle that his eight thousand-man garrison could not be trusted in open battle. Behind secure walls, with artillery in support, they were reliable enough, but he estimated that he had fewer than a hundred who could be trusted not to bolt at the first shot on a battlefield. Thus the fighting was confined to a duel of artillery shelling on one side, and volleys of rifle-fire on the other until the early summer. All the while, however, the Arabs were slowly tightening their grip.

In mid-April Gordon was able to get a message to Berber, which was then sent on by telegraph to Cairo. In it he said that he had provisions for at least five months, and that he was confident that if he were given two thousand or three thousand "reliable" (i.e. British) troops, he would be able to drive the Madhi back into the heart of the Sudan and quickly "settle" the rebellion. Gladstone, of course, was still adamant at this point about not sending a single British soldier to the Sudan, but it is curious to note that when, four months later, he did finally agree to send a military force up the Nile, he envisaged no more than three thousand troops being committed to the expedition.

Money soon became a problem, as the Egyptian soldiers expected to be paid, and the merchants in the city still expected likewise for whatever supplies Gordon purchased. On April 26, he began issuing paper notes against British credit in Cairo. They were made to look like Egyptian pound notes, the first printing being the sum of £2,500, and were redeemable at their face value six months from their date of issue. Subsequent issues raised the outstanding debt to £25,000 by July 30, and at the same time Gordon borrowed some £50,000 from the city merchants. Yet such was the confidence that the people had in him that despite the opportunity for rampant inflation, the notes held their value until almost the end of the siege.

All the while, Gordon was well aware that the garrison and the city both looked to him as the central pillar of their somewhat fragile morale, so he did what he could to maintain a semblance of normality under the circumstances. He tried to set a personal example of courage and endurance. In a classic display of British phlegm, when a shell fired by an Arab gun crashed through one of the walls of the Governor's Palace—fortunately it was a dud—he ordered the date of its arrival to be inscribed above the hole. He also enforced a stern discipline on everyone in the city, declaring, "I am an advocate of summary and quick punishment!" At one point, on the evidence of Frank Power, four sheikhs who were accused of plotting to betray the city to the Madhi were shot on Gordon's orders.

Gordon understood a basic truth that later generations of "leaders" would try to discredit: fear can be an essential part of ensuring obedience among reluctant followers. It was a lesson he had been willing to impose as far back as his days in China while commanding the "Ever Victorious Army." Still, an intimidating pose was not one with which he was ever thoroughly comfortable. "It is quite painful to see men tremble so," reads one passage in his journal, written in September, "when they come and see me, that they cannot hold the match to their cigarette."

Yet the need for such harsh discipline was made clear on April 27, when Valeh Bey, one of the tribal chieftains who had proclaimed himself loyal to Gordon, suddenly surrendered himself and his followers to the Mahdi at Mesalimeh, a small port on the Nile between Berber and Metemma. It was a significant blow to Gordon's prestige among those Arabs whose loyalty was wavering, and it was also costly in the material sense, for when Valeh capitulated he also surrendered one of the precious river steamers, seventy boatloads of provisions, and two thousand rifles.

But if he could be stern, even harsh, in enforcing his discipline, Gordon could also be generous with his praise. In April he commissioned several jewelers in the city to begin striking medals to honor distinguished service in the defense of Khartoum—silver for officers, silver-gilt and pewter for other ranks. The medals were shaped in the form of a crescent moon encircling a star; in the center of the star they bore an inscription from the Koran, a date, and the words "Siege of Khartoum" engraved over the image of an old-fashioned "flaming onion" grenade. Nor did he neglect awards for the civilians. "Schoolchildren and women," he wrote in his journal, "also received medals; consequently, I am very popular with the black ladies of Khartoum."

Gordon's residence, the Governor's Palace, was a flat-roofed, three-storey structure on the north side of the city, just a few hundred yards from the river. On a whim, Gordon had placed his telescope on the Palace roof, and discovered that his field of view was amazing. He had direct lines of sight across the Blue Nile, up the Nile proper to the north, and over to the west to Omdurman. It became his habit to spend several hours there each day, for not only could he see his troops in every part of the city, they could see him as well, and their knowledge that his eye might be upon them at any given moment helped him maintain discipline. If left unwatched, sentries would fall asleep and posts would be neglected. At times Gordon's despair over the wretched quality of the average Egyptian soldier sounds almost comical: "I certainly claim to having commanded, more often than any other man, cowardly troops, but this experience of 1884 beats all past experiences. . . . A more contemptible soldier than the Egyptian never existed. Here we never count on them; they are held in supreme contempt, poor creatures. They never go out to fight; it would be perfectly iniquitous to make them." Yet despite his frustrations with his Egyptian troops, Gordon never gave thought to abandoning them. By the end of October, having decided that the majority of the garrison were simply useless mouths to be fed if they remained in the city, he packed them into his five remaining steamers and sent them down to Metemma with orders not to return to Khartoum. Now the defenders numbered less than a thousand, but they were all, at least so Gordon believed, reliable.

For the Mahdi, when Valeh Bey changed allegiance in April it was yet another great moral victory, as Arab tribes all over the Sudan and southern Egypt were rallying to his call for a *jihad* against the foreigners, their Turkish clients, and their Egyptians vassals. By now the Mahdi was the absolute ruler of all of the Sudan, parts of Abyssinia, and the south of Egypt. His domain was as large a territory as all of Europe from Germany west to the British Isles. Tremors were felt as far north as Cairo, where the recently suppressed Arabi revolt left still-simmering resentments among the common people that threatened to boil over again in open revolt and mutiny. His proclamation of *jihad* had been heard throughout the marketplaces of the Middle East, threatening the security of the Ottoman Empire. No longer was he just another desert mystic suffering from delusions of grandeur; he was now perceived as a genuine threat as far away as Constantinople.

There, the Sultan, who had barely escaped being toppled from his throne when much of the Ottoman Empire's European territories had been stripped away in the Russo-Turkish War just six years earlier, was still looking nervously eastward, as the Russian border was only a few days' march from his capital. Such a revolt would be all the distraction the Tsar's armies would need to launch an offensive toward Constantinople, which the Russians had coveted for centuries. The Sultan did not have enough reliable troops of his own to be able to defend the city and at the same time put down a rebellion. This was a concern in London as well, for the British government had entered into an alliance with the Ottoman Turks in 1878, with the express

purpose of keeping the Russians out of Constantinople. Should the
Mahdi's rebellion spread beyond the Sudan, it had the potential to precipitate a major European war.

There is no way to know if the Mahdi was aware of any of this.
Just how extensive were his education, his knowledge of the larger
world, and his grasp of politics can only be estimated. Certainly he
had some knowledge of the geography of the Middle East, as well as
an understanding of the literally Byzantine politics of the Ottoman
Empire. But what he truly knew of Europe and Asia, as opposed to the
legend and myth that was—and often still is-part of the "education"
process in the Islamic world, cannot be determined. What was evident
to anyone who had any dealings with him at length was that
Muhammed Ahmed possessed a first-class intellect. Here was no
"noble savage" as was often the Europeans' characterization of the
peoples of Africa, nor was he simply a rabble-rousing demagogue. By
all accounts he possessed a charisma equaled in European leaders only
by Napoleon Bonaparte and Adolf Hitler. That is not to lump him
together with either of them, because though they did share many
common traits, in other ways the Mahdi stood apart. He never
descended to the depths of unbounded ambition or malignant prejudice as did the two European leaders. Though the Mahdi thought his
calling divine, and his person semi-divine, he still bowed before Allah,
and it could be argued that nothing he ever undertook was entirely
inconsistent with the will of Allah as presented in the Koran and
hadiths. If the Mahdi had one overarching fault it was excess—he carried his sense of mission to an extreme interpretation. While he might
seek to make himself the equal of the Prophet, he never sought to
usurp the position of the Prophet or rewrite the Koran.

It was in May that the Mahdi's charismatic nature revealed itself
to General Gordon, as the two men began one of the most peculiar
episodes in the entire history of the Mahdi's rebellion: their correspondence. There was little in its content that was actually novel or
unique: for the most part it was the expected exhortations and urgings
of each to the other to give up their vain effort and either surrender or
depart. What made it notable was the mutual respect, possibly even
admiration, that the two men developed for each other. Each recognized their mirror image and at the same time a kindred spirit: their

deep spirituality, their shared sense of mission, their loyalty to their respective causes, their determination not to capitulate to the other. While it might not be entirely correct to say that Gordon and the Mahdi each perceived that the other was an honorable man—the concepts of "honor" in their respective cultures were too different for such an appreciation to have fully developed—they certainly recognized that they were two opponents worthy of mutual respect, and so it was given. A passing remark in his journal reveals how well Gordon understood the Mahdi's ability to inspire his followers: "The meanest of the Mahdi's followers is a determined warrior, who could undergo thirst and privation, who no more cared for pain or death than if he were stone."

In Arabic culture there is a wonderfully telling phrase: "It is written." Its implication is that there are aspects of life—events, characteristics, fates—that are ordained by God or Allah that cannot be changed, no matter what the efforts of men to do so. In all of its power and import this phrase applied to the Mahdi and Gordon. Each would be firm, even forceful, in their statements and positions, and there was little acrimony or antagonism in their exchanges. It was as if they recognized that they were fated to be foes, even enemies, but that could not and would not prevent them from coming to respect each other. It was written. . . .

At the end of July the Arab tribes around the town of Shendy, directly across the Nile from Metemma, halfway between Khartoum and Berber, finally rose up and openly sided with the Madhi. Berber soon followed, but while the capture of Shendy had been achieved quickly and with relatively little bloodshed, the fall of Berber was a far different affair. Because of its loyalty to the Egyptian government, the city was sacked in an orgy of looting, rape and slaughter that lasted for days. When the town fell, the telegraph line to Cairo was permanently cut, and for months nothing more would be heard directly from Khartoum.

Gordon was now entirely cut off from the outside world and compelled to rely entirely upon his own resources. Knowing this, he was willing to try any stratagem, any subterfuge, that might increase the odds of the city holding out until the relief expedition—in which he passionately believed—could arrive. At one point he sent out black

Sudanese to mingle with the slaves of the Arabs in the Mahdi's camps, encouraging them to run away or even come into the city, assuring them that they would be given their freedom once the siege was lifted. The threat of rebellion or desertion among their slaves might, he hoped, prompt defections among the Arab sheiks who supported the Mahdi. The effort accomplished little, for among the slaves the fear of retribution by the Mahdi and his followers was for the most part more powerful than the lure of what might only be a temporary freedom.

While he was exchanging letters with the Madhi, Gordon was carrying on a separate correspondence with one of the Mahdi's European captives, Rudolf Slatin, the Austrian officer who had been Governor of Darfur. Given the Egyptian rank of Bey, Slatin had fought the Mahdi for almost four years in the western Sudan. Having been wounded several times, his courage was unquestionable, as had been his determination to hold out as long as possible. In the end, he had been defeated by the same fearful weapon that had subdued El Obeid and was slowly eroding Khartoum's will to resist—starvation. Somehow, though, Gordon felt that Slatin's capitulation at Darfur was something disgraceful, and as a consequence he held little respect for the unfortunate Viennese. He might have paid closer attention, for Slatin's experience could have been instructive.

During the fighting in Darfur, after suffering a series of setbacks, Slatin's Moslem soldiers became demoralized, attributing their defeats to the fact that they were fighting fellow Moslems, and, what was worse, were being led by an infidel. It seemed to them that in resisting the Madhi they were fighting for a Christian cause against their own faith. Sensing that a revolt or an outright mutiny was brewing, Slatin suddenly announced that he had chosen to follow the way of the Prophet and, outwardly at least, embraced the practices of Islam. This simple act—which Slatin would maintain, until the end of his life, was nothing more than an elaborate charade—inspired his rather simple-minded troops, and they defended Darfur with a renewed belief in themselves, their leader, and their cause.

But Slatin's stratagem only delayed the inevitable, and in January 1884 Darfur fell. Slatin, taken captive, was brought before the Madhi, who was sufficiently pleased to learn of his alleged conversion as to allow his life to be spared, but not sufficiently impressed by it to allow

Slatin's release. Instead, the young Austrian would spend the next twelve years a captive of the Madhi and his successors, some of that time in chains. When the Madhi made his encampment south of the city of Khartoum, Slatin was compelled to accompany him, and it was there he began his correspondence with General Gordon.

In his letters he attempted to explain the reasons for his surrender, while at the same time excusing his conversion to Islam. At several points he begged Gordon for permission to escape into the city. Gordon, however, wasn't inclined to be sympathetic or accommodating, questioning just how desperate conditions in Darfur had become before the city was surrendered. He noted in his journal that, "The Greek [one of the city's merchants] . . . says Slatin had 4,000 ardebs [measures] of dura [wheat], 1,500 cows, and plenty of ammunition." Before the correspondence between the two began, he made slighting references to Slatin in his journal, at one point writing, "One cannot help being amused at the Mahdi carrying all the Europeans about with him—nuns, priests, Greeks, Austrian officers—what a medley, a regular Etat-Major!"

It is possible that Gordon didn't understand the danger in which Slatin had placed himself with his letters; certainly they confused him. Ordered by the Madhi and the Khalifas to write demanding the surrender of the city, Slatin instead wrote a carefully worded appeal to Gordon for permission to escape into Khartoum, but when the first arrived on October 16, Gordon's only comments were: "The letters of Slatin have arrived. I have no remarks to make on them, and cannot make out why he wrote them." While admitting "one feels sorry for him," Gordon was adamant in his refusal to allow Slatin into Khartoum: "I shall have nothing to do with Slatin's coming here to stay, unless he has the Mahdi's positive leave, which he is not likely to get; his doing so would be the breaking of his parole which should be as sacred when given to the Mahdi as to any other power, and it would jeopardize the safety of all these Europeans, prisoners with Mahdi."

Where Gordon gained the impression that Slatin was an officer released on parole is unknown, for he was clearly being treated as a prisoner of war in the enemy camp. As such, he had the right, if not the actual duty, to try to escape. Sudanese and Egyptian soldiers who had been captured in the Mahdi's earlier victories and then forced to fight in his army were daily escaping to the city and being welcomed into it. Why he perceived Slatin's circumstance as different Gordon never explained, nor did he give any reasons for his presumption that Slatin's escape might endanger the rest of the Europeans being held by the Madhi. In point of fact, the Madhi never took reprisals against any of his European prisoners whenever one of them attempted to escape, or even succeeded.

The whole of Slatin's correspondence with Gordon reflects little credit on the General, which makes the entire episode worth noting, for it seems out of character with Gordon's widely-recognized generosity. Gordon's animosity toward Slatin seems to have stemmed more from his apparent conversion to Islam than to his surrender of Darfur. Slatin sensed this, and endeavored to explain that he had feigned becoming a Moslem in order to maintain his troops' morale and prolong their resistance. In his heart, he declared, he had never abandoned his allegiance to Christianity. "Whether by my conversion I committed a dishonourable step is a matter of opinion—it was made more easy to me, perhaps, because I had, perhaps unhappily, not received a strict religious education at home." If the source of Gordon's disapproval was that Slatin ultimately surrendered to the Mahdi, the young Viennese was prepared to answer that charge as well:

> Does your Excellency believe that to me, an Austrian officer, the surrender was easy? It was one of the hardest days of my life. By submission and obedient behavior I have attained a certain degree of confidence amongst the local magnates and thus have received permission to write to you, because they are of the opinion that by these lines I am requesting your Excellency to surrender. Should your Excellency not despise my feeble services and small knowledge of tactics, I beg to offer you my help, with no desire for a higher post of honour, only from a devotion and friendship with your Excellency. I am ready to serve with or under you, for victory or death. . . .

When Gordon did not respond, Slatin again tried to make his case to the General, writing a few days later:

Your Excellency, I have fought twenty-seven times for the government against the enemy, and they have beaten me twice, and I have done nothing dishonorable, nothing which should hinder your Excellency from writing me an answer, that I may know what to do. . . . If there are letters from Europe for me at the post I beg you to send them me, because it is almost three years since I have had any news of my family. I entreat your Excellency to honour me with an answer.

There would be no answer from Gordon, and no further exchanges between the two men, as Slatin's correspondence with Gordon was discovered by one of the Khalifas. He was immediately thrown into chains, where he remained for several months, while for some days he was threatened with execution—not for writing to Gordon, but for failing to write what the Madhi had instructed him to set down. News of Slatin's misfortune reached Gordon, but the General had little sympathy for him. Yet he could never completely suppress acknowledging Slatin's abilities or bravery: "What one has felt so much here is the want of men like Gessi, or Messadaglia, or Slatin, but I have no one to whom I could entrust expeditions. . . ."

Little news of the situation within the city was reaching the outside world. On September 29, a telegram from Khartoum dated July 31 was received by the *London Times*. From it the circumstances in the Sudanese capital became a bit clearer, although decidedly dated. Gordon was now entirely on the defensive, his only aggressive action being trying to clear a route up the Nile to reestablish communications and evacuate anyone who wanted to leave, and launching the occasional sortie intended to bring supplies into the city from the surrounding countryside. Otherwise he was trapped, with no way out. If he had possessed a single reliable regiment, he said, the Mahdi's lines might have been cleared with ease, but his impotence encouraged the Arabs, and they were gathering in ever-increasing numbers. To Gordon it was only a matter of time until at last they crushed his resistance under the weight of their numbers.

By the first week of September, the endless war of nerves between the besieged and the besiegers had begun to take its toll on Khartoum's defenders. Food was hardly an issue—so much grain had been laid in according to Gordon's orders and so many cattle taken in raids on Arab camps that the price of foodstuffs had actually dropped below what merchants were charging before the siege began. What was gradually wearing away the defenders' will to resist was the lack of news from the outside world. Rumors were spread by Mahdist sympathizers who remained behind in the city claiming that Khartoum had been abandoned by both Cairo and London, and that the relief expedition was a myth. Gordon, the whisperings ran, had been forgotten by his own government.

More critical to the city's morale was the outcome of a skirmish on September 4, when one of Gordon's cattle-raiding parties was overtaken by a horde of Arab horsemen. Dispersed in open country, the Egyptian soldiers were quickly ridden down, some eight hundred being lost in this single action. It was a heavy blow to Gordon's pride as well as the garrison's strength, for up until this moment it had been a point of pride for him that his soldiers could carry out such raids with near-impunity. The effects of the raids themselves had been twofold: not only were they a source of fresh meat for the city, they also gave the garrison and populace a means of striking back at their besiegers, alleviating some of the feeling of being trapped and helplessness. Even Gordon was at times overtaken by melancholy: watching the hawks that soared and swooped above the palace reminded him of a passage from Proverbs, Chapter 30, verse 17: "The eye that mocketh at his father and despiseth to obey his mother, the ravens of the valley shall pick it out, and the young eagles shall eat it." "I often wonder," he confided to his journal, "whether they are destined to pick my eyes, for I fear I was not the best of sons."

Apparently it was this action that caused Gordon to decide to try and force a passage of the Nile past Berber. The Nile had risen to the point where a steamer could safely negotiate the Sixth Cataract above Berber and sail down the river into friendly waters. Determined to make his case before the authorities in London and Cairo for remaining behind to defend the city, a cache of documents was prepared, including Colonel Stewart's diary of the siege, along with a personal appeal from Gordon to all the European powers, asking for assistance. The steamer *Abbas* was given the task of carrying the package, along with the English and French consuls and the rest of the Europeans who had remained in the city after the siege began. Also boarding the *Abbas* was Colonel Stewart, Gordon's second-in-command, who had come to share his General's passion for defending Khartoum and who was expected to make a forceful case before the Cabinet—and the House of Commons if need be—for a relief column to be sent up the Nile. Gordon, careful to protect Stewart's reputation, gave him written orders to depart on the *Abbas*, so that no one would question whether Stewart had abandoned his post. Four extra steamers would sail with the *Abbas*, protecting her until she was out of danger from attacks by the Mahdi's troops.

Extra baulks of wood and whatever bits of metal plating could be found were placed around the vulnerable spots of the *Abbas*' hull and superstructure. As long as the steamer stayed in mid-channel, she would be safe from nearly any weapon the Arabs possessed. Only if she neared the shore was there a danger that the Ansar's small arms might be able to do serious damage. As much cordwood for the boilers as could be carried was brought aboard, and the steamer's pilot, one of the most experienced men on the river, was urged to stop only at deserted parts of the river when it became necessary to collect wood to refuel. As darkness fell on September 10, the small convoy of steamers pulled away from the Khartoum waterfront and headed down the river. Though he had no way of knowing it, Gordon would never see anyone aboard the *Abbas* alive again.

While he never explicitly said so in his Journals, Gordon appears to have discounted the possibility that he would share Slatin's fate should Khartoum be taken. He expected no mercy from the Madhi, who, Gordon believed, would have him executed, no matter what the teachings of the Koran. He was aware of the ghastly fate that had befallen another European who had become a prisoner of the Madhi: a Frenchman by the name of Clavier Pain.

Pain, an adventurer at heart who had fought with the Paris Commune during the Franco-Prussian War, had been exploring the western Sudan when he was captured by the Mahdi's followers sometime in late 1883. It's unclear whether Pain was already unwell when he was captured or fell ill after he was taken, but in any case, as he was shuffled from encampment to encampment, a fever he had contracted became progressively worse. Forced to ride a camel on which he could barely sit, he was being carried to the Mahdi's camp outside Khartoum when he passed out and fell to the ground. Orders were given to bury him immediately, and within minutes Pain's body was lost to sight under a mound of sand. Witnesses later said they were convinced that Pain had been buried alive.

With Stewart gone, the burden of command began to weigh heavily on Gordon. Again and again he confided to his journal his need for subordinates he could trust. He was expected to be everywhere, to make every decision. "Nearly every order has to be repeated two or three times. I am weary of my life." And yet the intrepidity of Charles Gordon was never more evident than in the last few months of the siege of Khartoum.

He continued to pass out medals to deserving soldiers and civilians; special rations were issued on Moslem feast days; cash bonuses were paid to soldiers who volunteered for hazardous duty. At his orders, bands would give public concerts and fireworks displays were arranged. The latest bit of encouraging news, no matter how slight, was posted in city squares and the marketplace. Still, morale sagged. When in early October word reached him that sixteen of Khartoum's leading citizens were planning a revolt of their own to deliver the city to the Mahdi, Gordon had the lot of them arrested and imprisoned. But he confided to his journal that night, "I confess I am more perplexed about these arrests than I like: is it a good thing? Or is it not? If I could be sure that the majority wished to go to the Mahdi, I could make up my mind at once what to do: it would be an immense relief to me, but does the mass wish it?"

On the next day, October 16, came what was probably the cruelest blow of all. Slatin, still vainly carrying on his correspondence with Gordon, informed the General that the *Abbas* had been captured and all aboard her had been slain. Gordon had heard a rumor to that effect a few days earlier, but discounted it. Now Slatin apparently confirmed it, and while Gordon clung to the belief for a few more days that the report was another attempt at Mahdist propaganda, he confided to his journal on October 21, "I am very anxious about the Abbas: it would be terrible, if it is true, that she is captured."

The next morning a letter from the Mahdi arrived. It began, in Muhammed Ahmed's classically florid style:

In the Name of Allah the Merciful and Compassionate: praise be to Allah, the Bountiful Ruler, and blessing on our Lord Muhammed with peace.

From the servant who trusts in Allah—Muhammed the son of Abdullah.

To Gordon Pasha of Khartoum, may God guide him into the path of virtue, amen!

Know that your small steamer, named *Abbas*—which you sent with the intention of forwarding your news to Cairo, by way of Dongola, the persons sent being your representative Stewart Pasha and the two consuls, French and English, with other persons, has been captured by the will of Allah.

Those who believed in us as Mahdi, and surrendered, have been delivered; and those who did not were destroyed—as your representative afore-named, with the Consuls and the rest—whose souls Allah has condemned to the fire and eternal misery.

Muhammed Ahmed then went on to catalogue what property had been taken from the steamer—Gordon's government cipher; the appeals for help to the Pope and the Sultan; Stewart's journals; and the documents containing the details of state of the garrison, the food, and ammunition reserves within the city; along with copies of all the telegraphic traffic that had passed between Khartoum and Cairo. "We have now understood it all," the letter went on. Once again the Mahdi invited Gordon to surrender and convert to Islam, declaring that he would be given no more such opportunities: "For, after the beginning of the battle were you to surrender, it would be from fear, and not willingly, and that is not to be accepted."

What had happened to the *Abbas*? Gordon had no way of knowing, though he suspected treachery. But a message from Kitchener smuggled into the city a few days later provided some of the details, which were far less dramatic but equally tragic.

The *Abbas* had successfully made her way past Berber, despite heavy fire from the banks of the Nile at a number of places. But when the steamer was sixty miles below Abu Hamed and less than one hundred miles from Kitchener's outpost at Debba, she struck an uncharted rock, which forced her to make for the south bank. There she was greeted by Sulieman Wad Gamir, sheik of the Monasir tribe, along with several lesser sheiks. Professing friendship, the Arabs offered to provide camels to take Stewart and the two consuls to Debba, but during the night, as the Europeans slept, the tribesmen rushed their tents and massacred them. The *Abbas* was then stormed, and all but fourteen of the passengers and crew still aboard were cut to pieces.

It was a cruel blow to Gordon, who had been counting on Stewart to make a compelling case for intervention in the Sudan to the Cabinet, the Commons, and the British people. He had no idea that an expedition had already been formed and was slowly making its way up the Nile. In the same letter in which he announced that the *Abbas* had been captured and those aboard her killed, the Mahdi informed Gordon that he intended to launch a full attack on the city soon, concluding with the words, "I have decided to take pity on some of my men and allow them to die as to obtain paradise."

Gordon's reply was, as could be expected, defiant: "Whether he [the Mahdi] has captured twenty thousand steamers like the *Abbas*, or twenty thousand Stewarts Pasha; it is all one to me. I am here, like iron, and hope to see the newly-arrived English." With that he ended the correspondence, informing the Mahdi that henceforth they would communicate only with bullets. The siege of Khartoum was about it enter its final stages.

The Mahdi's declaration was a revealing look into the soul of a man who some would later claim was merely leading a nationalist fight for freedom. It was made with such passion and such utter conviction that there was no doubt that he still believed that he was answering a divine calling, and those who followed him were helping him fulfill a holy mission. At the same time it revealed a portion of that soul that was a portal into hell, for the cruelty inherent in sending thousands of men to their death in the name of pity, attempting to characterize their slaughter as an act of mercy, was the pronouncement of a madman.

It cannot be questioned that Muhammed Ahmed was still bound by his vision of Islam; what had happened was that the vision had changed. The Mahdi himself was growing corpulent, as years of living in austerity had given way to a life of sensuality and pleasure. Yet he still knelt toward Mecca five times a day and said his prayers. The details of his mode of living still adhered to the prescriptions and pro-scriptions of the Koran; according to all the fundamental teachings of Islam, he was still a holy man, a respected, scholarly imam. But a darkness was overtaking him. Gone was the austere, strict but benign Islam that Muhammed Ahmed had preached as an itinerant *imam* in the Sudanese desert; in its place was an austere and strict Islam now devoid of mercy or tolerance. The Mahdi was Allah's tool, the vessel by which the truth and glory of pure, unpolluted Islam would spread throughout the world, and in turn his followers were the Mahdi's tools, to be used and used up as he saw fit, with no regard to their wishes, hopes, or beliefs.

It was a cold contrast to Gordon's perception of himself as God's tool, to be discarded when the Almighty chose to do so. The Mahdi saw himself as indispensable; Allah could not achieve His will without him. Gordon saw himself as entirely expendable; God's will was not dependent on any single human being. The contrast in how each man viewed himself was a microcosm of the profound differences in their faiths: Gordon believed in a merciful Christianity, the Mahdi in a mer-ciless Islam.

It was in early November that some of the most encouraging news yet reached the city, which went far to relieve the despair that had set-tled over Khartoum with the loss of the *Abbas*. One of Kitchener's messengers slipped into the city with a packet of letters for Gordon, wrapped in a copy of the September 15 London Standard. Reading it eagerly, Gordon learned that Gladstone had finally been compelled to agree to a relief expedition and that it had already sailed for Cairo.

The details of the planned operations were a source of great excitement not only for Gordon but for the city as well. "Lord Wolseley seen off at Victoria Station, for the Gordon relief expedi-tion!!! NO! for the relief of the Sudan garrison.... I declare positively, and once and for all, that I will not leave the Sudan until every one who wants to go down is given the chance to do so, unless a govern-ment is established which relieves me of the charge; therefore if any emissary or letter comes up here ordering me to come down, I WILL NOT OBEY IT BUT WILL STAY HERE; AND FALL WITH THE TOWN, AND RUN ALL RISKS."

With this news, the overriding question for Gordon now was when would the Madhi decide the time had come to mount a major assault on the city. Judging the situation as the engineer he was, he concluded that the attack would come toward the end of the year, when the Nile began to drop. Would the relief column arrive in time? he wondered. Did Wolseley truly understand how different was war in the Sudan desert from war anywhere else in Africa—or the Empire for that matter? Would Wolseley follow the same pattern of methodical, plodding campaigning he had employed against the Zulus five years earlier, or would he strike with the dash and drive that Gordon knew was the key to campaigning in the African desert? Sensing that the Mahdi feared the approach of a British Army, the General got word to Kitchener that when the relief column arrived, the troops should wear their traditional red tunic rather than the khaki-colored ones that were now standard issue in the British Army. So potent had the image of redcoated infantry become among the peoples of Africa and Asia that their appearance would leave no doubt among the Mahdi's followers as to the identity of their new foes.

The same day that the news from Kitchener arrived, the Ansar were finally able to bring some of their guns to bear on the city itself. While their shells did little damage, the intermittent but never-ceasing bombardment became more enervating with each passing day. One of the four remaining steamers ran aground on the north bank of the Blue Nile, and the Mahdi's artillery soon set it afire. It had been one of the more reliable steamers, and its loss was soon felt, as Omdurman came under steadily increasing pressure and their was no chance of further reinforcement or resupply for the hapless garrison there. Surrounded and cut off from the river, devoid of any artillery of its own, the fort came under a steady barrage of small arms fire from the Ansar, and casualties mounted daily.

Despite careful rationing and the raids on Arab camps during the summer and autumn, food was beginning to run low and everyone within the city began to feel the effects of malnutrition. The war of nerves escalated, as an Ansar gun was sited across the river from the Governor's Palace and began an intermittent shelling that lasted day and night. The shells did little damage, for the building was constructed of heavy sandstone, but the noise made it impossible to sleep.

When the guns weren't firing, a large drum sited on the north bank kept up a steady beat, pounding heard in almost every quarter of the city. Little by little the morale of Khartoum was crumbling.

Though he was able to keep the boatyard working and had it build a replacement steamer for the one that had been lost—in a moment of black humor Gordon named it the *Zobeir*—there was little room left for his river flotilla to maneuver. The level of the Nile was falling, and as it fell vast stretches of mudflats on either bank allowed the Mahdi's forces to approach closer to the city than ever before. More ominously, as the Nile fell, so did the level of the moat, and by December 13, Gordon was beginning to worry that it was no longer deep enough to provide a barrier to a determined assault.

It was on that day that he wrote what would be the last reliable communication the world would ever receive from him or Khartoum. "NOW MARK THIS, if the Expeditionary Force, and I ask for no more than two hundred men, does not come in ten days, the town may fall; and I have done my best for the honor of my country. Good-bye. C. G. Gordon." Bundling up this note with his journal and papers, along with the telegrams sent and received during his ten months in Khartoum, he attached a note to it that read: "Events at Khartoum. General Gordon's Journal. No secrets as far as I am concerned. To be pruned down if published. C. G. Gordon." The bundle was given to the captain of the steamer *Bordein*, who was then ordered to make for Metemma and the Relief Expedition.

CHAPTER 9

THE RELIEF COLUMN

Everything now hung on General Garnet Wolseley's plans for his relief expedition to Khartoum. The fate of the city, of Gordon, and the Mahdi's revolt would be determined by Wolseley' success or failure. The greatest enemy was time: despite Kitchener's best efforts, the information coming out of Khartoum was sketchy at best, and often contradictory. Consequently Wolseley was unsure of how secure—or perilous—was Gordon's true position. He thus hesitated to make a decision as to whether it was urgent that he risk a rush to the city's relief, or whether he had time to make the careful, methodical approach he preferred. Whether he was willing to acknowledge it or not, the specter of the massacre of William Hicks' army in the desert still loomed darkly over any plans for campaigning in the Sudan.

While he was still in England, Wolseley had called on the talents of a young officer by the name of William Francis Butler to solve an essential part of his problem: transport up the Nile. Butler had made the acquaintance of then-Colonel Garnet Wolseley fifteen years earlier when, as an officer of the 69th Infantry, he had been posted to Montreal, Canada. There he had procured boats for Wolseley's Red River campaign, which the General was now using as a model for his Nile expedition. Butler had become something of an expert on small boats to be used for military operations, and so was given the responsibility of finding the right boats in sufficient numbers to carry the expeditionary force up the Nile.

Just two days after the relief column was authorized by Parliament, Butler and a Colonel Alleyn of the Royal Engineers went down to Portsmouth to inspect standard-design lifeboats for possible use. These were determined to be unsuitable, primarily because they drew too much water: the expedition would be trying to sail up the Nile at a time of year when the level of the river would be falling. Deciding that they could produce a design that met their exact needs and which could quickly be produced in the numbers required, the two men conceived of a thirty-foot boat they called the "Nile whaler." Fitted to mount a dozen oars, it could also step a small mast which would support a lug sail. Each whaler could carry ten soldiers and two crewmen, plus a half-ton of stores and ammunition.

Satisfied with their design (it was endorsed as sound and practical by no less an authority on African rivers than the world-famous explorer Henry Stanley), the two officers placed orders for four hundred of their distinct watercraft with a total of forty-seven boatyards. In four weeks all four hundred of them were stowed aboard eleven steamers bound for Alexandria. As plans for the expedition progressed, growing more detailed and elaborate at each stage, it became apparent that the original number of boats would be insufficient, and another four hundred were quickly built and shipped out.

While procuring a sufficient number of boats was easily handled, another problem less readily resolved was finding crews for them. Again turning to his Red River experience, Wolseley sent word to Ottawa that he was seeking to employ four hundred Canadian riverboatmen, known as *voyageurs*, at the then-handsome wage of $40 per month. Recruits flocked to the government offices, and soon a rather curious collection of trappers, hunters, boatmen—even Meti and Iroquois Indians—were gathered and shipped east to Suez. Before long, the seemingly chaotic buildup for the expedition became known as the Circus on the Nile.

As confused and confusing as the preparations may have appeared, there was an overall sense of organization to it, the hallmark of any undertaking to which Wolseley put his hand. His plan of campaign was based on the use of two columns of troops, one mounted on camels—a "camelry" was Wolseley's rather peculiar term—moving across the desert to Dongola, the other moving up the Nile in Major Butler's boats towed behind a flotilla of river steamers. The two columns would converge on Dongola and advance from there to

Korti, less than a hundred miles overland from Khartoum, where they would prepare for the final advance. Lt. General Sir Redvers Buller was named Chief of Staff and at the same time given command of the forces that would sail up the Nile, while Brigadier Sir Herbert Stewart (no relation to the late Colonel Stewart who had been Gordon's second in command) was given command of the Desert Column, the troops who would move overland to Dongola. Major Henry Brackenbury was appointed the Deputy Adjutant and Quartermaster, while Sir Evelyn Wood was assigned to keep open the expedition's lines of communication.

Wolseley and his troops spent nearly a month in Cairo and Alexandria, Wolseley spending the time planning, while the troops trained and became acclimated to the harsh Egyptian climate. The most difficult challenge lay in organizing the Camel Corps. It was hard enough for men fresh from England to adapt to the strength-sapping heat, but making camel-riders out of soldiers proved an even more daunting task. Cavalrymen, accustomed to their elegant chargers at Wellington Barracks, were hardly enthusiastic about their new dromedarian mounts, while infantry privates whose only experience mounting animals harked back to old Bessie and Dobbin from their days on the farm in Yorkshire or Kent, were absolutely baffled by the bellowing, spitting, vile-smelling and foul-tempered creatures. Yet the Camel Corps was destined to play a decisive role in the coming campaign, and even as public and politicians alike in London murmured about what they regarded as Wolseley's unnecessary delays, the time given to acclimation and training would prove well spent.

By the time he left Cairo, Wolseley had decided that Gordon's most recent, generally reassuring messages meant that there was little need for urgent haste. Consequently the expedition would be a carefully paced affair. When the two columns reached Dongola, "the situation," in Wolseley's words, "would be reviewed" and a decision made as to how to proceed to Khartoum. As events turned out, the land column's progress began as a relatively swift, uneventful passage across country to the Sudanese border. The mocking title, the "Circus on the Nile," had been well earned, for some of the senior officers in the column had personal baggage trains that numbered as many as forty camels. It was hardly the lightly burdened, swift-moving force that Kitchener had envisioned and for which he had pleaded in Cairo.

Once the Desert Column entered the Sudan, conditions became more trying. As the desert sun beat down, the column made its increasingly difficult way across the scree-strewn terrain, edging past the knife-edged rocks and boulders that lined the Valley of the Nile. As the force approached Dongola, sickness began to become a problem, as isolated cases of cholera, scurvy, and typhoid appeared; without constant attention, they could become epidemics that would lay low the entire force.

For General Buller and the River Column, the progress up the Nile was steady but exhausting, and often as painful as that of the Desert Column. The "Nile whalers," laden with troops and supplies, were towed behind paddle-steamers as far up the Nile as Aswan, just below the First Cataract. The Cataracts were stretches of the river too rocky or shallow to be successfully navigated by the steamers, and it was here that the River Columns' real slogging began. While the cataracts were supposed to be passable by light boats, by this time the water level was dropping at a rate of six inches a day. Sandbars, shallows, and shoals would appear overnight, rendering what had one day been a navigable stretch of river into an impassable tidal flat the next.

It was two hundred miles from Aswan to Wadi Halfa, site of the Second Cataract. No steamers were available on this section of the river, so the passage would be made by muscle-power alone. First the troops had to portage their boats and equipment past the First Cataract, then once the boats were re-launched, they had to be rowed to Wadi Halfa. At times the sails helped, but the winds in the Valley of the Nile were capricious and unreliable, so most of the two hundred miles of river passage was accomplished through back-breaking work. It was little wonder that, with the mocking humor that was so often the hallmark of the British soldier, Wadi Halfa became known as "Bloody Halfway."

By day the boats would pass through a harsh, bleak landscape, often barren of any sign of life aside from scattered desert scrub. The men would row their boats against the strong Nile current under an increasingly powerful sun, its heat and glare magnified as it was reflected from the water. Often the soldiers and crews wore improvised goggles to avoid desert blindness. As darkness fell the boats would push ashore where the soldiers would set up bivouacs and light small fires of driftwood. The nights were almost enough to make up for the days, as a coolness would descend upon the desert and the cloudless skies would reveal the stars, uncountable in their number and unimaginable in their brilliance. The men would sleep, and then stand-to just before dawn, which would burst across the desert like a silent thunderclap.

The portage at Halfa was, if anything, more difficult than that at Aswan. The rapids of the Second Cataract, which stretched for over twenty miles, ran through Bab-el-Kebir, the Belly of Stone, a ravine fifty yards in length and only thirty feet wide. Through this narrow portal the entire flow of the Nile poured, bursting out of the ravine in a raging torrent. There was a railway at Halfa which skirted the cataract, but there were no railway cars capable of carrying the whalers. This meant that the boats had to either be hauled through the Bab-el-Kebir or carried around it. Buller chose to portage them around the rapids, as the risk of losing any of the boats was too great to run. As they had done at Aswan, the troops unloaded the boats' supplies and gear, and somehow managed to manhandle them around the Cataract, where they were reloaded and re-launched. At Gemai, upriver from the worst stretch of the Second Cataract, the column halted for several days to set up a supply base and a boat repair yard, while General Buller rested his nearly exhausted troops.

Leaving Buller to his work at Gemai, Wolseley, who had gone up the Nile with the river column, now rode ahead with his staff to Dongola and there set up his headquarters. The sketchy reports coming out of Khartoum told him that his initial estimates of Gordon's position had been overconfident. The garrison at Khartoum was becoming weaker with each passing day, and the slow pace of the expedition's advance began to alarm Wolseley. For all of his meticulous planning, he had underestimated the challenge of moving his columns up the Nile. Most seriously, he had failed to anticipate how debilitating the desert heat would be to troops who had only just left the cool climate of the British Isles, and the sheer physical strain imposed by movement across the terrain. Distances of three hundred, six hundred, or twelve hundred miles may look the same on a map of Europe as they do on maps of Egypt and the Sudan, but what the maps cannot convey is that the effort required to move one mile in the desert can be as much as three-fold that needed to cover the same distance in Spain or Russia.

The heat saps the strength and will of men while flies torment and irritate them; sand and grit create jamming and malfunctions in machinery and equipment, while bringing up supplies can require more effort than the actual operations. Sanitary conditions are rudimentary at best, and sleep is a precious commodity. Water is worth its weight in gold, and the apparently endless landscape seems to barely change from one day to the next, creating a mind-numbing monotony. Since Wolseley's campaign, two World Wars and two wars fought in the Persian Gulf have demonstrated that men can adapt to and even fight in these conditions, but such adaptation takes time, and time, Wolseley was coming to discover, was now a rapidly diminishing luxury. He chafed at the delays imposed by the need to portage around the cataracts, fretted at the slow progress of the Desert Column, and worried about was happening at Khartoum. In his despatches and in the talks he had with the journalists accompanying the expedition he did his best to appear assured and confident, but in the privacy of his journal he vented his frustration at Gladstone's procrastination in authorizing the expedition.

Doubtless much of Wolseley's anger at Gladstone was justified, but in fairness some of it should have been directed at himself. While the memory of the massacre of Hicks' column continued to exert an influence on Wolseley in his plan of campaign, the fact that he commanded a force of more than ten thousand British regulars, rather than the motley dregs and leavings of Egyptian jails, could have inspired bolder and swifter action.

From Wadi Halfa it was three hundred miles to Dongola, with the Third Cataract to be negotiated just below the town. Given the exertion required, altogether the River Column's progress had to be judged as impressive. The column had left Alexandria on September 27, arrived at Aswan on October 5, reached Wadi Halfa on October 19, and finally joined the Desert Column at Dongola on November 8. The river force might have made even better progress had not a shortage of coal for the steamers in Alexandria kept scores of whalers from being brought up to Aswan, a delay that eventually proved costly.

Meanwhile, the Desert Column was being reorganized as the Camel Corps. It was to be a self-contained unit of infantry, cavalry, and artillery, capable of striking out across the desert on its own if need be, possessing sufficient strength of arms to defend itself against enemies several times its number, and swift enough to be able to withdraw to the River Column should it be faced with overwhelming odds. However, from Dongola to Korti the Camel Corps would move up the Nile alongside the River Column, acting as a scouting force. The formation of the Camel Corps owed much to Major Kitchener, whose perseverance with Lord Wolseley finally compelled the General to see the wisdom of the concept. At the same time, it came as something of a disappointment to Kitchener, for he would neither command nor accompany the Camel Corps if and when it made a dash for Khartoum. Wolseley regarded the young major as too valuable to his intelligence service to risk in the wastes of the Sudanese desert; Kitchener would remain at Debba.

Back in London, almost from the day Wolseley left for Alexandria, an anxious public was kept abreast of the Relief Expedition's preparations by an equally anxious press; then when the troops left Cairo, their apparently agonizingly slow progress up the Nile was followed just as avidly. In the House of Commons, Prime Minister Gladstone remained impassive and imperturbable, still unhappy about being forced into authorizing the Relief Expedition at all, but content that no matter what the outcome of events he had done everything he could to answer the dictates of his conscience and the responsibilities of his office. Lord Hartington regularly briefed the Queen on the latest news from the expedition.

In Cairo, Sir Evelyn Baring was watching Wolseley's progress as keenly as anyone in London. While hardly the schemer that Gordon believed him to be—Gordon's journals would later be found to contain page after page of scathing, though often witty, comments about Baring and his diplomatic posturings—the Consul-General had come to believe that he had probably made a terrible mistake in agreeing to Gordon's appointment to Khartoum. Once he arrived in Khartoum, Baring felt, Gordon had essentially ignored his orders, and with his presence in the city had forced the British government, by mounting an expedition to rescue him, into the very course of action he had been sent to the Sudan to avoid.

In the ten months since Gordon had left Cairo, Baring had come to see that the General was, at times, "extremely pugnacious . . . hot-headed, impulsive, and swayed by his emotions. . . . In fact, except in personal courage, great fertility in military resource, a lively though sometimes ill-directed repugnance toward injustice, oppression and meanness of every description, and a considerable power of acquiring influence over those . . . with whom he was brought into personal contact, General Gordon does not appear to have possessed any of the qualities which would have fitted him to undertake the difficult task he had in hand." The irony of Baring's words were that their very accuracy made his disapproval ring hollow. Gordon's qualities which Baring deplored were the very qualities that made him such an effective soldier, and in fact were the very qualities that recommended Gordon to the mission to Khartoum in the first place. Baring was lamenting the fact that Gordon was not a diplomat; in essence, he was lamenting that Gordon was not a man like himself. True, there have been few men as unlike as Gordon and Baring, but the fact remains that Gordon came within a hair's-breadth of accomplishing what Baring wished he could have done: saving Khartoum and smashing the Mahdi. That, however, was a task for which Baring lacked the emotional or moral fiber to achieve; his criticisms of Gordon, leveled a quarter-century after the event, would smack more of sour grapes than a legitimate condemnation of ill-considered actions. In the meantime, with the Relief Expedition on its way up the Nile, Baring knew that should the city fall and the General be lost, no small portion of the blame would fall on his shoulders. It would be inevitable that Gladstone, who would first feel the wrath of Parliament and people alike should the Relief Expedition fail, would attempt to defend himself by pointing out Baring's initial opposition to Gordon's mission, then his later endorsement of it, and claim that he had acted on the best advice available. If Gladstone were to be accused of failing Gordon, then Baring would be made a party to that failure.

Once it arrived at Korti, the expedition was less than three hundred miles overland from Khartoum. By now the power of the Mahdi in the surrounding country was palpable, and it was here that the expedition entered its most critical phase. Each British soldier, all of them long-service veterans of multiple campaigns, was armed with a Model 1871 Martini-Henry .455/.577 rifle. If the Remingtons with which some of the Mahdi's followers were armed was a powerful weapon, which it was, the Martini-Henry, popularly known as simply the Martini, was a man-stopper. The big .577 caliber cartridge fired a .455 caliber round, which weighed over an ounce and was made of soft, unjacketed lead. On striking its target the round would deform, mushroom, and sometimes fragment, expending its considerable energy within the target—and if that target was a man, it could often literally knock him off his feet. The British soldier, known even in that day as "Tommy," was drilled endlessly in the art of volley fire— massed ranks of infantry two, three, sometimes four deep, firing simultaneously on command. If ever the cliché "hail of fire" was warranted, it would be when an enemy faced a British regiment in square, each face numbering close to three hundred men, firing as many as six or seven times a minute. It was this sort of volley fire that William Hicks had hoped would save his column—and himself—three years earlier, but which his Egyptian conscripts lacked the training and discipline to be able to produce or sustain.

But volley fire was a British specialty. Foes ranging from French infantry columns in Portugal and Spain, to Bonaparte's cuirassiers at Waterloo, to Russian heavy horse in the Crimea, to Zulu impis in southern Africa could attest to the devastating effects of the steady, rolling volleys of British musketry. How the Ansar would fare when confronted by such firepower no one knew.

For the Mahdi's followers in this part of the Sudan were mainly from the Hadendoa tribe, popularly if somewhat incorrectly known as Dervishes, almost primitive Arabs, fanatically Moslem, who still fought with sword and shield. They weren't a people to be taken lightly, however, for their huge, two-handed swords could dismember a victim in one stroke, while the shield each Dervish warrior carried could be a weapon in its own right, smashing and bashing an enemy senseless before the death-stroke of the sword fell. Wearing their distinctive, bushy hair, the Dervishes would soon become known throughout the British Army, not in derision but with a hard-won respect, as "Fuzzy-Wuzzies."

At Korti the Nile changes course, bending back to the north, then swinging around eastward then southeastward, like a huge question-mark stretching for two-hundred fifty miles until it finally runs down to the south, toward Khartoum. If the relief column remained on the Nile, its progress would actually be taking it farther away from the city, creating further delay at a time when Wolseley had come to real-ize that Gordon had only days left, not weeks. At the same time, if the expedition set out directly across the desert to Khartoum, it would risk serious supply shortages, as there were too few camels, mules and horses to carry the column's ammunition, rations, and equipment. It would also be moving into the same sort of terrain where William Hicks' army had come to grief at the hands of the Mahdist forces. Wolseley had to make a choice between swift action and secure progress.

Not surprisingly, he compromised. The bulk of the expedition would continue up the Nile, while the Camel Corps would set out across the desert for Metemma, where, it was hoped, more definite word could be gained of the situation at Khartoum. If the city still held out when the Camel Corps reached Metemma, it could serve as a valu-able reinforcement for Gordon, not to mention a huge boost to the morale of the garrison and citizens alike. Should the news at Metemma be bad, the Camel Corps would be strong enough to defend itself if it had to withdraw back to Korti or down the Nile to Abu Hamed. Should the city still be holding out but the Mahdi's forces encircling it prove too strong for the Camel Corps to break through, they could wait until the rest of the column arrived at Metemma so that the combined forces could attack the Mahdi's army en masse. In contrast to most compromises, this one appeared to be not only work-able, but would satisfy all the strategic circumstances that might arise.

Officially comprised of four regiments, the Camel Corps' strength totaled some sixteen hundred officers and other ranks, along with three hundred native servants and interpreters, the lot of them mount-ed on twenty-eight hundred camels. In addition to the rifles carried by each ranker and the officers' sidearms, the column was armed with three light cannon manned by a contingent of the Royal Artillery, and a five-barreled Gardner gun, crewed by men from the Naval Detachment. The Gardner gun was an early form of machine gun, similar to the American Gatling, and was an impressive weapon: in a public demonstration while the Gardner was first being evaluated by the British Army, the prototype had fired ten thousand rounds in twenty-seven minutes. Command of the Desert Column was given to Brigadier Stewart, with Colonel Frederick Burnaby as second-in-command.

Stewart was one of the more promising officers in the British Army, which he had entered in 1863. He first served in India and later South Africa, where he fought against the Zulus in 1879, and then in the first Boer War. He had been captured by the Boers at Majuba in 1881, and held for three months before being released when a peace settlement was reached. He was no stranger to Egypt, for like many of his fellow officers, he had taken part in putting down the Arabi revolt. In August 1882 he was serving of the cavalry division in Egypt, and after the battle of Tel-el-Kebir he led the advance upon Cairo, capturing the city. His personal bravery as well as his leadership caused him to be mentioned in despatches three times, and he was promoted to brevet-colonel, made a Companion of the Bath, and appointed an aide-de-camp to the Queen. He next saw action in January 1884 when he fought at Suakin, commanding Sir Gerald Graham's cavalry, which earned him promotion to brigadier. When Wolseley began assembling his staff for the Relief Expedition, Stewart, on the strength of his experience as well as personal courage, was one of the first officers he requested. Stewart's combination of cavalryman dash and steady common sense, shown in his previous actions, made him the ideal candidate for command of the Camel Corps.

Of all the remarkable characters who played a part in the story of the siege of Khartoum, few were as colorful—which is a diplomatic way of saying "controversial"— as the column's second-in-command, Frederick Gustavus Burnaby. A colonel of the Royal Horse Guards (known as the Blues from their distinctive blue tunics, the only British heavy cavalry regiment so clad) he was much like a kindred spirit to Gordon. Standing six feet, four inches in height, he was the tallest soldier in the entire British Army. A born adventurer, explorer, traveler, and soldier, he had worked as a military correspondent for the *London Times* in the early 1870s, and in late 1874 was transferred to Africa where he went to Khartoum to report on Gordon's work as governor of the Sudan. Two journeys made on horseback in the late 1870s, the first through Russian Asia to Khiva, the capital of Uzbekistan, the second across Asia Minor from Scutari to Erzerum, led to the publication of two popular books by Burnaby, and made him a household name throughout Great Britain.

Burnaby served as an observer for the Red Cross in the Russo-Turkish War of 1877, dabbled briefly in politics, and in 1882 became the first person to cross the English Channel alone in a hot-air balloon. Without bothering to obtain official leave he went to the eastern Sudan in early 1884 as an intelligence officer for General Baker, and was wounded in the action at El Teb. When plans were announced for the relief expedition to Khartoum, Burnaby was one of the first to volunteer. Wolseley, who valued his experience among Moslem peoples, quickly accepted his services, initially appointing him second-in-command to the Relief Expedition's intelligence section before naming him second-in-command of the Camel Corps.

Wolseley's orders, reinforced by periodic reminders from London, were for himself to remain at Korti and leave any action further upriver to his subordinates. With these instructions in mind he ordered the Camel Corps to begin its advance on January 1, 1885. But rather than march directly to Khartoum, it set off for Metemma, in order to secure the small riverfront town as a base for the remainder of the Relief Expedition, which would be sent up the Nile in its whalers. That force, which numbered twenty-nine hundred men, mostly infantry, actually set out from Korti before the Camel Corps, leaving on December 28 under the command of Major General William Earle. Earle, as methodical as Wolseley, was taking no chances: in the two-hundred seventeen whalers he was employing, his troops had loaded supplies for one hundred days, three times the estimated span it would take to arrive at Khartoum. A small mixed force of British and Egyptian cavalry would accompany Earle's force, acting as a scouting screen along the banks of the Nile. The journey from Korti to Metemma was a far from easy task, accompanied by more than the usual share of grumbling and griping which is the private soldier's God-given right. The complaints were well-deserved, for this stretch of the Nile was essentially unmapped, particularly that stretch of the river between Korti and Abu Hamed, and as a consequence Colonel Butler had no prepared plans for dealing with its cataracts and canyons, but had to improvise the solution to each new challenge.

The remainder of the Relief Expedition, just over five thousand troops, remained at Korti, tasked with securing the passage of the Nile for both Stewart and Earle. Wolseley was determined that there be no chance of his command being cut off deep inside the Sudan with no secure route of withdrawal. Once again, as the ghost of William Hicks hovered over the map-tables where Wolseley made his plans, the General both overestimated the Mahdi and underestimated the men under his command, having no way of knowing that in less than three weeks, a battle would be fought which would throw the strengths and weakness of the opposing armies into stark relief.

The desert track from Korti to Metemma was marked by a series of wells and watering holes, and it was at these spots the Camel Corps would halt at night, set out pickets, and rest and water their animals. January 16 found the Corps at the wells of Gakdul, having spent the last two weeks searching in vain for any sign of the enemy. The next morning, they left Gakdul behind, making straight for the wells at Abu Klea. It was there that the sixteen hundred soldiers of the Camel Corps would suddenly be met by eight thousand of the Mahdi's followers. On January 17, 1885, the steadiness of the British Tommy was challenged by the fanaticism of the Mahdi's army, and the decisive action of the campaign was fought.

As it approached Abu Klea, the Camel Corps had no idea that any of the Mahdi's forces were near. Their first intimation that they faced action was when outriders of the column saw ranks of red, green, and black banners, some embroidered in gold with quotations from the Koran, waving above a hidden ravine. Dashing back to the column, the scouts had barely made their report when hordes of Mahdists began swarming over the top of the ravine, less than a thousand yards away. "All of a sudden," Captain Charles Cochrane of the Scots Greys would write, "the banners were in motion towards us at a rapid pace, led by spearmen on horseback. The enemy advanced against our square at a very rapid pace and in a dense black mass, keeping perfect order."

The Mahdi's force—a collection of Arab cavalry and Dervish foot-soldiers, the "Fuzzy-Wuzzies"—were mostly armed with swords or javelins, with a sprinkling of Remington rifles captured from Egyptian troops. In theory, what happened next should have been a rout, but instead the next twenty minutes saw what Winston Churchill was to describe as "the most savage and bloody action fought in the Sudan by British troops." A skirmish line was quickly thrown out to delay the onrush of the Arabs long enough to allow the column to deploy into square.

As the skirmishers came in, the troops of the northern face of the square opened ranks to allow them to pass, but before they could close up again, the Dervishes were upon them. With their big, two-handed bronze swords and coffin-shaped shields, chopping, slashing, and shrieking in their fury, the Fuzzy-Wuzzies literally flung themselves upon the British infantry. The Tommies, no strangers to ferocious rushes by determined natives, grimly stood their ground and the impact when the two met was terrible. The Martini-Henry rifles, prone to overheating in the desert sun, jammed as the cartridges swelled in their breeches, and sand caused the Gardner gun and the artillery to malfunction, while the bayonets, made of inferior-grade steel, buckled and bent when striking the bronze shields of the Ansar.

But what happened next was not due to jamming rifles or bending bayonets. It was at this moment that the Ansar showed the world the stuff of which they were made, and gave the lie to those who said that they were fighting for freedom, or independence, or for the "nation" of the Sudan. What the Dervishes were about to accomplish could only have been achieved by men who were fighting for eternity, for Paradise; men fighting for their God and a vision of their salvation given them by their leader, a belief worth dying for. For the Dervishes, soon to be immortalized by Rudyard Kipling's poem "Fuzzy Wuzzy," did the impossible—they broke the square.

They broke the square! No other army that ever faced a square of British infantry, at any time, in any place in the world, had ever done such a thing. No tide of French cuirassiers riding to their doom at Bonaparte's command, no wave of Russian horse in the snow and mud of the Crimea, nor the horsemen any of the Indian princelings battling Clive or Wellesley, not even the awesome Zulu impi, had ever accomplished the feat. Catching one outer face of the square in the brief moment of disorder as it tried to close ranks, the Dervishes broke into the square's interior, and began wreaking havoc.

Within seconds the interior of the square was chaos. Men shouted, officers and sergeants bellowed commands, the Dervishes wailed their war-cries, horses reared, and camels bolted. Dervish warriors slashed viciously at anyone or anything in their path, striking with both sword and shield, indiscriminately hacking down men and animals. The center of the square became filled with roiling clouds of dust and smoke as individual British soldiers fought for their lives, desperately trying to distinguish friend from foe in the split-second before a mistake could prove fatal. Unless the Dervishes could be thrown back and the broken face of the square reformed, the entire formation was doomed.

It was in these desperate moments that the awesome discipline of the British Tommy made itself felt. The years of spit-and-polish, of tongue-lashings from sergeants and corporals, of punishment details given for performance of duties judged unsatisfactory, the cuffings, the curses, the sweat, the endless drills, all coalesced in a moment as the men heard their officers shouting out commands, responding almost reflexively with the movements and actions practiced a hundred, a thousand times in the barrack-square and on the parade ground.

The infantry on the broken side of the square fought ferociously, and slowly reformed their ranks, all the while firing into the charging Dervishes at point-blank range, the big Martini-Henry slugs dealing horrible, gaping wounds. Others fought hand-to-hand, sometimes with their bayonets, others with their fists and even their teeth. The Fuzzy-Wuzzies were equally fierce, hacking off heads and limbs with their long swords and yelling out their defiance. For some minutes the melee surged back and forth as the issue hung in doubt and the entire square was threatened with annihilation should it fail to reform. The decisive moment came when the men in the rear ranks of the face opposite the one that had broken did an about-turn and at the direction of their colour-sergeants, who were carefully choosing their targets, began picking off the Dervish attackers. At the same time, those troops not firing into the Dervishes inside the square were steadily firing into the masses outside it, driving the Arab cavalry back, buying precious seconds for British soldiers to reform their ranks and begin closing the gap in the square. At some point in this melee, Colonel

Burnaby, who had strode into the thick of the fighting, rifle in hand, was killed by a spear-thrust through the heart.

Within moments it was all over—the last of the Dervishes lay dead or dying inside the square, their comrades outside falling back in confusion and dismay, driven off by the intensity of the British musketry. It had been a costly victory for the British and a costly defeat for the Ansar. The Camel Corps suffered some one hundred and sixty-eight dead, with another two hundred and eighteen wounded, while the Dervishes left behind more than eleven hundred bodies. The number of their wounded would never be known.

The battle had a dramatic effect on both the Mahdi and Wolseley, although neither knew of the other's reaction. The Mahdi, who had long feared the appearance of British troops, knew of their reputation for battlefield steadiness but apparently disregarded it, in part because he had not yet come face-to-face with the British army. Thinking the Tommies little better than the Egyptian conscripts of William Hicks, the decimation of the blocking force he had sent to Abu Klea was a shock to Muhammed Ahmed, and hardened his resolve to take Khartoum by storm before the British column arrived at the city. He had no idea whether the Relief Expedition had been sent to rescue Gordon or crush the Moslem revolt, but he knew that it would be far better to face the British from within the security of Khartoum's walls than risk another battle in open country.

For Wolseley, Abu Klea confirmed his worst fears: another Hicks disaster was in the offing if he lingered in the Sudan one day longer than absolutely necessary. The casualties suffered by the Camel Corps weighed heavily on him. That the circumstances under which they were incurred were exceptional in the extreme appears to not have made any impression; that his troops had held and driven off the Ansar with dreadful losses was lost on him. He had been given strict instructions by Gladstone before leaving London that the sole purpose of his expedition was to bring Gordon out of Khartoum, not to begin a war with the Mahdi. There were moments when it seemed that Wolseley had come to appreciate what Gordon had perceived at Khartoum: that the surest, quickest, and least costly way, both in blood and treasure, to eliminate the threat of the Mahdi was to decisively defeat him now rather than wait for future events. After Abu

Klea, Wolseley seems to have abandoned any thought of a final, crushing confrontation with Muhammed Ahmed.

After Abu Klea, the Camel Corps counted its losses, buried its dead, tended its wounded, and then set out for Metemma. General Stewart, now determined to reach the Nile as quickly as humanly possible, had his men ride through the nights of January 17th and 18th. On the morning of the 19th, at Abu Kru, just as the Corps was drawing to within sight of the Nile, it was attacked again by the Mahdi's followers. The fighting was as fierce as at Abu Klea, with the Dervishes charging the British square with the same courage and fanaticism, but there was no repeat of Abu Klea–the square held, and the measured volleys from the Martini-Henrys tore huge holes in the Dervish ranks. After fifteen to twenty minutes of bloody struggle, some of it hand-to-hand, the Arabs withdrew, leaving another thousand dead behind. The British suffered one hundred and eleven casualties. Among the wounded was Sir Herbert Stewart, the Camel Corps' commanding officer, who had suffered a spear-thrust in his side that would take his life ten days later. And so, with Colonel Burnaby having been killed at Abu Klea, command of the Corps fell upon Col. Charles Wilson, an intelligence officer who had never before commanded troops in the field.

His lack of experience may have exerted a cautionary influence on Wilson, who chose to rest his weary men at Abu Kru, with Metemma almost in sight. The following morning, when the Camel Corps finally reached the river just outside the town, they were met by four of Khartoum's river steamers, sent down from the city by Gordon three days previously, carrying some two hundred or so of the garrison's black riflemen, who had been singled out by the Mahdi to be put to death as infidels when the city was taken. Closely questioning some of the soldiers, Wilson learned that the situation in Khartoum was rapidly approaching desperation, with food supplies running low and the morale of both the garrison and the populace failing. Gordon's repeated reassurances that the Relief Expedition was on its way were beginning to wear thin. As an intelligence officer, Wilson was undoubtedly aware of the last communication from Gordon, sent up the river on the steamer *Bordein* on December 13: "NOW MARK THIS, if the Expeditionary Force, and I ask for no more than two hundred men, does not come in ten days, the town may fall; and I have done my best for the honor of my country. Good-bye. C. G. Gordon." Wilson also knew that Wolseley had received a message from Khartoum, allegedly from Gordon, on December 29, which read, "Khartoum all right, could hold out for years," but Wolseley regarded it as a ruse, meant to deceive the Arabs should the message fall into their hands.

Clearly the situation was urgent, but Wilson inexplicably chose this moment to halt the Corps' advance outside Metemma, which was still held by the Arabs, to set up his headquarters and establish a bivouac. The engines of two of the Khartoum steamers were torn down and overhauled, in expectation of using them to ferry troops to the city, but three days were lost while this work was undertaken and a reconnaissance of the river was carried out. It may be that some of Wilson's hesitation was due to the emotional shock of the two battles that had just been fought, but his inexperience was certainly a factor, as his actions at this point were strictly "by the book," not those of a seasoned officer confronted with an urgent situation. Ultimately the delay would prove critical.

When the steamers were finally readied, on the morning of January 24, two of them, the *Bordein* and the *Tel Hewein*, were loaded with the two hundred Sudanese riflemen that had sailed down to Metemma, along with the detachment of the Naval Brigade that had accompanied the Camel Corps, and twenty men from the Royal Sussex regiment, all of the latter wearing, as Gordon had requested, the British infantryman's traditional red tunic. With them went Colonel Wilson. The river was falling, slowing the steamers' progress as previously unsuspected rocks and shoals became evident, and often channels that appeared to be clear passages were found to be dead-ends. The little ships had to stop frequently for fuel, and do so in sections of the river which seemed deserted, lest they be ambushed as was the *Abbas* four months earlier. Though both steamers were armed with small brass cannons and a pair of Gardner machine guns, they were too lightly armed to withstand an attack of the kind launched by the Arabs at Abu Klea or Abu Kru. Indeed, the significance of this little expedition to Khartoum was intended as more of a gesture to reassure Gordon that help was truly on the way than any attempt to relieve the city or raise the siege.

As the steamers neared Omdurman, Arabs on both banks of the Nile began calling out to those aboard that they were too late: Khartoum city had fallen. Wilson refused to believe it and ordered the two ships to continue onward. As they drew closer to Khartoum, they came under intense rifle and artillery fire from both riverbanks as well as the city itself, and Wilson noted that there was no flag, British or Egyptian, flying above the Government House. Wanting there to be no mistake, Wilson ordered the *Bordein*'s captain to put the ship against the riverbank, and once there, Arabs confirmed the news. Gordon was dead; the city had fallen. The relief column had arrived two days too late.

CHAPTER 10

THE FALL OF KHARTOUM

In the center of Khartoum a tower had been erected, a vantage point where Gordon was able to keep a sharp lookout for the Mahdi's forces. They were daily growing in numbers, and by the beginning of October it was clear that the city was not merely cut off but completely surrounded. While never really unexpected, this development had an unfortunate consequence—the raids to steal cattle and grain that had proven so successful in the previous months in augmenting the city's food supplies would no longer be possible, a point that was made emphatic by the disastrous raid in September when eight hundred of Gordon's soldiers were trapped outside the city and lost. Now all Gordon could do was wait—and hope. He made every exertion possible to keep up the morale of the city and its defenders, but although by the end of September he had definite news that a Relief Expedition had been authorized and was making its way up the Nile, with each passing week with no sign of British soldiers approaching Khartoum, the defenders' faith in Gordon's ability to triumph over the Mahdi began to erode and grow brittle.

There was, in point of fact, little Gordon could do except wait it out. Surrender was never a possibility for him, either personally or as the commander of the garrison and governor of the city. It wasn't that Gordon possessed a martyr complex, rather that it simply wasn't in his character. Certainly if he had ever regarded capitulation as an honorable alternative, he had good reason to do so. By the end of December, nearly all the grain that had been so carefully hoarded had been consumed, along with every camel, horse, donkey, monkey, dog, and rat

183

in the city. In late November a large store of grain, concealed by a group of merchants who had planned to sell it to the highest bidders when the shortages became acute, was discovered, and the day of reckoning was delayed for a few more weeks.

But by the end of the year, nearly all that was left was an almost inedible form of palm fibre, and a sort of gum made from tree sap that caused severe intestinal pains some hours after it was eaten. Starvation was beginning to set in, and soon the sight of dead bodies lying by the hundreds in the streets became common. Those still alive lacked the strength and the will to bury them. In late December nearly five thousand of those civilians who could still walk were sent out to the Mahdi's lines under a flag of truce, one of them bearing a letter from Gordon to Muhammed Ahmed, begging for them to be treated humanely. Instead they became more fodder for the slavers.

When the contents of Colonel Stewart's papers, captured when the *Abbas* was ambushed and Stewart killed, were translated for the Mahdi, the game was up, to all intents and purposes, for the city and its populace, unless the Relief Expedition arrived very shortly. Muhammed Ahmed realized that with conditions as grave as they had become in Khartoum the time had come to force a conclusion. Having made his camp to the west of Omdurman in October, he brought up fresh reinforcements so that the non-stop fusillades of rifle and cannon fire were doubled. November 30th—the date Gordon had named in one of the captured despatches as the last possible day the city could hold out—came and went with no sign of the Expeditionary Force. The Mahdi's army daily grew more aggressive, the skirmishes along the lines around the city becoming sharper, the casualties mounting. Every eye among attackers and defenders alike, from Gordon and the Mahdi to the lowest private and Ansar, was directed daily toward the Nile, where the water level grew lower with each passing day, and the moat to the south of Khartoum became less and less of an impassible obstacle.

There were still sporadic exchanges of letters between Gordon and the Mahdi, though these accomplished little for by now the Mahdi knew that he fully held the upper hand. The relief column, the Mahdi knew, was moving with almost deliberate sluggishness up the Nile. As his guns kept up a harassing fire on the city, lacking the power to do real damage, they could still prove disruptive, depriving the garrison of sleep at night, causing incidental casualties, and further wearing down morale. Gordon did what he could, making nightly rounds of the fortifications, cheering his men on when possible, chivvying and cajoling them to action, reprimanding and punishing slackers when they were found. The threat of the lash was always available to Gordon, but as the days grew shorter and the situation became increasingly grim, he came to realize the futility of such harsh punishment—the threat of shame and disgrace was a much more powerful incentive to duty.

Always he kept the men on the alert against sudden attacks, for he had no idea what strategy the Mahdi would pursue. Both men were aware that they were in a race against time, the Mahdi hoping that the city would fall before the Relief Expedition arrived, Gordon determined to hold on until it did. Treachery was always his greatest dread. Despite the thousands who had left the city in February, as well as those sent out in December, many people still within Khartoum's walls secretly sympathized with the Mahdi; he knew that with each passing day he could depend less and less on the loyalty of his remaining troops. When definite news of the relief column's departure from Cairo reached Khartoum, Gordon ordered an illumination of the city and fired salutes in honor of the news. Two hundred of his black Sudanese troops, who had already been condemned to death by the Mahdi should the city fall, were loaded aboard four steamers and given instructions to sail down the Nile to Metemma, the obvious staging ground for any attempt to relieve the city. There they were to wait for the Relief Column and once it arrived guide it up the Nile into Khartoum. Meantime, morale soared within the city for a time, but plummeted again when there was no sign of the approaching column.

In the bundle of papers the *Bordein* carried down the Nile to Wolseley was a letter Gordon wrote to one of his friends in Cairo. In it he gave expression to a fatalism that had never before surfaced in any of his correspondence or journal entries. "Farewell. You will never hear from me again. I fear that there will be treachery in the garrison, and all will be over by Christmas." The melancholy tone of this note, so different from the Charles Gordon whom Wolseley had come to know and admire over the years, seemed to act as a spur to him, and he quickly ordered the Camel Corps to begin its march to Metemma.

That tone was repeated in the farewell letter Gordon wrote to his sister, Augusta: "I decline to agree that the expedition comes for my relief; it comes for the relief of the garrisons, which I failed to accomplish. I expect Her Majesty's Government are in a precious rage with me for holding out and forcing their hand." In this confession Gordon demonstrated that he had indeed divined the true character of his original mission as well as the consequences of his stubborn refusal to leave Khartoum under any circumstances. It was a significant admission, for its implications were twofold.

First was that while Gordon was aware of the ambiguous nature of the mission given him—if he had succeeded in evacuating Khartoum and the northern Sudan, Gladstone and the Cabinet could declare that they had achieved a great foreign policy success without having to resort to another imperialistic adventure. If Gordon failed, however, the Prime Minister would be able to claim that he had only been acting as an agent of the Egyptian government, without sanction or commission from Her Majesty's government. Second, there was the subtle inference that Gordon had played a game of his own, in which his intention was never to evacuate the Sudan or abandon Khartoum, but rather to compel Great Britain into a confrontation with the Mahdi to stop him cold.

If this was the case—and the evidence certainly supports the idea—it is remarkable for what it reveals about Gordon. While at first glance, and even at second and third, he appears to be a typical Victorian adventurer and soldier of fortune, it becomes evident that there was a far more complex individual residing within. While he bore all the outward trappings of a stereotypical imperialist, he was anything but one. The great irony of Gordon's life and death is that he and Gladstone shared a similar dislike of imperial adventures. It was unfortunate that Gladstone, who normally was a very perceptive judge of character, could not see deeper than Gordon's uniform and reputation, and consequently was unable to see how congruent were their attitudes and beliefs. Both were moral, Christian men in the best sense of those terms, each keenly interested in improving the station of those whose birth had denied them opportunities for improvement.

Where they diverged was in each their comprehension of Gordon's assignment to Khartoum. Gladstone could only think of it in terms of an imperial adventure—to Gordon it was a moral mission. At no point did he express a desire to see the Sudan become a part of the British Empire—indeed, unlike many of his more glamorous contemporaries, such as Cecil Rhodes, Gordon had never acted as an agent of imperial expansion. He did not bring British institutions, laws, or ways of life with him, did not advocate the introduction of Western technologies or business interests into the lands where he served. In both his terms as Governor-General in Khartoum, he was careful to work entirely within the framework of the Egyptian legal system.

Rather than being intrusive, as Gordon saw it, his mission to Khartoum was protective in nature. Not the "protection" of the White Man's Burden: he had no intention of trying to "civilize and Christianize these people," as William McKinley would later claim as America's mission in the Philippines.

To Gordon, the people of Khartoum were already civilized, and as they chose to be Moslem, they were entitled to remain so. For all of his Christian zeal, Gordon was no thundering missionary, converting all and sundry in sight. Instead he saw himself as protecting their particular civilized ways and their choice to follow Islam as they saw fit from a tyranny that would eradicate both. If Khartoum fell, the whole of the Sudan would be submerged in the rule of an oppressive theocracy that was becoming almost indistinguishable from the corrupt regime it was attempting to supplant. Some semblance of law and order must be maintained in the Sudan if the country was not to be swallowed up in chaos—or worse, religious tyranny. If the Egyptian government in Cairo was incapable of maintaining civilized rule in the Sudan, which it clearly was, then it was up to Great Britain to provide the means to do so. This meant British troops confronting and "smashing" the Mahdi, as Gordon had written so many months before, but without the motive of adding the Sudan to the Empire. Once order was restored, Gordon seems to have believed, Her Majesty's forces could withdraw and the Egyptian government be allowed to continue to administer the land—after a stern admonishment to not allow such a state of affairs to develop again.

Curiously, Gordon came to this conclusion without developing any deep abiding affection for the Sudanese, or they for him. There was superficial admiration and respect on both sides, but there was also a distance—Gordon could never be one of the Sudanese, nor did they ever expect him to be so. He never attempted to, in the mot of the time, "go native." In fact, there were moments when Gordon's attitude toward the Sudanese and Egyptians was almost contemptuous. Nevertheless, he seems to have felt some sort of moral obligation to them, or perhaps more precisely to what the city of Khartoum represented. The letter to his sister Augusta closed with this farewell:

> This may be the last letter you will receive from me, for we are on our last legs, owing to the delay of the expedition. However, God rules all, and, as He will rule to His glory and our welfare, His will be done. I fear, owing to circumstances, that my affairs are pecuniarily not over bright...your affectionate brother, C. G. GORDON.
>
> P.S. I am quite happy, thank God, and, like Lawrence, I have TRIED to do my duty.

On January 6, Omdurman fell. The fort had been putting up a surprisingly stout resistance since the summer, particularly in light of its lack of artillery. As long as the Mahdi's hold on the banks of the Nile remained tenuous, the defenders could count on periodic support from one of Gordon's river steamers. But since October, when the fort was cut off from the river and surrounded by the Ansar, there was no longer any hope of resupplying the garrison, neither of relieving or withdrawing it. All Gordon could do was offer what little encouragement he could, urging the defenders to hold out as long as possible. The volume of small arms fire that the Arabs brought to bear on the fort increased and so did the little garrison's casualties.

On December 16, the Mahdi's army launched a determined attack on the town, which was thrown back with heavy losses; but that would prove to be the Omdurman garrison's last hurrah. Though there were no more large-scale assaults, three weeks later the Egyptian officer commanding the fort signaled to Gordon that he could no longer hold out. Gordon, bowing however reluctantly to the inevitable, gave his permission to surrender, trusting the garrison's fate to the Mahdi's mercy.

By the middle of January, the strain and fatigue were finally beginning to take their toll on Gordon. The fatalism of his farewell letters sent off on the *Bordein* in mid-December gave way to the beginnings of despair: "I have given 6,000 pounds of biscuits to the poor. Half will be stolen. The shells fall about 200 yards short of the palace. I am worn to a shadow with the food question. Five men deserted today." In another passage he recorded bitterly that the remaining Egyptian officials were utterly incompetent and the soldiers were cowards— hardly a fair judgment, perhaps, as these men still retained the courage to remain within the city. There are also touches of admiration for the Mahdi's followers, the meanest of whom, he said, was "a determined warrior, who could undergo thirst and privation, who no more cared for pain or death than if he were stone."

Still, he was able at times to make a show of fearless defiance. Bordeini Bey, a merchant in Khartoum and a close friend of Gordon who managed to survive the siege, recounted how he was the reluctant participant in one such demonstration.

In spite of all this danger by which he was surrounded, Gordon Pasha had no fear. I remember one night some of the principal men of Khartoum came to my house and begged me to ask Gordon Pasha not to light up the rooms of the Palace, as they offered a good mark for the enemy's bullets. When I mentioned this to Gordon Pasha he became very angry, saying, "Who has said that Gordon was ever afraid?" A few evenings afterward I was with Gordon in the Palace, and as the rooms were still lighted up I suggested that he should put boxes full of sand in front of the windows to stop the bullets. He called up the guard, and gave them orders to shoot me if I moved; he then brought a very large lantern which would hold twenty-four candles. He and I put the candles into the sockets, placed the lantern on the table in front of the window, lit the candles, and sat down at the table. The pasha said, "When God was portioning out fear to all people in the world, at last it came my turn, and there was no fear left to give me; go, tell all the people in Khartoum that Gordon fears nothing, for God created him without fear.

For his part, the Mahdi had come to what would be the great crisis of his meteoric career, though of course he couldn't of known it. He did have a growing sense of urgency, however, as Wolseley's Relief Expedition gradually made its way up the Nile. With his scouts informing him daily of the progress of both the Camel Corps and the River Column, Muhammed Ahmed was able to develop a sense of how much time remained for him to take the city. He knew that he had two, perhaps three, weeks left before Wolseley arrived. Ordering some of his followers northward to delay the advancing British columns as best they could, he gave instructions to prepare for the final assault on Khartoum.

The great mystery in these last days of the siege, as events were rapidly approaching their climax, is Gladstone. Just why had he chosen to act as he did throughout the entire Sudan affair? He had been adamantly opposed to any sort of "adventure" that would see Great Britain become deeply involved in the affairs of the Sudan, had been reluctant to send Gordon to Khartoum when it became clear that the Egyptian government had lost control of the situation, had resisted with all his strength and for as long as possible sending troops to the Sudan—and had only permitted that with the understanding that the Relief Expedition was not to actually relieve Khartoum but merely bring the Gordon out.

What is never explained, particularly because he never openly, specifically addressed the issue, is what Gladstone would have done if, after taking Khartoum, the Mahdi had moved further down the Valley of Nile and invaded Egypt. That Muhammed Ahmed might not be content with just the Sudan—and from all of his proclamations and pronouncements he clearly would not have been—never seemed to have occurred to the Prime Minister. While it may be that he genuinely believed his assertion that the revolt in the Sudan was that of "a people struggling to be free," he certainly knew of Gordon's letter in which the General asserted that the great danger of the Mahdi was not that he might extend the reach of his power, but that his success might catalyze a popular Islamic uprising throughout the Middle East. It was a shortsightedness that Western politicians would continue to share for the next century and a quarter—a willingness to assign benign motives to radicals in the face of all evidence to the contrary, and a resistance to acknowledging the possibility that they could present a continued, wider, or spreading danger.

While his latter-day colleagues may arguably be excused for their lack of prescience, Gladstone was the latest of a long line of British Prime Ministers trained to think in terms of global responsibilities and the security of the Empire. His failure to appreciate that the Mahdi posed a threat to the Empire was little short of dereliction of duty, or at the least an abrogation of responsibility. The political balance of the Middle East, Afghanistan and India would be fundamentally altered if the Suez Canal were lost to Great Britain: the defense and security of the Canal had, in little more than a decade, become one of the critical strategic demands on Imperial defense policy. To simply assume, without reason, that the Mahdi would not or could not threaten Britain's hold on the Canal was a risk of enormous proportions.

The looming danger was Russia, seemingly far from the Sudan but very much a factor in the consequences of whatever transpired at Khartoum. Should the Mahdi take the city and continue to advance down the Nile, and an uprising similar to that led by Colonel Arabi three years earlier erupt, the closure of the Suez Canal that would certainly result would mean that Great Britain would be compelled to reinforce India by means of the long and dangerous Cape of Good Hope around the southern tip of Africa. Russia had been contesting control of Afghanistan, which was the northern gateway to India, with Great Britain for nearly half a century. With control of the Suez Canal lost and the time for reinforcements to reach India from Great Britain increased from two weeks to two months, a Russian army could lunge across Afghanistan and into the Khyber Pass before Britain could bring up sufficient troops to stop it, leaving the "jewel in the Imperial crown" in peril.

There was also the added complication of the need for a military operation to recapture the Canal, which would be a difficult undertaking if only because of its complexity. By trying to avoid one "imperial adventure" in the Sudan, Gladstone was risking more prolonged, extended, and expensive military adventures and operations in widely separate parts of the Empire. It was not only bad politics, it was foolhardy, and Gladstone would indeed shortly pay for his political and ideological myopia.

On the morning of January 20, the entire city of Khartoum was roused when what sounded like a full-scale bombardment began, only to discover that it was a hundred-gun salute fired off at the orders of the Mahdi. It was a ruse on his part, an elaborate bluster to deceive Khartoum's defenders into believing that the Ansar were celebrating a great victory over the approaching Relief Expedition. The truth became evident when the wailing and mourning of the Arab women widowed the previous day by the action at Abu Klea were faintly heard floating across the Nile from the Arab camps.

Abu Klea came as a shock to the Mahdi. Heretofore he had a great respect for the fighting skills of the British soldier, but when he learned of the appalling cost of the battle at the wells, and that the Arabs had been defeated by a force little more than a tenth the size of their own, Muhammed Ahmed was badly shaken. Calling a council of war with his Khalifas, he suggested that the Ansar break camp and fall back to El Obeid, or even into Kordofan. He recalled that he had once had a vision in which he had been told by Allah to make a Hegira—a flight into the desert, just as the Prophet Muhammed had done—and that the time for such a flight had come.

The Khalifas were vehemently opposed to the idea of any such withdrawal. They pointed out that starvation had already taken a severe toll on Khartoum's defenders; more importantly, the falling Nile had now left the moat along the south side of the city hardly more than a wide ditch in places, rapidly filling with mud. Gordon's men, exhausted and hungry, no longer had the strength to build new earth-works or even adequately man the defenses already in place. The time had come, they argued, to take the city by storm; if the assault failed, the retreat to El Obeid or even Kordofan was still possible. Success at this point, however, would compel the advancing British column to fall back into Egypt, where it could be disposed of in time, but with Khartoum lost it would have no reason to remain in the Sudan. For five days the arguments ranged back and forth, but by the afternoon of January 25, Muhammed Ahmed had recovered much of his nerve and self-confidence, and he ordered the attack on the city to take place in the pre-dawn hours of the next morning.

The Egyptian merchant, Bordeini Bey left behind a poignant por-trait of the penultimate night of Gordon's life:

At last, Sunday morning broke, and Gordon Pasha, who used always to watch the enemy's movements from the top of the Palace, noticed a considerable movement in the south, which looked as though the Arabs were collecting at Kalakala (one of the forts on the ditch to the south of the town). He at once sent word to all of us who had attended the previous meeting and to a few others to come at once to the Palace. We all came but Gordon Pasha did not see us. We were again addressed by Giriagis Bey, who said that he had been told by Gordon Pasha to inform us that he had noticed much movement in the enemy's lines, and believed an attack would be made on the town; he therefore ordered us to collect every male in the town from the age of eight even to the old men, and to line all the fortifications, and that if we had difficulty in getting this order obeyed we were to use force. Giriagis said that Gordon Pasha now appealed to us for the last time to make a determined stand, for in twenty-four hours' time he had no doubt the English would arrive; but that if we preferred to submit, then he gave the commandant liberty to open the gates and let all join the rebels. He had nothing more to say. I then asked to be allowed to see the pasha, and was admitted to his presence. I found him sitting on a divan; and I came in he pulled off his fez, and flung it from him, saying, "What more can I say, I have nothing more to say, the people will no longer believe me, I have told them over and over again that help would be here, but it has never come, and now they must see I tell them lies. If this, my last promise, fails I can do nothing more. Go and collect all the people you can on the lines and make a good stand. Now, leave me to smoke these cigarettes." I could see he was in despair, and he spoke in a tone I had never heard before. I knew then that he had been too agitated to address the meeting, and thought the sight of his despair would dishearten us. All the anxiety he had undergone had gradually turned his hair a snowy white. I left him and that was the last time I saw him alive.

At one point during the siege Gordon had an immense store of powder laid under the cellars of the Governor's Palace and a fuse prepared which he could light from his quarters, anticipating that the city might fall and the palace be stormed by the Ansar. The idea was to wait until the last possible moment and then blow himself and as many of the Mahdi's followers as possible to atoms. But in the end he reconsidered: blowing up of the palace and himself with it would have, he thought, "more or less the taint of suicide"—in a way, "taking things out of God's hands."

Up to the very moment the end arrived, he remained undecided as to what he would do when the city fell. One of the small river steamers, armed and armored, was kept ready on the waterfront, with steam up, day and night, to transport him south to the wilderness of Equatoria province, though to what purpose apart from survival he never made clear. Ultimately the sudden appearance of the Arabs within the city walls and the complete collapse of Khartoum's defenses took the decision out of his hands.

Events reached their inevitable climax as past, present, and future—the Sudanese rebellion, Gordon's defense of the city, the Mahdi's revolt, the mission of the Relief Expedition—all came together in the early morning of January 26, 1885. In the still grayness of the pre-dawn, Faraz Pasha, an Egyptian lieutenant whose loyalty Gordon had doubted, opened the main gates of the city. Forewarned of his actions, the Mahdi's army was waiting below the walls, and when the portal was opened, rushed in and spread out down the streets and alleys of Khartoum. Exhausted and weakened by months on reduced rations, the defenders could put up only a feeble resistance. Soon they were overwhelmed by a flood of Arab warriors, hacked to death by scimitars or run through by Dervish spears. It took three hours for the Mahdi's followers to overrun the whole of the city, and even as they were advancing toward the Governor's Palace the looting, plunder, rape and murder had begun. Shrieks and screams, pleas for mercy or forgiveness, cries of agony and despair, sounded down the alleys and streets. The Ansar were making good on the Mahdi's promise of a torrent of blood in Khartoum once it fell.

Gordon himself had been sleeping when the Mahdi's army broke into the city. The sound of gunfire awakened him, and he dashed up to the roof, where he saw a mob surging toward the palace. For a while he was able to hold them off with a Maxim gun mounted there, but eventually the crowd got so close to the building that he couldn't depress the muzzle sufficiently to fire on them. He then went back to his quarters, quickly changed into the white uniform by which he was known throughout the city, buckled on his sabre, and picked up two revolvers. Stepping out onto the head of the stairs leading up from the courtyard, he waited for the Arabs to burst in. Gordon had long debated with himself what his action should be at the supreme moment. He had once told Sir Evelyn Baring, "I shall never be taken alive." Now that moment had come.

What happened next is still debated. The Mahdi's followers had hesitated to enter the Governor's Palace, fearing both the possibility of mines on the palace grounds and the chance that the entire building might blow up in their faces if Gordon indeed lit the fuse to the tons of powder stored in the palace cellars. A few of the braver among them finally charged into the palace and were quickly followed by hundreds more. The Palace Guard, fighting desperately and selling their lives dearly, were massacred. When the Arabs at last pushed into the courtyard, they found Gordon waiting, still at the head of the stairs leading up to his quarters. One version of the next few moments has Gordon rushing down the stairs, charging into the midst of his attackers, emptying both revolvers before drawing his sword and hacking at them until he was overwhelmed in a flurry of spear thrusts.

Another version tells of Gordon fleeing the Governor's Palace and attempting to reach the American Consulate, where, it is said, he believed he would find sanctuary. As this story has it, Gordon was recognized by the Arabs while still in the streets of the city and was killed in a flurry of rifle fire.

The most popular telling of how General Gordon met his end has him standing motionless at the top of the steps of the Palace courtyard, his icy blue eyes staring down his assailants, who suddenly halted their headlong rush when they caught sight of him. For a moment, there was a silence as still as death, as Gordon surveyed his attackers. They were led by four of the Mahdi's fiercest Dervish warriors, swords gleaming and spearpoints glittering in the torchlight. Gordon met them at the top of the staircase. They all stood motionless for several moments, until one of the Dervishes cried out, "O cursed one, your time has come!" Gordon is supposed to have said nothing in reply but merely made a dismissive, almost scornful gesture, and began to turn away. It was then that one of the Arabs threw a spear at him, driving it deep into Gordon's chest and through his heart. The General's body toppled off the stairs and was immediately set upon by the jubilant Ansar, who hacked at it for some minutes until they were sure he was dead.

While this latter version of Gordon's death was immediately immortalized in the lore of the Empire—and as a display of heroic disdain in the best "stiff upper lip" British tradition, it was inevitable that it would be so—later observers came to believe that the version of Gordon's death which had him, revolvers in hand, submerged in a sea of hacking, slashing enemies was more likely the way the General had actually met his end. Certainly it would have fit his character, for someone of Gordon's personality could only go down fighting. The idea of Gordon seeking sanctuary in the American consulate is simply impossible to believe given his strong fatalistic streak. Having many years earlier expressed his belief that he was God's tool to be used or discarded when and as the Almighty saw fit left no room for such efforts at self-preservation. If Khartoum fell, Gordon could only believe that his usefulness had ended, and so with it should his life.

And yet, there is an element about the third version, with Gordon standing atop the steps, staring down his would-be assailants, which has a certain ring of truth to it as well. Most certainly it was an almost stereotypical Victorian demise: the victim, noble but flawed, looking Death squarely in the eye, without the slightest evidence of fear or dismay, showing only disdain for the fate that was about to overtake him. It was an image that Victorian Britain embraced without question or shame, for it was the portrait of the death of a man who was perceived, with some justification, to personify all that Victorian Britain stood for.

And while there is an element of romanticism in this vignette, there is also an element of validity: Gordon could have died in exactly this manner. The steely-eyed stance at the top of the stairs, the contemptuous dismissal of his would-be executioners, the sheer theatricality of the entire scene, is one that would have appealed to Gordon, who understood the dramatic gesture better than most of his contemporaries. Given the sort of man he was, it would have been a fitting death.

Whichever version is true, what happened next is unquestioned. Gordon's head was cut off and placed atop a pike, where it was paraded through the Arab camps and then taken before the Mahdi as a trophy. The body was left to lie in the street, where any passing Ansar was encouraged to jab his spear into it; later, that afternoon, it was thrown into a well. When the head was brought to the Mahdi, Muhammed Ahmed was horrified. He had given, he thought, strict orders that Gordon's life be spared, and had no wish to see his antagonist's body mutilated. Whether this decision was made out of a grudging respect for Gordon or because he wished to have the General join his other European captives, as one more living trophy and proof of his invincibility, is unknown. What is known is that the Mahdi feared that he would be accursed because Gordon's death had come at the hands of his followers.

The pillage and plunder, rape and murder, lasted the better part of a day. Exactly how many lives were lost is unknown, although some figures run as high as thirty thousand men, women, and children being either executed out of hand and or sold into slavery, which was hardly the better fate.

Two days later, the steamer *Bordein* chugged up the Nile and came within sight of the city. Heavy rifle fire and some artillery shells greeted the boat, which was, of course, carrying the advance party of Relief Expedition. The sheer volume and intensity of the Arabs' fusillade, along with the absence of any British or Egyptian flag flying from the roof of the Governor's Palace, convinced those aboard that the worst had happened, the rumors were true. The city had fallen and Gordon was either dead or a captive of the Mahdi. In any event, the little force aboard the *Bordein* was far too small to take on the whole of the Mahdi's army, and recapturing Khartoum was never part of Wolseley's orders or the instructions he gave Sir Herbert Stewart when the Camel Corps set out from Korti. Reversing her engines, the *Bordein* made a hasty retreat back down the Nile to Metemma.

In the meantime, on instructions from Wolseley, General Buller had taken two regiments, the Royal Irish Regiment and the West

Kents, to Korti, where he assumed command of the Desert Column. Setting out from Korti on January 29, 1885, his plan was to attack Metemma. The town itself was still held by the Ansar, and an earlier attack by the Camel Corps had failed, although losses were thankfully light. Once he arrived on the scene, Buller surveyed Metemma and its defenses, and concluded that it was too strongly held to be taken by the force under his command. With Khartoum lost, there was no need for the town and its waterfront, which in the original planning had been designated as the staging area for the final push into the Sudanese capital. In fact there was no longer a need for the Relief Expedition at all, and Buller immediately began pulling his troops back toward Korti.

At the same time, though, the River Column continued to advance. On February 24, just twenty-six miles below Abu Hamed, with the Nile Cataracts behind them and the passage to Khartoum seemingly open before them, the men of the column, by now all veterans of desert campaigning, heard the news: Khartoum had fallen and Gordon was dead. The River Column put about, and now began gently drifting down the river up which it had just so laboriously muscled its way. Upon reaching Cairo in March, the British soldiers would once again board transport ships, this time bound for Afghanistan, where Russia was suddenly threatening war. Apart from the handful of British soldiers aboard the *Bordein*, the officers and men of the "Gordon Relief Expedition" never came within sight of the city of Khartoum.

The Mahdi's victory in capturing Khartoum, coupled with the sight of a retreating British army, caused most of the remaining desert tribes of the northern Sudan to flock to his banner. He was now the undisputed master of the whole of the country from Equatoria in the south to the Egyptian border in the north, from the Red Sea in the east to the Saharan wastes in the west. What he would do next was anyone's guess, but certainly it could not be expected that he would stop there. He had threatened to carry his *jihad* into the heart of Islam and the Ottoman Empire, and then turn on Europe: there was no reason to believe that he would not attempt to do just that. London was worried and Cairo was frightened.

When the news of Khartoum's fall and Gordon's death reached

Great Britain, the outcry was deafening. Memorial services were held the length and breadth of the country, as Britons of every class, but particularly the middle and working classes, felt that a symbol of the Empire had been destroyed. Many felt as though they had lost a personal friend. Ministers found inspiration for innumerable sermons in Gordon's "gallant death," and Queen Victoria, writing to the General's sister Augusta, gave voice, as she did so many times during her reign, not only to her own sentiments but also those of the nation:

> HOW shall I write to you or how shall I attempt to express WHAT I FEEL! To THINK of your dear, noble, heroic Brother, who served his Country and his Queen so truly, so heroically, with a self-sacrifice so edifying to the World, not having been rescued. That the promises of support were not fulfilled—which I so frequently and constantly pressed on those who asked him to go—is to me GRIEF INEXPRESS-IBLE! Indeed, it has made me ill . . . Would you express to your other sisters and your elder Brother my true sympathy, and what I do so keenly feel, the STAIN left upon England, for your dear Brother's cruel, though heroic, fate!

The British public's grief was equaled only by its indignation. Gladstone found himself being booed in public as the British people blamed him and his prevarication for what they saw as a disaster and humiliation for the Empire. By spring a growing crisis in Afghanistan, where Russian expansionism had been encouraged by what Moscow saw as Great Britain's preoccupation with Africa, would begin to erode his base of power in the Commons, and by the end of the summer the Conservatives, joined by the Irish Nationalists who had previously been staunch Gladstone allies, would maneuver him out of office. The "imperial adventure" that Gladstone had never wanted, and into which he had been forced when his attempt at a clever political solution—sending Gordon to Khartoum as a gesture, to give the appearance of "doing something"—fell apart, had played a major part in his fall from office. In the meantime, both in London and Cairo, government officials waited anxiously for the Mahdi's next move. He in fact had only one place to go: down the Nile into Egypt.

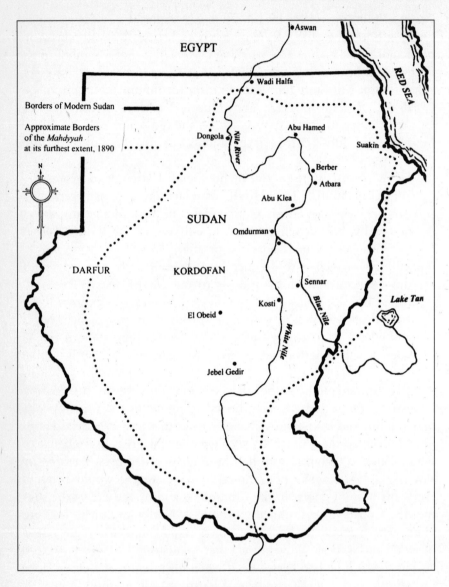

THE MAHDYYAH IN 1890

CHAPTER 11

THE DEATH OF
THE MAHDI

With the fall of Khartoum and the death of Gordon, a sea change took place in the politics of the Middle East, although it would require more than a century for its nature to become fully evident. While British and Egyptian officials blithely spoke of "Mahdism" when addressing the revolt in the Sudan, they failed to grasp the true significance of Muhammed Ahmed's accomplishment. Within their frame of reference, the Mahdi was merely another desert adventurer seeking to carve a name for himself among the Arabs of northern Africa. What they failed to see—though for his part Muhammed Ahmed appeared to have perceived it on some level—was that the Mahdi had turned Islam itself into a potent political force. Such a thing had not happened since the days of the Prophet Muhammed himself.

The Arabian and Ottoman Empires from the 8th to the 17th centuries had merely used Islam as a pretext and excuse for their expansionist ambitions—their goals were gain and aggrandizement under the guise of spreading the faith. The Mahdi, on the other hand, like the Prophet Muhammed, who never ceased to be his inspiration and model, for better or worse, had no use for nor interest in temporal power or the accumulation of wealth, save only as it would further the spread of Islam. For the Mahdi, the goal of simultaneously cleansing and spreading Islam transcended ethnic identities, national boundaries, and political divisions. The Egyptians in the service of the Ottoman Empire were lumped together with their masters as "Turks," not because the Mahdi had any particular antipathy toward the Turks, but because all those who opposed him were perceived as a single

201

common enemy, in this case the corrupt and decadent Ottomans. Likewise, even though the Egyptians and Turks were nominally Moslems, because their following of the faith did not correspond to his determination of what was true Islam, they were considered infidels. Christians, of course, whether Coptic, Orthodox, Roman Catholic, or Protestant were in their entirety regarded as beyond the religious pale, while Jews held no standing in his eyes whatsoever.

Both London and Cairo were at first surprised and then suspicious when the Mahdi did not immediately follow up his victory at Khartoum with a sweeping advance down the Nile and into Egypt. Even though the Relief Expedition was conducting an orderly withdrawal down the Nile and could have delivered a serious check to the Mahdi's army had it advanced along the river, it was neither organized, equipped nor supplied for a prolonged defense. At the same time the fall of Khartoum had amply demonstrated the erratic quality and unreliability of the Egyptian Army. It would be a month to six weeks before Great Britain could send additional reinforcements to Cairo, and when in March 1885 the Russians began acting aggressively in Afghanistan, it became uncertain if those reinforcements would be available at all.

It would be incorrect to describe the atmosphere in either capital as anything near panic, but there was a marked degree of apprehension in London and outright dread in Cairo. Suddenly the Mahdi seemed far more powerful and threatening than he had been before Khartoum was captured. However, as Muhammed Ahmed seemed content for the moment to simply consolidate his gains, for the moment both the British and Egyptian governments settled into a posture of watchfulness.

What the British and Egyptians did not comprehend was that the Mahdi's apparent hesitation to advance down the Nile into Egypt was in part the same strategy that had served him so well in the previous three years. Headlong rushes into battle were to be avoided; rather it was better to patiently wait for the enemy to make a mistake, as Egypt had done when sending the Hicks Expedition into the Sudan, or else gradually surround and cut off strategic points of his enemies' territory, forcing them into battles of his choice and timing. That had been the strategy that had succeeded at Khartoum, for the Mahdi had played a waiting game, waging a war of nerves with Gordon and Gladstone while blockading the city, and he had won, albeit by a margin of only two days.

Part of the consolidation the Mahdi was undertaking was a swift restoration of order in Khartoum. When the news that the Relief Expedition was indeed retreating down the Nile reached the Mahdi, he quickly asserted his authority and ordered a halt to all plundering and looting, as well as an end to the killing. Little significant damage had been done to the city during the siege, and soon shops and businesses were reopened, some by their original owners who had survived the sack of the city, others by the Mahdi's followers. The shipyards were quickly put to work repairing Gordon's little flotilla of steamers, while more than £55,000 worth of gold coins of various mintings were restruck with Muhammed Ahmed's image. No sooner had the coiners gone to work than a lucrative counterfeiting business sprang up, and despite the Mahdi's best efforts at suppressing it, including such drastic penalties as lopping off hands or heads, it was never completely put down. Within weeks, Khartoum was again a functioning city, albeit a somewhat empty one, a condition that was not improved when smallpox broke out soon after the end of the siege.

Thousands died, both among the surviving inhabitants and within the ranks of the Mahdi's followers. Hundreds more languished in Khartoum's dungeons, where they were thrown after being convicted by one of the Mahdi's ecclesiastic courts. In yet another foreshadowing of the totalitarian states of the 20th century, a flourishing subculture of spies and informants thrived by keeping the population in a state of abject subjugation through intimidation and terror. To be reported as an infidel, denounced as a "Turk"—which came to include anyone who had cooperated in any way with the Egyptian authorities—or merely suspected of disloyalty was an assurance of being hauled before one of the harsh and usually arbitrary Islamic courts.

The Mahdi himself was not content in Khartoum. For reasons never adequately explained, he felt ill at ease in the city. It was said that this was due in part to the fact that Gordon had been killed within its walls, contrary to the Mahdi's express orders that he be spared, and so Muhammed Ahmed felt the city to be cursed. At times he even gave voice to the belief that he himself had been cursed by Allah because of Gordon's murder. Whatever the real reason, in February the Mahdi withdrew his household from Khartoum, crossing the Nile to Omdurman and there making a new home.

By now he unquestionably led a luxurious existence. The ascetic traits that Muhammed Ahmed had shown in his youth and early manhood had all but vanished, and as middle age overtook him, the lean, predatory figure he had presented to the world had grown fat and decadent. In the privacy of his own tents and house, the patched and tattered jibba, which he had so long worn as a way of identifying himself as one of the faithful, gave way to scented drawers, shirts, and robes of fine cotton and linen, and he took to wearing makeup in order to enhance his appearance. Stretching out on elegant pillows, surrounded by thirty or more of his wives at any given time, Muhammed Ahmed was waited on literally hand and foot. While some of his concubines would gently fan the reclining figure, others would massage his feet and hands, while still others stood by awaiting his instructions as to what whim or pleasure he desired fulfilled.

Ethnically, the Mahdi's harem encompassed the spectrum of peoples living in the Sudan. Father Ohrwalder wrote that "Almost every tribe in the Sudan supplied its representative." There were even Turkish girls, some younger than ten years old, who had been captured when El Obeid fell and Khartoum was taken, and had been brought into the Mahdi's harem. The only interruptions permitted to this daily routine of sensuality were the ever-shorter councils of war he held with the Khalifas.

This was not, however, the face the Mahdi presented to his followers. Whenever the Ansar demanded that he present himself, in particular during the holy month of Ramadan, when all Moslems were expected to fast during the daylight hours, Muhammed Ahmed would once again don his jibba, girdle, and turban, and present himself to the faithful as their devout and fiery leader. His corpulence could not be disguised, yet such was the power of his personality that his charisma remained. The path he would follow to the Omdurman mosque for daily prayers would be lined with near-hysterical crowds; women would throw themselves to the ground behind him, prostrating themselves across his footprints, believing that their image would bring health, fertility, and a multitude of other blessings. The Mahdi's public appearance was a grand performance, yet it begs the question: was that all it really was, a performance?

It is easy, perhaps too much so, to dismiss the Mahdi at this point as being exactly what Cairo and London believed him to be: a desert rogue, an Arab scoundrel, an adventurer seeking to accumulate power and wealth but no more. Had he actually degenerated into a poseur, maintaining the fiction of his dedication to his holy mission of purifying Islam and bringing *jihad* to the infidel wherever he could be found? Had he succumbed to the very luxury, opulence, and ostentation that he had once so fiercely condemned? Had he confirmed Lord Acton's dictum about power and corruption?

While it is undeniable that in the last months of his life the Mahdi allowed himself to enjoy the trappings of power earned through his success, it would be incorrect to say, as some historians have maintained, that he descended into debauchery. His lifestyle was not significantly different from that of any other Arab tribal leader or chieftain of similar rank. While Arab culture respects the ascetic holy man, it also demands that its leaders surround themselves in a certain level of luxury as a method of establishing their status and importance.

The victory at Khartoum caused large numbers of minor tribal chieftains who were yet undecided as to where their loyalties should lie to suddenly throw in their lot with the Mahdi. Thousands of new followers began drifting toward Khartoum and Omdurman, settling in the cities and along the banks of the Blue and White Niles. For the most part they clustered around Omdurman, as Khartoum began to fall into decay. Fervor for the Mahdist cause remained high, and even grew after the fall of Khartoum, and had he chosen to advance into Egypt, the Mahdi would have commanded a willing force of more than a hundred thousand fighting men.

Then, in midsummer 1885, came an event as sudden and unpredictable as the rise of the "Expected One" four years earlier. On June 22, five months after the fall of Khartoum, while at the pinnacle of his power and influence, Muhammed Ahmed died under mysterious circumstances. There were rumors at the time and in the years to follow that he had been poisoned by a member of his own household in retribution for his increasingly harsh rule. Others speculated that an early demise was to be expected of a middle-aged man worn out by sensu-

ality and the physical strain of attending to his growing harem. Both
are possible, though not likely, and most historians believe he simply
died of typhus, which, along with smallpox, broke out in Khartoum
in the weeks following the massacre.

When Muhammed Ahmed died, his dream died with him—his
vision of purifying what he saw as a corrupt and decadent Islam, and
then sweeping all of Christendom before him in the cleansing fury of
jihad. With his death the driving power behind the Mahdyyah was
lost. While his successor, the Khalifa Abdullahi, would maintain the
existence of a Mahdist regime for another fourteen years, aside from
an abbreviated war with the kingdom of Ethiopia, a few attacks on his
neighbors, and one brief excursion into Egypt in 1888, its expansion
ceased. The Khalifa was too preoccupied with securing his position to
be able to devote time and energy to continuing the jihad.

While the Mahdi quickly became an historical figure of almost myth-
ical proportions among militant Moslems and Sudanese Arabs, he was
soon all but forgotten outside of the Sudan and the Middle East. This
was in no small part because of cultural differences: while the Mahdi
was—and remains—a charismatic, almost romantic, figure of mystery
to Arab Moslems, there is little about him that moderate Moslems or
Westerners find appealing. His devotion to his faith, his sense of
honor, his values and morals, all in some way seem alien, as if their
basis and perspective were just slightly out of focus or misaligned. He
seems to have enjoyed the harshness and frequent cruelty of his rule,
and the ecclesiastical justice it dispensed, just a bit too much. It is
almost as if he knew he was a despot, however divinely motivated or
appointed he believed himself to be, and took a perverse pleasure in
that knowledge. It's not that he was corrupted by his power, but rather
that he reveled in it; instead of reluctantly assuming the burden of
leading his jihad and regretting the blood shed and lives lost, he gloried in all of it. Even his death just months after his greatest triumph
has often been regarded among his followers and descendants as a sort
of divine justice, particularly as a retribution for the death of Gordon.

It is Gordon who over the decades has had his reputation bur-
nished and his historical place secured as a tragic figure of political
betrayal who nevertheless faced death with courage and dignity. He

has become the quintessential Victorian hero—and as such, a figure of tragedy. It's not an undeserved reputation, for Gordon's tragedy—which translated into tragedy for Khartoum—was that he could not conceive that respectable men who occupied positions of great authority and responsibility could stoop to playing petty political games with human lives. Sacrificing lives, figuratively and sometimes literally, is at times an unfortunate part of the political process even under a democracy, yet the very nature of a democratic system places a responsibility on those who must make these hard choices, believing they will do so for the very noblest of reasons. Gordon's tragedy is that he expected those to whom he looked for leadership and support to do exactly that.

Yet, it has to be said that if Gordon is a tragic figure, as he has almost invariably been depicted in print and film, the Mahdi was one as well, for it is difficult to perceive him as being much more than a grand failure. Ultimately nothing to which he aspired came to pass and endured long beyond his lifetime. True, the Sudan had been freed of the burden of Egyptian rule, but Cairo would reassert its authority over the country within a few years; the cleansing of Islam to which he had originally dedicated himself was never completed, and in truth was never sought outside the circles of extreme fundamentalist Moslems even in his day. Perhaps if he had lived long enough to carry his *jihad* into Egypt, the widespread Moslem revolt so feared by Gordon might well have come to pass, but there is no way to be certain of it. At the end of his life, which was by any standard abbreviated, the Mahdi had little to show for having expended so much effort. A passage in one of the Scandinavian Eddas reads: "All things pass away but death and the glory of deeds." For the Mahdi, his tragedy was that after his death, whatever glory his deeds had accrued would eventually fade away.

Although the *Mahdyyah*—the Mahdist state—was established by his successor, Abdullahi, who styled himself "the" Khalifa rather than simply "a" Khalifa—there would be no *primus inter pares* with the other two Khalifas for Abdullahi— the Sudan soon sank back into the chaos it had known under Egyptian rule as the *Mahdyyah* became a barbarous parody of itself. Abdullahi was the first Khalifa chosen by

Muhammed Ahmed, and long before the Mahdi's death his position as successor to the leadership of the *Mahdyyah* was proclaimed. Thus when the Mahdi died, there was none of the bloody quarreling and open warfare that had marked the death of the Prophet Muhammed and which left such a bitter legacy to Islam. Abdullahi himself came from the Ta'A'Ishi branch of the Baggara tribe, one of the most loyal of all those following the Mahdi. He was said to be tall, dark, and imperious-looking, much like the Mahdi himself; however, what might have been a handsome visage was marred by the scars of smallpox. Though he was intelligent, he was more shrewd than intellectually gifted. He was fundamentally ignorant and functionally illiterate, with little or no knowledge of the world outside the Sudan.

He was also ruthless and opportunistic. He had buttressed his position as the Mahdi's successor by marrying one of Muhammed Ahmed's daughters, and after the Mahdi's death he was careful to avoid asserting his authority by governing in the Mahdi's name, as if he were only a steward or caretaker. Even so, he essentially banished any member of the Mahdi's family who might have been a rival to power. Meanwhile, the Baggara tribe gradually assumed a position of pre-eminence in the Mahdist ranks, becoming something of a ruling clique as they took over every significant office within the *Mahdyyah*, further solidifying the Khalifa's grip on power.

While Islamic law was harsh—and harshly applied—under the Mahdi, its application was for the most part even-handed. Under his successor, Islam's laws were applied at the whim of the magistrate charged with its enforcement. The only appeal from the ecclesiastical courts' judgements was to the Khalifa himself, and he rarely intervened. The usual punishment for all but the most minor offenses was death by beheading. The slave trade was not only resumed, it grew in scope and numbers. Zobeir Pasha never returned to the Sudan, but at their worst his activities paled in comparison to those of his successors under the Khalifa. Order in the Mahdist realm was maintained only through constant, ever-looming terror, or by incessant internecine warfare. Typical of all tyrants, the Khalifa felt most secure when he could keep those whom he suspected of disloyalty under close scrutiny. Consequently, during his years of power, the city of Omdurman, which he made his capital as the Mahdi had done, became the center of life in the Sudan, while Khartoum continued its decline into ruin. Sometime in 1886 the Khalifa ordered the whole city abandoned, save for the boatyard and the arsenal. At the same time Abdullahi ordered an elaborate tomb constructed in Omdurman for the Mahdi, surmounted by a white dome eighty feet high, visible to travelers still three days out of the city. Before long, for Moslems in the Sudan, a pilgrimage to the Mahdi's tomb became as holy an undertaking as the traditional pilgrimage to Mecca.

It was beside this tomb that an open-air mosque was built, and this became the center of the Khalifa's government. Sheikhs and emirs wishing to prove their loyalty were conspicuous by their daily attendance at prayers, while Abdullahi would announce what dreams and visions he had received from Allah and the Mahdi for the purpose of leading the faithful of the *Mahdyyah*. Among these was one which told him that money was a distracting and corrupting influence, therefore no man should possess more than he required for his needs. The excess was to be "donated" to the Mahdist state, where it became in essence the Khalifa's personal fortune. The injunction against acquiring and keeping wealth did not, of course, apply to him.

Abdullahi began to embrace all the trappings of petty despotism. He surrounded himself with sycophants, and visitors to his court were expected to approach him on all fours and prostrate themselves when they spoke. His personal bodyguard numbered five hundred horsemen, while some four hundred concubines were added to his harem. He took a particular delight in humiliating and tormenting the handful of European captives he had inherited from the Mahdi: Father Ohrwalder and four nuns from his mission; the German merchant Neufeld; Rudolf Slatin, one-time governor of Darfur; Martin Hansal, the son of the Austrian consul, captured at Khartoum; and a number of Greeks. Slatin was employed as an interpreter, but the others spent much of their time in chains, while the nuns in particular were tortured for their refusal to embrace Islam. One of the captives, Frank Lupton, was worked to death in the Khartoum boatyard.

The Khalifa attempted to extend the Mahdi's *jihad*, but with none of the success that Muhammed Ahmed had achieved. While the Ansar and the Dervishes remained as brave as always, the Khalifa lacked the charisma that enabled the Mahdi to inspire his followers to feats of

arms that seemed almost superhuman. Abdullahi's first venture into
the realm of foreign policy came in 1886 when he rejected an offer of
an alliance against the Europeans made by the King of Ethiopia,
Yohannes IV, on the grounds that, as a Christian, Yohannes was an
infidel and therefore not worthy of an alliance with the faithful.

A year later the Khalifa sent a sixty thousand-man army to invade
Ethiopia, and it reached the ancient capital of Gondar, which was
sacked. The war would flare up intermittently for the next three years,
but in 1889 the Khalifa withdrew his army and instead sent it down
the Nile to Wadi Halfa, under Abd ar Rahman an Nujumi, his best
general. British-led Egyptian troops met the Ansar at Tushkah and
soundly defeated them, ending the Mahdist threat to Egypt. Next the
Khalifa turned south, trying to conquer Equatoria, only to be turned
back by the Belgians, and in 1893 the Italians repulsed an Ansar
attack in Eritrea.

None of these setbacks diminished the Khalifa's arrogance, however. A quartet of Arab envoys was sent to Cairo with letters for the
Sultan of the Ottoman Empire, the Khedive of Egypt, and Queen
Victoria. In the letter to the Queen he reminded her of the deaths of
Hicks and Gordon, and assured her that a similar fate awaited any
other British general who dared oppose the faithful. He then invited
her to make a pilgrimage to Omdurman in order to embrace Islam,
and submit to his authority.

Thy soldiers thought only of retreat from the Sudan with dis-
comfiture and defeat, whereof they have had more than
enough. . . . Thus thou hast erred in many ways, and art suffering great loss, wherefrom there is no refuge for thee save by
turning to Allah the King, and entering among the people of
Islam and the followers of the Mahdi, grace be upon him. If
thou wilt do thus, and yield all matter to us, then shalt thou
achieve thy desire of perfect felicity and true repose, which is
salvation before Allah in the blissful and enduring Dwelling,
the like of which the eye has not seen, nor ear heard, or heart
of man conceived. But if thou wilt not turn from thy blindness
and self-will, continue to war against the hosts of Allah thy-
self, with all thy armies and war-like equipment. So shalt thou

behold the end of thy work. Thou shalt be crushed by the power of Allah and his might, or be afflicted by the death of many of thy people, who have entered on war with the people of God, by reason of thy Satanic presumption.

The letters were returned to the envoys with a simple message for the Khalifa: none of the three monarchs could be bothered to make any reply. Nothing could have more clearly demonstrated that the *Mahdyyah* no longer possessed the strength or momentum to be able to challenge the European powers or any of their client states.

Among the British public there was still running a current of discontent over the failure of the Relief Expedition to arrive in time, as well as regret for Gordon's death. The people weren't unmindful of Gladstone's prevarication and the near-certainty that it was the cause of so much of the delay that eventually led to the expedition being a fruitless effort. While the issue of the Sudan was not one that could have brought the Gladstone government down, it did lose the Prime Minister a few key political allies in the House of Commons.

The desire to "avenge Gordon" still ran strong in much of Great Britain, as did the hostility toward the Mahdi and his successor. The Anti-Slavery Society in particular took great pains to ensure that every rumored atrocity and alleged barbarous act attributed to the Khalifa received wide press. Yet none of these sentiments were powerful enough to compel the British government to retake the Sudan and bring an end the Mahdist regime. When that decision was finally made, it would be for entirely different reasons.

In early 1892, Herbert Kitchener, now a major-general, was appointed Sirdar, or commander, of the whole of the Egyptian army, which had been thoroughly reformed and reorganized in the years following the fall of Khartoum. About this same time the British government under Lord Salisbury decided to occupy the Sudan, and ordered Kitchener to begin preparations for the expedition. Circumstances had changed very dramatically for Britain since 1885, both domestically and internationally.

Gladstone had been forced to resign as Prime Minister in the summer of 1885 as a direct consequence of his efforts to get a Home Rule Bill for Ireland passed by both the Commons and the House of Lords.

To many, there was a certain element of revenge for the Khartoum fiasco in the vote that brought his government down.

Lord Salisbury, the last British Prime Minister to sit in the House of Lords rather than the House of Commons, was a protégé of Benjamin Disraeli, and like him firmly believed in the Empire. Simultaneously filling the offices of Prime Minister and Foreign Secretary, Salisbury was emphatic about the direction that British foreign policy would take under his leadership: "France," he said in 1888, "is, and must always remain, England's greatest danger." Consequently it came as no surprise that when British, French, and Belgian colonial claims unexpectedly clashed at the Nile headwaters in the southern Sudan, Salisbury was determined to assert Britain's authority in the region and prepared to back up its claims, if need be, with force. The aggressiveness of the Khalifa did not bother Lord Salisbury; rather it was the instability of his regime that was cause for concern. The British were worried that the other colonial powers would take advantage of the muddled state of the Sudan's politics to carve off territory that was, nominally at least, annexed to Egypt.

In addition to these political considerations, plans for an irrigation dam to be built at Aswan were already in hand, which when built would transform the entire southern half of Egypt, more than doubling the available farmland and making the region an even more attractive prize for an adventurer such as the Khalifa. The region, and even the dam itself, would be under constant threat if the *Mahdyyah* were allowed to continue. And as always any threat to the Suez Canal, however remote, could not be ignored. Lastly, as Britain carved out a string of colonies along the eastern spine of Africa from the Cape of Good Hope to the Nile Delta, maintaining the security of these colonies made control of the entire length of the Nile a necessity. As long as the Mahdist state continued to exist, it presented threats to all of these imperial ambitions. The *Mahdyyah* would have to be swept aside, not because of its continued hostility toward Egypt and Britain, but simply because it had become an inconvenient obstacle.

In 1895 Kitchener was formally authorized by the British government to prepare a campaign to reconquer the Sudan, with Britain providing men, equipment and supplies, while Egypt contributed troops and underwrote the costs of the expedition. When his plans were completed, the simply-styled "Anglo-Egyptian Nile Expeditionary Force" included twenty-six thousand soldiers, of whom eighty-six hundred were British. As with Wolseley's expedition, there were contingents from the Royal Artillery, the Royal Engineers, and the Royal Marines, along with the Camel Corps, while a flotilla of half a dozen gunboats manned by the Royal Navy would accompany the force up the Nile. The balance of the expedition's strength was made up of Egyptian units that included six battalions of black Africans recruited in southern Sudan.

The entire expedition was to be methodical in the extreme. Rather than being driven by the urgency to relieve a beleaguered garrison, which fourteen years earlier had forced Wolseley to drive his men at an exhausting pace, Kitchener's advance up the Nile would take two years. Steamers hired by the Thomas Cook Company brought the army to Wadi Halfa, old "Bloody Halfway," where an army headquarters was set up while the border defenses were extended and reinforced. In March 1896, the campaign officially began as the column moved slowly and majestically into the Sudan, brushing aside an Arab blocking force at Ferket on June 7. In September, Kitchener captured Dongola, less than two hundred miles from Wadi Halfa. Then, in order to eliminate several hundred miles from the journey up the river, the British constructed a rail line from Wadi Halfa to Abu Hamed, cutting off the huge U-shaped bend in the Nile that held Debba, Korti, and the Fourth Cataract. From Abu Hamed an extension of the rail line ran parallel to the Nile down to Berber. When it was complete it became possible to move troops and supplies at nearly four times the best speed that steamers could make up the river.

The Sirdar's Anglo-Egyptian forces continued their leisurely advance, meeting no real opposition until they encountered a few thousand Arabs at Abu Hamed on August 7, 1897. A short, sharp action was fought before the Arabs withdrew, realizing they were badly outnumbered. The army halted at Abu Hamed and built up a supply base before moving on again; there was little other significant resistance until Kitchener reached Atbarah, not far from Abu Klea.

There the Emir Mahmoud, one of the Khalifa's better generals, met the British and Egyptians in a carefully prepared position. But Mahmoud had not reckoned with the destructiveness of modern weapons, and as the Royal Artillery and the Nile gunboats bombard-ed the Ansar, the British and Egyptian infantry attacked and drove the Arabs in disorder into the desert. Mahmoud was captured and in a victory parade a few days later in Berber was forced to walk in chains before Kitchener, who was mounted on a splendid white charger.

It was a calculated humiliation for Mahmoud, made all the more galling because it was Kitchener who had personally devised it. Even then Kitchener was an enigmatic character. Intelligent, insightful, a curious combination of by-the-book orthodoxy and imagination, he was distant, extremely reserved, and not at all popular among either his officers or his men, all of whom were nonetheless ready to concede his gifts for strategy, tactics, and especially logistical planning. While eminently practical and methodical—it was Kitchener who drew up the plans for the Anglo-Egyptian army's careful advance up the Nile—he was sometimes capable of the most profound insights and intu-itions. In August 1914, when Kitchener had become Secretary of State for War, in the middle of a staff meeting where all the other officers present were—like their French and German counterparts—discussing the likelihood of the war being over in six weeks, Kitchener suddenly declared that the war would last three or four years and require armies of millions of men. It was this sort of chilling genius that kept men at arm's length from Kitchener.

He was unmarried (rumors would circulate over the years that he was a homosexual, but it seems more likely that the death of his fiancé many years earlier had left him emotionally scarred), and had little or no social life with his officers, although he was certainly popular in the best Establishment houses in Britain. He cultivated friendships with people who could be useful to him and his career, yet at the same time he was a consummate professional soldier who refused to rely on "connections" to make up any shortcomings in the performance of his duties or his battlefield leadership. The confrontation with the Khalifa that both men knew was shortly inevitable would establish Kitchener as Great Britain's most distinguished soldier.

In mid-summer, the expedition reached Metemma, where they found the remains of positions dug by Wolseley's troops fourteen years earlier, along with the graves of those who had died at Abu Klea and Abu Kru. Supplies were again built up, and the troops, Egyptian and

British alike, were spoiling for a fight. By the end of August Omdurman was almost in sight, and on September 1, 1898, the Sirdar halted his army on the bank of the Nile fifteen miles above the city. There he began preparing for the battle that would seal the fate of the *Mahdyyah*.

As dawn broke that morning, Kitchener sent the British and Egyptian cavalry, with the Camel Corps and Horse Artillery in support, out in advance of the army, where it quickly formed a screen for the infantry and advanced toward Omdurman for a distance of about eight miles. The 21st Lancers took up positions on the left flank, anchoring the line on the Nile, while the Egyptian horse covered the front and right flank, deploying in a vast arc that stretched back into the desert. At the same time the gunboat began chugging up the river, keeping pace with the land forces.

As the cavalry advanced, just ten miles north of Omdurman, they came up to the Kerreri Hills, which to their surprise were undefended, although an abandoned Dervish camp was found. It had evidently been shelled by the gunboats the day before. It was about this time that the men of the 21st Lancers noticed that a flock of enormous vultures, numbering as many as a hundred, had suddenly begun hovering over the regiment. The belief was widespread throughout the Sudan that this was an ill omen, a sign the troops over which the birds circled would suffer heavy losses. The regiment halted at the foot of the hills, and the senior officers and a party of scouts made their way to the highest crest. From there they could behold a sight no British soldier or civilian had seen for thirteen years: Khartoum. The advance resumed and shortly every man with a pair of field-glasses or a telescope could make out not only Khartoum but also the now-yellowish dome of the Mahdi's Tomb and the city of Omdurman.

The cavalry screen began its descent from the Kerreri Hills and onto a wide, gently rolling sand plain, some six to seven miles wide, interrupted here and there with patches of coarse grass and straggling bushes. On the left, to the east, was the Nile, with a small, deserted mud-hut village perched on its bank. The remaining three sides of the plain were surrounded by low, rocky hills and ridges, while a single low black hill and a long, low ridge running from it bisected the plain from east to west. The ground behind the ridge, that is, to the south of it, was invisible to the British and Egyptian cavalry.

Sharp-eyed observers among the Lancers noticed a long black line with white spots running along the ridge. It appeared to be a dense zeriba, or barricade, of thorn bushes. The cavalry continued to move forward in a vast line, khaki-colored on the left where the 21st Lancers were positioned, black in the center where the dark-skinned Egyptians sat on their black horses, and mottled on the right, where the Camel Corps and Horse Artillery jostled for position. As they closed with the zeriba, they could make out enemy horsemen riding about the flanks and front of the Ansar line.

It was now nearly eleven o'clock and the sun was getting hot. Suddenly the whole black line which had seemed to be the zeriba began moving—it wasn't a thornbush barricade, it was a mass of fighting men. Behind it thousands upon thousands of Ansar and Dervish soldiers began to appear over the crest of the ridge. It was the whole of the Mahdist army. Stretching across a front of four miles, formed into five huge divisions, it moved with astonishing swiftness. A cloud of banners—black, white, and green, embroidered in gold with inscriptions from the Koran—floated above them, while their spearpoints glittered in the noon sun. It was an army of more than 50,000 men.

The Khalifa had assembled every able-bodied fighting man he could muster at Omdurman, determined to achieve the victory over the British that had eluded Muhammed Ahmed. But remembering only the victory over William Hicks' Egyptian conscripts in 1883 and forgetting the slaughter at Abu Klea three years later, he ordered his soldiers forward into the attack rather than make a stand on the plains of Kerreri. On August 30 his scouts informed him that the enemy was nearing Omdurman, and the next day he assembled his army. Some sense of what was to come seeped through his forces, however, and nearly six thousand men deserted the night before the battle. Still it was an imposing force that advanced toward the British and Egyptians, forty-eight thousand foot soldiers and four thousand horse.

The first shots of the battle were fired at just after 11:00 AM by the gunboats on the Nile. Spotting batteries of Mahdist artillery on the riverbanks, the Royal Navy gun crews immediately opened fire on them. The Arab batteries replied as best they could, as did the forts along the river. It was a one-sided exchange, for though the Arabs had some fifty guns that could be brought to bear, the Royal Navy's weapons were heavier and better served, and the combination of better accuracy and greater weight of shells soon took the Arab guns out of the battle. Rifle pits along the riverbanks were swept by machine-gun fire. Under cover of this barrage, the Arab Irregulars under Major Wortley began clearing out the forts and their outlying villages, which were defended by Dervishes. Most of the Irregulars refused to move closer to the buildings than five hundred yards, but Wortley's reserve—Jaalin tribesmen who despised the Dervishes—moved in and began methodically clearing out each building, executing every Dervish they captured.

A battery of the Royal Artillery began shelling Omdurman, scoring at least three hits on the Mahdi's Tomb. The damage to the tomb was an unfortunate consequence of its proximity to Omdurman's arsenal, but the Arabs took it as a deliberate insult, and in their anger they sped up their advance. The Egyptian cavalry and the Horse Artillery began to withdraw, followed by the Camel Corps; the 21st Lancers remained on the army's left flank. The Mahdist army maintained its order and began to close with the six brigades of infantry that made up the main body of the British force. The collision of the two armies, if it came, would be shattering.

Kitchener quickly issued orders that drew up the British and Egyptian infantry in lines of parade-ground precision, anchoring each flank on the Nile, the whole of the army forming an arc along the river. When a junior officer named Winston Churchill reported to the Sirdar that the advancing Arab army would be within range within the hour, Kitchener informed his staff: "We want nothing better. Here is a good field of fire. They may as well come today as tomorrow."

As soon as the troops' mid-day meal was finished the whole of the army stood to arms, awaiting the approaching Arabs. But instead, just before 2:00 PM, the Dervish army halted. Their riflemen loosed a single volley into the air, then the entire force went to ground. There would be no engagement that day, but it was certain that the battle that both Kitchener and the Khalifa wanted would take place on the morrow.

CHAPTER 12

OMDURMAN

The rest of that day and night were marked by a handful of desultory skirmishes between small groups of British infantry and Ansar on the Kerreri Plain. The steamers took up positions on the Nile to cover the flanks of the army, and throughout the night shone their searchlights up and down the riverbanks to prevent any surprise attacks.

Kitchener had ordered his troops to bed down for the night in the positions they had occupied during the day, so rather than establishing the checkerboard arrangement of brigade squares which had been typical of the British Army at night, each brigade had constructed rough zeribas of thorn bushes about its position and posted double sentries, while patrols roamed the intervals between brigades. It was a tactic through which Kitchener displayed his intimate knowledge of the Arab way of making war. Knowing that they despised night attacks, he gave himself the advantage of having his units sleep in their lines, which in the morning would save valuable time by not requiring the brigades to maneuver into position in the face of the enemy.

As the pre-dawn grayness crept across the sky on September 2, 1899, bugles sounded the morning stand-to across the British camp. Cavalry patrols were sent out, and by 6:30 AM the first reports were coming in: the Khalifa's army had spent the night in the same place it had halted the day before. Suddenly the cavalry scouts realized that the entire Mahdist army was on the move. A roar of righteous fury arose from the Arab mass as they rode and marched to the attack, a sound so loud that it was faintly heard in the British camp, still nearly five miles distant.

The British and Egyptians were ready. As the morning light grew, the banners of each Khalifa and Emir became visible to the waiting infantry: on the extreme left the bright green flag of Ali-Wad-Helu; next to his followers flew the dark green flag of Osman Sheikh-ed-Din, surrounded by a mass of spearmen, preceded by long lines of warriors armed presumably with rifles; on the right a host of Dervishes surged forward under a collection of white flags, while visible among them was the red banner of Sherif; in the center flew the sacred Black banner of Abdullahi himself. Within the ranks of this army were, as Churchill later described it, "Riflemen who had helped to destroy Hicks, spearmen who had charged at Abu Klea, Emirs who saw the sack of Gondar, Baggara fresh from raiding the Shillooks, warriors who had besieged Khartoum—all marched, inspired by the memories of former triumphs and embittered by the knowledge of late defeats, to chastise the impudent and accursed invaders."

While the Khalifa was committed to attacking Kitchener's army, he had no intention of simply flinging his Dervishes and Ansar into a headlong assault. Instead he formulated a clever plan that, had he not so greatly underestimated the destructive power of modern weaponry, might actually have succeeded in driving Kitchener's army into the Nile. His first move was to send fifteen thousand of Osman Sheikh-ed-Din's Dervishes forward to deliver a frontal attack on the Anglo-Egyptian line. He waited with a similar force near a rise known as Surgham Hill to watch the outcome.

Though he almost certainly didn't expect it to succeed, if it did the assault would have been followed by Abdullahi's own bodyguard, the elite of the Arab army. As every man in the British and Egyptian Armies knew by now, the Dervishes were extraordinarily brave men and dangerous opponents. The purpose of this attack was two-fold: it might actually succeed in breaking the enemy line, and at the same time it would cover a movement by the rest of Osman Sheikh-ed-Din's soldiers, who were to move to the northern flank and swing around to strike at the Egyptian brigade, not by any means Kitchener's best or most reliable troops. But that was not the most clever part of the Khalifa's plan. Ali-Wad-Helu had been instructed to keep some twenty-two thousand men in reserve behind the Kerreri Hills, out of sight and out of range of the British. If the first two attacks failed—and by his planning it seems that Abdullahi was to some degree anticipating that they would—when the Anglo-Egyptian army advanced on Omdurman, believing they had won an easy victory, the remaining Ansar would swoop down from the hills, catching the enemy out in the open plain, in marching order, unable to form their habitual square. Caught by Ali-Wad-Helu's twenty-two thousand to the north and the Khalifa with sixteen thousand to the south, with the Nile behind them and the open desert before them, the British and Egyptian soldiers would be doomed. It would be the Hicks disaster all over again.

But it was not to be. The British artillery opened up when the Dervish center came within range. Four batteries began firing at a range of about 3,000 yards. Gaps momentarily appeared in the Arab ranks. They were quickly filled, and the advance continued. The gunboats joined in the cannonade, and soon shells were bursting all along the Arab line. Still the Arabs closed with their British and Egyptian foes.

At a thousand yards the infantry opened fire, the crash of their massed volleys of rifles punctuated by the chatter of machine-guns. The gaps in the Arab lines grew larger and were filled less quickly now, the approach becoming a bit ragged—yet they still came on. The artillery was firing shrapnel shells over the heads of the advancing Dervishes and Ansar, the fragments raining down on them. It was here that two mistakes caught up with the Khalifa, dooming his plans. The first was that in one of those quirks of fate which can often decide battles and which no commander can ever completely avoid, both divisions of Dervishes attacked simultaneously rather than in succession. This meant that the Anglo-Egyptian infantry would only confront a single charge, rather than being forced to divide their fire, and would only have to endure a single shock action if the Arabs were able to come to close combat instead of the succession of impacts that Abdullahi had anticipated. It also meant exposing them to the devastating rifle volleys of British and Egyptian troops and the raking fire of the Maxim guns. The second mistake was the Khalifa's apparent ignorance of the effectiveness of his enemy's weapons.

The British Army and its Egyptian counterpart, now thoroughly reorganized along British lines, were now equipped with the .303 cal-

ibre Lee-Metford, a bolt action rifle which had replaced the old
Martini-Henrys. The Lee-Metford fired a round at nearly twice the
velocity and twice the range of the Martini, with almost double the
rate of fire. When the Arab army advanced toward the Anglo-
Egyptian lines, they marched into a veritable wall of fire, as the 300
rounds-per-minute rate of fire of the Maxim guns was added to the fifteen rounds per minute each infantryman was capable of producing.

The effect was devastating. Entire ranks of Ansar and Dervishes
were brought down in bloody heaps before they could get within
range with their own weapons. With each volley the charging Arabs
seemed to draw a little closer to the British ranks, but in ever dwindling numbers. Finally, at about 800 yards from the British lines, the
Dervishes could do no more—it was impossible to advance another
foot against such firepower.

On the Anglo-Egyptian right, a force of cavalry, the Camel Corps,
and Horse Artillery, supported by the Egyptian Brigade, brought the
Dervish left to a halt, preventing the turning movement that Abdullahi
had thought possible there. The fighting was fierce and the British suffered significant casualties, though the Dervish losses were just awful.
Several British officers would recall how the Dervishes continued to
close relentlessly, heedless of the artillery shells exploding within their
ranks. When one of the gunboats stood in close to the shoreline and
began firing at the Dervish soldiers at almost point-blank range, the
situation became unbearable even for those incredibly brave men, and
they fell back in confusion, harassed by the British cavalry, effectively
out of the battle.

The Dervish frontal attack on the center continued, but still could
make no headway against the fearsome British firepower. Though they
quickly learned that the dense ranks in which they advanced presented targets impossible to miss and so began advancing in more dispersed formations, eight hundred yards was the closest any of the
Ansar could approach to the British lines. Yet, though they were
unable to advance, they were unwilling to retire. Here and there Arab
riflemen would find a fold of ground that allowed them to take shots
at the British troops, but the range was long, their weapons old, and
their effect was negligible. Slowly, reluctantly, the Arabs withdrew.
Their courage had been unquestionable, but it hadn't been enough

against the measured volleys of a modern army supported by machine guns and artillery. By eight o'clock more than four thousand of the Dervish warriors lay dead or wounded on the open ground before the British lines.

As the Arabs withdrew, artillery started picking off the small groups of riflemen who were still doing their best to harass the British line. Small pockets of warriors, seeking shelter from the British volleys, were flushed into the open and, deciding that they had endured enough for the moment, quickly fled the field. Lee-Metford and Maxim fire followed them, until they were lost to sight behind the far ridge of the Kerreri plain.

Once the Arab attack had been broken, Kitchener and his officers agreed that they had to occupy Omdurman before the Dervish army could retreat into the city. The British unit on the extreme left of the Anglo-Egyptian position, the 21st Lancers, was sent orders to ride for the city and cut off the retreat of the Arab army: "Advance and clear the left flank, and use every effort to prevent the enemy re-entering Omdurman."

Initially facing the Lancers was a small force of seven hundred Arabs, positioned to prevent any blocking movement of the Khalifa's line of retreat to Omdurman. As soon as the Lancers began moving toward Omdurman, Abdullahi sent an additional twenty-four hundred of his fighting men to support the blocking force. While the Arabs raced to get into position, the 21st methodically went through the drill preparatory to advancing against an enemy—or if need be, charging one.

This was not a demonstration of British dedication to military orthodoxy or the commanders' lack of imagination or sense of urgency. To be truly effective, cavalry charges had to be carefully organized and staged: in real life they were a far cry from the spectacles depicted in countless motion pictures, where a bugle sounds the "Charge" and a mass of horsemen spring forward in a mad, headlong gallop. The success or failure of a charge came down to one single moment—the instant when the horsemen met the foot soldiers. Unformed infantry, that is troops not in a column or square, were vulnerable at all times to cavalry, but formed troops could only be defeated if the cavalry met them in a single, cohesive mass, relying on the shock of the impact to break the infantry formation. Maintaining that cohesion and mass was the purpose of the careful preparations the 21st Lancers were now undertaking.

They first formed into line of squadron columns, and continued forward at a walk until they came to within three hundred yards of the Arabs. Wheeling left, the squadrons broke into a trot as they moved across the Dervish front. The Arabs quickly opened fire on the cavalry, inflicting casualties among the troopers and the horses. The order rang out, "Right wheel into line," and at that, four hundred horsemen swung round into a single line and began working up to the gallop.

It was the first charge the regiment had ever made in its history. The fact that the unit had never before been in battle was an embarrassment to all of its officers and troopers. Though the regimental motto was "Death or Glory," cynical officers from other cavalry units scorned the 21st by declaring that its actual motto was "Thou shalt not kill." Now the 21st was given a chance to prove its mettle. What was about to happen would be a costly demonstration of regimental pride.

The horsemen were still some two hundred and fifty yards from the Arab riflemen who were still firing away at them, when the rising, ten-note bugle call of the "Charge!" was sounded and the regiment broke into a full gallop. Before half the distance to the riflemen had been crossed, a khor—a dry watercourse—appeared that had been invisible until the riders were virtually on top of it. Out of it sprang a screaming, surging mass of white-clad Arabs, the twenty-four hundred reinforcements the Khalifa had sent to support the blocking force.

The Lancers crashed into and through the Arabs, down into the khor and up the other side. Seventy-one officers and troopers fell in that first clash, and as its impetus carried it through the Arab position, the regiment wheeled about-face, reformed, and charged once again. By this time, though, the unit had lost much of its cohesion and the pace of the charge was slower. Soon a hand-to-hand melee was underway between Dervish and trooper, and it was only decided when one squadron of the Lancers drew off, dismounted and opened fire on the Arabs with their carbines. It was the last cavalry charge ever made by the British Army, and it was over in barely ten minutes.

It had been a desperate, ferocious, and ultimately needless action.

Winston Churchill, who had not only been an eyewitness to the charge but a participant, painted a memorable picture of the aftermath of one of the last stands of the Mahdi's army:

> The Lancers remained in possession of the dearly bought ground. There was not much to show that there had been a desperate fight. A quarter of a mile away nothing would have been noticed. Close to, the scene looked like a place where rubbish is thrown, or where a fair has recently been held. White objects, like dirty bits of newspaper, lay scattered here and there—the bodies of the enemy. Brown objects, almost the color of the earth, like bundles of dead grass or heaps of manure, were also dotted about—the bodies of soldiers. Among these were goat-skin water-bottles, broken weapons, torn and draggled flags, cartridge cases. In the foreground lay a group of dead horses and several dead or dying donkeys. It was all litter.

It had been a costly action. The seventy-one dead and wounded Lancers amounted to nearly a fifth of the regimental strength, while close to a thousand Arabs lay dead or dying on the field. The remainder fled while the surviving Lancers collected their casualties and reformed their ranks. At about the same time, a heavy barrage of cannon fire began and seconds later the crackle of small arms could be heard from behind the ridge. It was just on 9:00 AM and the whole of the British Army had swung over to the attack.

As soon as the Mahdist soldiers in the center began to withdraw, Kitchener had ordered his British and Egyptian brigades to advance toward Omdurman. It was a bold move, for there were still more than thirty-six thousand Ansar and Dervishes on the field, many of them mounted—more than sufficient forces to block Kitchener's advance and inflict heavy losses in the process.

The infantry brigades wheeled left in echelon formation and began marching toward Surgham Ridge. At the same time, the Khalifa's reserves, fifteen thousand horsemen and foot-soldiers, turned on the northernmost British brigade, that is, the last in the line. Surging over the ridge, the Arabs charged with as much ferocity as the Dervishes had shown earlier. Seeing the looming threat, Kitchener instantly responded with a series of crisp orders that completely realigned his army. Whereas it had begun the fight facing to the southwest, it was now facing almost due north.

The Khalifa, watching from the far side of the plain as his warriors attacked the British line, saw a possibility that his original plan might still come to pass—catching the British and Egyptians in the open desert—if his widely separated divisions could manage to attack both British flanks simultaneously. It would create a crisis for Kitchener, compelling him to divide his reserves, denying him the opportunity to move units from one part of the line to support threatened sections. But even as he watched he saw that the assault against the British left would begin too soon. On the other side, the divisions of Ali-Wad-Helu and Osman Sheikh ed-Din were still reforming on the Kerreri Hills, and their attack on the British right would come too late.

The British front was nearly a mile in length, and all along it the Lee-Metfords and Maxims took a savage toll of the Arabs. Many of the Ansar and Dervish leaders lay dead in the sand, surrounded by their bodyguards and warriors. Field batteries ranged artillery fire up and down the Arab ranks. With the Sirdar in the center, the entire Anglo-Egyptian line began to move forward against what was left of the Mahdist army. Shiekh Yakub and his bodyguards made a defiant stand under their Black Flag, refusing to give up their ground, and were killed where they stood. The remnants of Abdullahi's other divisions began to dissolve, fleeing into the desert. Thousands straggled toward Omdurman, where survivors of the 21st Lancers harried the flanks of the fugitive column. One group of some four hundred Arab horsemen formed up and charged the British brigade on the far left of the line, only to be shot down to a man before they reached the khaki-clad infantry.

Kitchener pressed his attack until the Ansar and Dervishes were driven into the desert, left in a state of chaos and confusion, and no longer a threat to his army. At 11:30 AM, the Sirdar turned to his staff and announced that the enemy had been given "a good dusting." He then gave orders that the march to Omdurman be resumed. The "Cease Fire" sounded up and down the line, rifles brought to the slope, and columns of march reformed.

As they departed the field, the British left behind nearly twenty thousand Arab dead, with another five thousand trailing behind under guard as prisoners. The Arab wounded totaled more than twenty-two thousand. British and Egyptian losses, in contrast, were forty-eight dead and less than four hundred wounded. Abdullahi had escaped, but his power was broken, his eventual capture a mere formality—at least, that was what Kitchener and his officers believed.

The Sirdar and his staff rode into Omdurman with their troops in the late afternoon. The rumor had been spread by the Khalifa that should the city be taken the British would massacre all the inhabitants as revenge for the murder of Gordon, but when this proved to be false there was a tremendous celebration in the streets. British troops were scouring the city, hoping to find Abdullahi, only to learn that as the Arab army was collapsing under the weight of Kitchener's final assault, the Khalifa had fled into the city, spent two hours in prayer at the Mahdi's tomb, and then just as Kitchener was entering the city by the north, Abdullahi mounted a donkey, took a Greek nun with him as a hostage, and fled out the southern gate. There he joined thirty thousand refugees, the remnants of his army, who were trudging their way south toward El Obeid.

Kitchener's troops did find Rudolf Karl von Slatin, the Austrian officer who had been a prisoner of the Mahdi and the Khalifa for fifteen years, along with Karl Neufeld, a German trader who had been held captive for twelve. Kitchener himself paid a visit to the Mahdi's tomb, which had been badly damaged when the British gunboats had shelled the city's arsenal, and initiated what was probably the most disturbing incident of his entire career. Arriving at the tomb, he ordered Muhammed Ahmed's body removed, its head cut off, and its remains thrown into the Nile. What he intended to do with the skull is unknown, although rumors later had it that he either intended to turn it into a drinking cup or send it to the Royal College of Surgeons as a curiosity. In any event, once word of this incident reached the public the outcry was fierce—even Queen Victoria expressed outrage at the desecration, remarking that it "savoured too much of the Middle Ages." Chastened, Kitchener then sent the skull to Cairo, where Evelyn Baring took possession of it and had it buried according to Moslem custom in a cemetery at Wadi Halfa.

In the meantime, Kitchener and his troops occupied Khartoum, now falling into ruin, and there found a handful of reminders of General Gordon. Though his body was never found, a funeral service for Gordon was held on September 4 with full military honors. As gunboats on the Nile fired a salute and three cheers were raised, first for the Queen, then for the Khedive, the British and Egyptian flags were once again unfurled above the Governor's Palace. Kitchener, who had long admired Gordon and had taken the news of Khartoum's fall fourteen years earlier very hard, was so moved by the ceremony that he was unable to give the order to dismiss the troops on parade, and had one of his subordinates issue the command. In the days to come he would be seen spending long hours in solitary contemplation walking in the courtyard where Gordon had met his death. When Queen Victoria received Kitchener's report of the funeral service, she confided to her diary with some satisfaction, "Surely he is avenged."

A part of Kitchener's solitary walks were no doubt devoted to a set of orders he had been given before departing Cairo, but was not permitted to open until he had taken Khartoum. Upon reading them, he discovered that he had been ordered to take his army further up the Nile into the Sudan to a small mud-fort called Fashoda, once held by the Eygptians but now occupied by a column of French soldiers who had marched out of the Congo. Once there, Kitchener was to remove the French and place the fort and the surrounding territory firmly under Anglo-Egyptian control.

Setting out from Khartoum in a small flotilla of riverboats on September 10, Kitchener reached Fashoda eight days later, and through a remarkable demonstration of tact and diplomacy, persuaded the French commander to leave the fort. It took two months for the details of the two officers' agreement to be settled by their respective governments, but on December 11, the French departed. Kitchener took his time returning to Khartoum, securing the Nile along the way by building small forts and leaving Egyptian garrisons to man them.

When he arrived in Khartoum at the beginning of March, he discovered that a grateful nation, by an act of Parliament, had awarded him the sum of £30,000, and that he had been elevated to an earl—styling himself "Kitchener of Khartoum," he would be known throughout the Empire as simply "K of K." At the same time he had also been given the authority to rebuild the Sudanese capital. Seven thousand new trees were planted as five thousand workmen began repairing the buildings damaged during the siege or allowed to fall into ruin during the *Mahdyyah*. Kitchener also raised a £120,000 public subscription for the establishment of Gordon College in Khartoum. To further commemorate the General, a statue of Gordon mounted on a camel was eventually placed in the square in front of the Governor's Palace.

But there was still one piece of unfinished business: the Khalifa. For more than a year Abdullahi had wandered in the dry hills of the central Sudan, among the Baggara, the tribe from which the Khalifa had come. British and Egyptian agents searched for him, but it wasn't until October 1899 that definitive reports of a camp near Jebel Gedir were received. An oasis more than four hundred miles south of Khartoum, Jebel Gedir was hardly a likely focal point for a new Islamic uprising, while the Khaifa had fewer than ten thousand followers who remained loyal. It is even arguable that Abdullahi himself had given up the cause of the Mahdi. Yet there was still a cause for concern among the British and Egyptians: Jebel Gedir lay just south of Abbas Island, where the Mahdi had been born and where he had begun his *jihad*. There remained strong undercurrents of pro-Mahdist sentiment in the region, and that alone was reason enough for Kitchener to choose to settle the issue with the Khalifa once and for all.

Sending eight thousand men up the Nile to the village of Kaka, where they began their overland trek to Jebel Gedir, Kitchener gave command of the force to Colonel Sir Francis Reginald Wingate, who had served as an aide to Field Marshal Wolseley on the Gordon Relief Expedition, spoke fluent Arabic, and was by all accounts an expert on Egypt, the Sudan and the Middle East. Moving swiftly, Wingate took part of his force westward and on November 21 overtook an Arab caravan carrying grain for the Khalifa. Two days later the Khalifa's camp was discovered near a well at Um Diwaykarat. Wingate brought up the whole of his force and Abdullahi was trapped. With the route to the north cut off by the British, the Nile to the east, the desert to the west and impassible scrub and brush to the south, a battle was inevitable.

It was Omdurman all over again, though on a far smaller scale. As the Arabs attacked in the early morning light, the crashing British rifle volleys and chattering machine guns chewed into the ranks of the charging enemy. It was over within an hour: a thousand Arab dead lay on the field, while nearly ten thousand more were taken prisoner, including the Khalifa's son, his designated successor. As the morning light grew brighter, an amazing sight greeted the British officers examining the battlefield. Wingate told the tale with simple dignity:

> Only a few hundred yards from our original position on the rising ground, a large number of the enemy were seen lying dead, huddled together in a comparatively small space; on examination these proved to be the bodies of the Khalifa Abdullahi, the Khalifa Ali Wad Helu, Ahmed-el-Fedil, the Khalifa's two brothers, Sennousi Ahmed and Hamed Muhammed, the Mahdi's son, Es-Sadek, and a number of other well-known leaders.
>
> At a short distance behind them lay their dead horses, and, from the few men still alive—among whom was the Emir Yunis Eddekin—we learnt that the Khalifa, having failed in his attempt to reach the rising ground where we had forestalled him, had then endeavoured to make a turning movement, which had been crushed under our fire. Seeing his followers retiring, he made an ineffectual attempt to rally them, but recognizing that the day was lost, he had called on his emirs to dismount from their horses, and seating himself on his "furwa" or sheepskin—as is the custom of Arab chiefs who disdain surrender—he had placed the Khalifa Ali Wad Helu on his right and Ahmed Fedil on his left, whilst the remaining emirs seated themselves round him, their bodyguard in line some twenty paces to their front, and in this position they had unflinchingly met their death. They were given a fitting burial, under our supervision, by the surviving members of their own tribesmen.

It was the end of the *Mahdyyah*.

Kitchener added a postscript to Wingate's report, saying, "The country has at last been finally relieved of the military tyranny which started in a movement of wild religious fanaticism upwards of 19 years ago. Mahdism is now a thing of the past, and I hope that a brighter era has now opened for the Sudan." As prophecies and predictions go, this was both prescient and naive.

Certainly the Sudan would prosper under British rule. Once the last remnants of the *Mahdyyah* were swept away the slave trade quickly withered and died, while railroads brought permanent connections to the outside world for the entire country; the Sudan would no longer be dependent solely on the Nile. Culturally the country would remain divided between the Arab, Moslem north and the African, Christian south, but as long as the British retained power, there was little friction between the two—the British simply did not tolerate it. When independence came to the Sudan in 1956, to all appearances the country, its administration, finances, industry, and agriculture were all in fine shape—the transition from colonial rule to home rule was smooth and uncomplicated.

As often happens, however, appearances were deceiving. As the Anglo-Egyptian co-dominium wound down, two political parties had emerged in the Sudan. One was the National Unionist Party (NUP), which had as its central policy a demand for a union of the Sudan and Egypt. The other was the Umma Party, backed by Sayed Sir Abdur-Rahman al-Mahdi, the Mahdi's grandson, which wanted no links with Egypt, but rather demanded complete independence. In December 1953, in the first elections held in the Sudan in preparation for the introduction of home rule, the NUP won a resounding victory, securing a majority in the House of Representatives with al-Aihari becoming the Sudan's first Prime Minister. The replacement of colonial officials and bureaucrats with their Sudanese counterparts proceeded smoothly, and British and Egyptian troops left the country for the last time on January 1, 1956.

Yet, less than two years later, on November 17, 1958, General Ibrahim Abboud toppled the Government of al-Aihari in a bloodless army coup. Suspending democratic institutions indefinitely, General Abboud ruled through a thirteen-member army junta until October 1964, when a popular uprising among the Sudanese drove Abboud and his junta from power. For the next five years, the Sudan once again functioned as a working, if somewhat troubled, democracy.

It was during this period, though, that a new set of troubles began to emerge, as rebellion broke out in the southern Sudan as a consequence of what was felt to be oppression of the black southern Christians by the northern Arab Moslems. The rebels were led by Major-General Joseph Lagu, who continued with his rebellion even when the civilian government fell to another military coup in May 1969 and installed Colonel Jaafar al-Numieri as the new head of state. Open warfare broke out between the north and south that same year, and the fighting continued until March 1972 when a peaceful settlement was reached between the government and the rebels.

The ghost of the Mahdi still haunted the Sudan, however, as in July 1976, al-Numieri, who now styled himself President, was almost removed from power in an attempted coup led by former finance minister Hussein al-Hindi and former prime minister Sadiq al-Mahdi, the Mahdi's great-grandson. More than two thousand heavily armed civilians were carefully smuggled into Khartoum and Omdurman, where, once the signal to act was given, they caused widespread destruction among both civilian and military targets. The Sudanese army remained loyal to Numieri, however, and gradually crushed the coup. The reprisals were swift and severe: several hundred suspects were summarily imprisoned, while ninety-eight were executed for their part in the plot. Al-Hindi and al-Mahdi returned to exile.

It was on September 8, 1983 that President al-Numieri brought the Sudan much closer to a return to the *Mahdyyah*, when he announced that the nation's penal code would be linked "organically and spiritually" to Islamic common law, called the Sharia. All criminal offences would now subject to judgment according to the Koran. The penalties for murder, adultery, and theft suddenly became the same as they had been a century earlier. Alcohol and gambling were once more prohibited.

In the 1980s, as drought overtook central Africa and famine set in, millions of refugees poured into the Sudan, particularly to the south. Massive aid by the United Nations kept a tragedy from escalating into a disaster, but thousands still died as the Sudan's agricultural base, though strong, was insufficient to support them all. Once regarded as the potential bread basket of the Arab world, there were now food shortages throughout the country, even in the capital of Khartoum.

Discontent with al-Numieri grew as the famine worsened and the southern provinces, now chafing under an Islamic legal system they did not recognize as legitimate, once again rose in open rebellion. In April 1985 al-Numieri was deposed in yet another military coup, this one led by Lt. Gen. Swar al-Dahab, who, in a departure from the norm for African and Middle Eastern politics, returned the government to civilian rule. The new Prime Minister was Sadiq al-Mahdi. A century after the Mahdi's death, his great-grandson ruled the Sudan.

Like an Arabian fairy tale, the story of the Mahdi has become a fixture in the folklore and mythology of modern Islam. The young religious scholar who became the great desert warrior, dedicated to cleansing Islam, who defied and defeated great armies and generals, and who caused powerful leaders in mighty nations to tremble at his name, still holds a powerful sway over the hearts and minds of countless Moslems. Well into the twentieth century, the Mahdi remained a central figure in Sudanese history and myth, symbolic of a poor nation's resistance to foreign aggrandizement and oppression. Nor was the lesson of his successes lost on all Western observers: historian Anthony Nutting offered an incisive analysis of how the Mahdi's appeal still remains potent: "A boat builder's son from the Nile had shown the world how a group of naked tribesmen, armed physically, at first, with sticks and stones but inwardly always with faith and unity, could be united and obtain superiority to a point where the greatest power on earth was held to ransom." In emulating the Mahdi's doctrines, his spirit, his intolerance, and his ruthlessness, it has been a lesson that modern militant Islam has taken to heart.

EPILOGUE

It was September 11, 2001.

The twin towers had fallen.

On that terrible morning, without warning, a score of militant Moslem fundamentalists, filled with what they felt was a righteous rage and a hatred for the Great Satan of the United States, had seized the controls on a quartet of airliners. They crashed them into the towers of the World Trade Center in New York City, into the Pentagon in Washington DC, and, when challenged by passengers who refused to be hapless pawns in the terrorists' scheme, plunged the last aircraft into the ground in rural Pennsylvania.

In New York, little more than an hour after the first airliner had struck, the South Tower crumbled, disintegrating in a shower of concrete dust, shattered glass and splintered steel. Less than thirty minutes later, the North Tower collapsed. The death-toll was nearly three thousand. In Washington an entire face of the Pentagon was engulfed in flames as civilian workers and uniformed military personnel struggled to escape suffocation or incineration. In Pennsylvania an aircraft smoldered in an empty field, all its crew, passengers, and hijackers dead.

In a very real sense, these acts of slaughter were part of the legacy of the Mahdi. Those responsible for the planning and execution of these terrible deeds soon came forward, the leaders of a militant Islamic organization that called itself Al Qaeda ("the Base"), a shadowy group of Moslems dedicated to bringing death and terror to the peoples and countries they perceived as threats to their own peculiar visions of Islam. They would prove to be the most dangerous of a surprising number of spiritual descendants of the Mahdi who have made their existence known in the last decade.

Like the Mahdi, the leadership of Al Qaeda is Sunni Moslem; most of them are also Wahhabis. It should be little wonder then that their vision of the evils of the world, as well as their concept of the source of those evils and what is necessary to correct or eradicate them, should differ little from that of Muhammed Ahmed in the 19th-century Sudan. Al Qaeda has declared that Islam has become morally lax and corrupt, succumbing to the extravagances and decadence of Western capitalism. It has also perceived the actual territories of the faithful to be under veritable occupation by infidels. It recognizes the only solution as a purging of all influences it deems dangerous to the faith. As it was with the Mahdi, tolerance is not permitted and persuasion is an alien concept—Al Qaeda can only comprehend, and thus embrace, a purging of sacred lands through blood. And much like him, while their pronouncements are laced with frequent declarations of the mercy and greatness of Allah, mercy is conspicuously absent in their actions: they define mercy only as a swift death, whether in the service of Allah or as a propitiation for unbelief. It is a chilling echo of the Mahdi's message to Gordon: "I have decided to take pity on some of my men and allow them to die as to obtain paradise."

When the United States-led coalition invaded Iraq in March 2003, a Shi'ite imam, Muqtada al-Sadr, chose to exploit the resultant chaos in the country to establish a semi-autonomous theocracy of his own. Offering a disjointed but still deadly resistance to the coalition forces, al-Sadr styled his militia "The Mahdi Army." It fought two pitched battles against Coalition forces, near the holy cities of Najaf and Karbala, and (ironically) now maintains a power bloc in the Iraqi parliament, because of free elections sponsored by the United States.

In the Sudan, the Mahdi's descendants—spiritual and literal—have sustained a genocidal civil war for nearly two decades. In 1988, Sadir al-Mahdi, Sudan's Prime Minister and Muhammed Ahmed's great-grandson, began a brutal civil war, as a century-long clash between the two cultures of the Sudan—one Arab-dominated and Islamic to the north, the other African and largely Christian in the south—once more burst into open flames, as millions of people were driven from their homes and at least two million were killed, most of them black Christians.

Empowering the Mahdi's medieval Islamic theocracy with the tactics of a modern police state, the Arab-dominated government established "ghost houses" where the enemies of the regime were subjected to whippings, electric shock, castration, branding, starvation, and executions. Tens of thousands of women were raped, children were kidnapped and sold into slavery (an institution that made its malignant reappearance in the early 1990s), and entire villages and towns were burned to the ground, their inhabitants often burned alive within. The only two crimes of which the African Sudanese are guilty are that they are not Arab and not Moslems.

In Darfur province, once the site of Rudolf von Slatin's spirited defense against the Mahdi, Baggara tribesmen, who still hold the memory of the Mahdi in deep reverence and take great pride in their tradition of being Muhammed Ahmed's most trusted and fearsome warriors, have extended the war against the Christian and animist black Africans to their fellow Muslims. Since its beginning in February 2003, this Sudanese holocaust has descended into what the United States government has openly described as genocide. By September 2006, estimates of the death toll in Darfur had risen to 400,000. When the United Nations attempted to intervene with an international peacekeeping force, officials of the Sudanese government—descendants of the Mahdi—absolutely refused to allow its intervention. (Though it did allow a feeble African Union force to operate near the border.) The government's opposition is hardly surprising, since it has been providing the tribesmen with arms, munitions, and supplies, tacitly giving the Baggara militias a free hand in their systematic slaughter of neighboring tribes. The Mahdi's war—along with his tradition of pointless bloodshed—continues in his homeland with as much brutality as ever.

Well over a century after his death, the Mahdi's spirit is still being invoked to call fanatics to the ranks of Al Qaeda, the Muslim Brotherhood, and other terrorist groups conducting campaigns of hatred and genocide. The Mahdi's deep and unquestioned devotion to Islam married the spiritual strength of his call to the faithful with powerful anti-colonial, anti-foreign, anti-Christian and anti-Semitic sentiments, a mix which modern Moslem terrorists such as bin Laden have embraced and propagated among their followers. In their decrees and pronouncements, both rail against the perceived corrupting influences of Western culture; both offer a focus for the common people of Islam to give voice and action to their resentment toward the "outsiders" or "foreigners" who they perceive draw believers away from the true faith; and both believe that in order to "cleanse" Islam, it must be washed in the blood of infidels.

The slaughter of thousands of innocents the day Khartoum fell gave the Mahdi's revolt a face of terror that no amount of latter-day revision will erase. When Osama bin Laden announced his own version of *jihad* against the world with atrocities on the morning of September 11, 2001, he was merely echoing the ideals and sentiments of the Mahdi. Bin Laden and his followers have become as convinced that their version and vision of Islam is the only true interpretation of the faith as Muhammed Ahmed had been a century and a quarter earlier when he was the "Expected One," destined to lead Islam back to its original purity.

Here then is a lesson for both the Western nations who have become the targets of militant Islam and the moderate and progressive elements within Islam—the majority of Moslems—who have renounced violence as an essential element of Islamic doctrine. The perception within the Moslem world that terrorists like bin Laden are carrying on the tradition of an Islamic hero such as the Mahdi cannot be allowed to continue giving such people a credibility and appeal that they do not deserve. Only when Islam itself chooses to make a determined effort to purge itself of its modern fanatics and ceases to glorify their spiritual forebears can civilized peoples from every continent hope to live in peace. Until then, the ghost of the Mahdi will still haunt the world.

But if the Mahdi's spirit still lives, so does that of Charles Gordon. Today, in Southampton, an old port city on England's Channel coast, where Gordon lived for many years off and on between his adventures, there is a memorial to Charles George Gordon in Queen's Park. An historical marker can be found on the house at 5 Rockstone Place, once Gordon's home. Gravesend is the site of a statue of the General in Fort Gardens, as well as a Gordon School and a Gordon Mission

Church, all of which were established in part as a remembrance of the General's spirit of kindness, generosity, and sense of social responsibility that were the products of his faith. Another school, the Gordon Boys School, was established in Surrey. There is still a statue of Gordon on the school grounds—it depicts the General seated atop a camel. The statue originally stood in front of the Governor's Palace in Khartoum, and was removed to Surrey after the Sudan became independent in 1956. Another statue of Gordon, this one in London, was erected in Trafalgar Square, later moved to the Thames Embankment.

And it is in London that perhaps can be found the great, fundamental, and irreconcilable difference between the Mahdi and Gordon and everything they represented—the contrast between their dreams for the world, their hopes for the future, and their visions for humanity. It can be seen in the words carved into a memorial tablet that sits in the nave of St. Paul's Cathedral. It reminds anyone who reads it that General Gordon was a man "who at all times and everywhere gave his strength to the weak, his substance to the poor, his sympathy to the suffering, his heart to God."

AUTHOR'S NOTE

As curious as it may seem, this book was not written as a reaction or response to the tragedies of September 11, 2001, or subsequent events, although its contemporary relevance is far greater now than I ever imagined it might be when I first gave thought to its writing back in 1999. My lifelong fascination with maritime subjects has been paralleled by an equally abiding—and equally deep—interest in military history. I knew of the story of the Mahdi, Gordon, and the siege of Khartoum long before I ever heard of Osama bin Laden or Al Qaeda, and for me it has always been a compelling tale.

But there was always an annoyance, which grew with the passing years, with the excessive—to me—emphasis that was always placed on General Charles Gordon, as if he were the only character of any significance or stature in the drama that unfolded at the confluence of the White and Blue Niles. I had always admired Gordon, particularly from the time I had grown up enough to be able to look beyond his obvious heroics and appreciate the underlying character of the man. Though he was frequently portrayed as the stereotypical, two-dimensional Victorian "hero," Gordon was simply too big a man to be bound by such conventions, and so the full dimensions of his persona, good and bad, always seemed to emerge no matter what. At the same time, however, the Mahdi was all too often cast in the role of the equally stereotypical, two-dimensional Victorian villian, the requisite "bad guy" to serve as the necessary foil to Gordon. There seemed to me to be something wrong with this inequity, not because of a commitment to political correctness, which I cordially despise as being intrinsically dishonest, but rather it seemed to me that an individual who could—and did—serve as the counterpart to a man of Gordon's moral and professional stature had to be someone of equally impressive character. As a consequence, I began looking deeper into the life of Muhammed Ahmed ibn-Abdullah—the Mahdi—and discovered an extraordinarily powerful historical figure.

Of course, much of the historical obscurity suffered by the is a direct consequence of the hero-worship that overtook Gordon after the fall of Khartoum at the hands of the Victorian biographers. Gordon's death was quickly transformed into a sort of "martyrdom" and because he was the agent if not the instrument of the General's demise, the Mahdi was instantly transformed into an incarnation of evil by those same biographers. It little helped his cause that the Mahdi was dark-skinned, belonged to a people who were colonial subjects of the European powers, and practiced a religion that was distinctly non-Christian and even openly hostile to Christianity.

So when I decided that the time had come for a retelling of the story of the siege of Khartoum, I made a determined effort to present a fuller picture of the Mahdi, and to present his rebellion in the light by which he led it, rather than the one it which is was perceived in Europe.

In doing so I discovered that the Mahdi was an extremely interesting individual, quite understandable if not exactly admirable. His ambitions and dreams were the products of his culture and his religion: he was in every way thoroughly Arab and thoroughly Moslem. This latter fact often upsets many of Islam's latter-day apologists, who prefer to gloss over their religion's violent history and doctrines much the same way Christians prefer to gloss over the Crusades and the European religious wars of the 16th, 17th, and 18th centuries.

In my research I discovered that the Mahdi has his own equivalent of Gordon's hero-worshipping biographers: even the most "objective" lives of the Mahdi written by Arab scholars are more hagiography than responsible biography. While records and documents from the *Mahdyyah* aren't exactly scarce, they are at times sketchy, and not always reliable: there is always the suspicion that some of them may have been altered long ago to please Egyptian and British colonial officials—or more recently to make them acceptable to whichever ruling faction was currently in power in the Sudan.

Consequently, the information available was sometimes ambiguous and frequently contradictory: a considerable mass of information available, but as any good historian will tell you, there is a vast difference between "information" and "knowledge." This made sorting the wheat from the chaff a sometimes formidable project, as the voices of racism and religious prejudice had to be filtered out of both British and Arab documents and sources.

It is with great pleasure then that I am able to acknowledge the assistance of His Excellency Khidir Haroun Ahmed, Ambassador of the Republic of Sudan to the United States, as well as his predecessor, His Excellency Mahdi Ibrahim Muhammed, who were gracious enough to initiate various contacts for me within the Sudan, particularly at the University of Khartoum and the International Islamic University in Khartoum, with which I conducted long and fruitful correspondences. The former Information Attache to the Sudanese Embassy, Mr. Elsadig Bakheit Elfaki Abdalla, was invaluable for his knowledge of just who knew what in his homeland, and who might have answers to specific questions about Sudanese history.

In the United States, Professors John Crossley and Megan Reid, both Assistant Professors of Religion at the University of Southern California, were invaluable for their insights into Islam, its ethics, and its morals, as was Dr. Charles Orr of Westwood Presbyterian Church. Professor Henry Vogt, retired from Hope College's Department of Religion, also made significant contributions to my understanding of Islam, its origins and practices. Dr. Maynard Pittendreigh gave me the benefit of his decades of religious scholarship, not only in Christianity but in Islam as well, and often provided intriguing and thought-provoking "real-life" counterpoint to the sometimes over-idealized perspectives and conclusions of academic religious experts.

The staffs at Hope College's Van Wylen Library, the Libraries of the University of Southern California, the Library of Congress, the Imperial War Museum, the British Museum, the British Public Records Office (PRO) and the Scottish National Records Office (SNO) were as always paragons of helpfulness. Deserving particular mention is the staff of the Sudan Archives at the University of Durham, in Durham, England, which possesses one of the most complete collections of both British and Arab correspondence and documents from the period of the Mahdi ever to be brought together in one place; the knowledge of the staff there is as amazing as their collection. All have my heartfelt gratitude for their efforts.

Mention should be made of the photographs and illustrations used in *The First Jihad*. I've collected militaria, photos and military artwork for more than a quarter-century, and have accumulated an extraordinary variety of them over the years from other collectors, antique shops, estate sales, and such. Quite a few were acquired while I was in the Army and haunting antique shops in Great Britain while on leave. One packet of photos that apparently dated from the 1930s was simply labeled "Khartoum" and appeared to be somebody's travel photos; others photos came from old regimental collections that were broken up and sold off. Though I do what I can to save images in my possession, knowing how years of neglect take a toll on many of them I can only imagine what photographic treasures have been lost: thrown into a dustbin, faded to nothing, or allowed to rot and crumble away because no one knew what they were, or cared.

As can be expected, during the research and writing of this book, many of the usual suspects showed up, along with some new faces. Scott Bragg has been, as always, a remarkably reliable resource for rooting out information and contacts through the Internet, as well as providing his own considerable knowledge of comparative religions. Where Trish Eachus found the time to do another one of her excellent proofreadings I have no idea: certainly she had to take time out from her own writing career to do so. She claims that proofreading is therapy for her in her ongoing battle with fibromyalgia, and if that is the case, I'm glad to have been of service—certainly she has done a great service for me! Kitty Bartholomew is at once the most energetic and most level-headed person I know: she's always a morale-booster without peer, and I value her for her common sense as well as her insight. She's never afraid to simply ask "Why?" over some point of discussion or conclusion, giving rise to much-needed reality checks as well as ensuring a sound basis for any arguments I may put forward. And no small credit goes to my editor at Casemate, Steve Smith, as well as to my publisher, David Farnsworth, for believing in and supporting this book.

Finally, I have to express my deep appreciation to Eily Wojahn. Her incisive thinking led to many a thought-provoking discussion, while her boundless cheerfulness was a source of constant encouragement to keep working on a sometimes difficult story. Ultimately she gave me reason to finish it.

In closing, let me repeat my gratitude to all of the institutions and individuals I've mentioned. In the case of specific persons, while my opinions did not always agree with theirs, not one of them ever made any qualification to their assistance as a consequence of our disagreements; this was true professionalism. While nearly every author at some point will state that they are personally responsible for the ideas and opinions expressed in his or her work, in this case, because some readers may take exception with some of my comments, observations, and conclusions I will state even more emphatically than usual that while all of these institutions and individuals made some contribution to the material presented in *The First Jihad*, the use of that material, as well as the conclusions and opinions drawn from it, are my responsibility alone. I wouldn't have it any other way.

—Daniel Allen Butler
Santa Monica, California

SOURCES AND BIBLIOGRAPHY

OFFICIAL RECORDS, MUSEUMS, AND ARCHIVES

Imperial War Museum, London
Institute of African and Asian Studies, University of Khartoum
International Islamic University, Khartoum
National Records Office, Khartoum
Public Records Office, London
Scottish National Records Office, Edinburgh
Archives of the Division of Guards, Wellington Barracks, London
Archives of the Royal Highland Regiment, Balhousie Castle, Perth
Sudan Archives, University of Durham

NEWSPAPERS

Edinburgh Review
Glasgow Herald
Illustrated London News
London Daily Express
London Daily Mail
London Daily Standard
London Morning Post

PERIODICALS

Ali, Abbas Ibrahim Muhammad, "Contemporary British Views on the
    Khalifa's Rule," *Sudan Notes and Records*, Khartoum, vol. li,
    1970, 31–46.

Holt, P. M. "Correspondence on Mahdiya Archives," *Sudan Notes and Records*, Khartoum, vol. xxxiii, 1, 1952, 182–86.

____"The Archives of the Mahdiya," *Sudan Notes and Records*, Khartoum, vol. xxxvi, 1, 1955.

____"The Source Material of the Sudanese Mahdia," St. Antony's Papers 4, *Middle Eastern Affairs*, 1. London, 1967.

Mirak-Weissbach, Muriel. "Why The British Hate Sudan: The Mahdia's War Against London," *The American Almanac*, September 4, 1995.

Peters, R., "Islam and the Legitimation of Power: The Mahdi-Revolt in the Sudan," *Zeitschrift der deutschen Morgenländische Gesellschaft*, Supplement: XXIV Deutscher Orientalistentag, 1980.

Sanderson, G.N. "The Modern Sudan, 1820–1956: The Present State of Historical Studies," *Journal of African History*, vol. iv, 1963.

BOOKS

abu-Shouk, Ahmed Ibrahim. *The Public Treasury of the Muslims: Monthly Budgets of the Mahdist State in the Sudan* (n.p., 1897).

al-Mahdi, Al-Athar al-Kamila li'l-Iman (Muhammad Ibrahim Abu Salim, editor). *The Complete Writings of the Mahdi of the Sudan* (Centre for Middle East & Islamic Studies, Universi, 1993).

Baring, Evelyn (as Lord Cromer). *Modern Egypt* (Routledge, 2000).

Bermann, Richard A., introduction by Sir Winston S. Churchill. *The Mahdi of Allah* (Simon Publications, reprint 2002, originally published 1932).

Chaillé-Long, Charles. *The Three Prophets: Chinese Gordon, Mohammed-Ahmed (El Maahdi), Arabi Pasha* (D. Appleton, 1884).

Churchill, Winston. *The River War* (Longmans Green, 1899).

Collins, Robert O. *The Southern Sudan 1883–1898* (Yale University Press, 1962).

Daniel, N. *Islam, Europe and Empire* (Edinburgh University Press, 1966).

Farwell, Bryon. *Prisoners of the Mahdi: The Story of the Mahdist Revolt Which Frustrated Queen Victoria's Designs on the Sudan, Humbled Egypt, and Led to the Fall of Gladstone* (W.W. Norton

& Company, 1989).

Featherstone, Donald. *Omdurman 1898: Kitchener's Victory in the Sudan* (Osprey Publishing, 1994).

Fradin, Murray. *Jihad: The Mahdi Rebellion in the Sudan* (Author's Choice Press, 2003).

Gordon, Charles. *Journals* (Negro Universities Press, 1969).

Holt, P. M. (ed. & trans.). *A Calendar of Correspondence of the Khalifa Abdallahi and Mahmud Ahmad, 1315/1897–98* (Khartoum, 1950).

____ *A Modern History of the Sudan* (Weidenfeld and Nicolson, 1961).

Ibn Warraq. *What the Koran Really Says: Language, Text, and Commentary* (Prometheus Books, 2002).

Keown-Boyd, Henry. *A Good Dusting* (Leo Cooper, 1986).

Lewis, Bernard. *The Crisis of Islam: Holy War and Unholy Terror* (The Modern Library, 2003).

____ *What Went Wrong? Western Impact and Middle Eastern Response* (Oxford University Press, 2001.

Mahdi, Muhsin. *Alfarabi and the Foundation of Islamic Political Philosophy* (University of Chicago Press, 2001).

Marlowe, John. *Mission to Khartum* (Victor Gollancz, 1969).

Moorehead, Alan. *The White Nile* (Harper-Collins, 2000).

Neillands, Robin. *The Dervish Wars* (John Murray, 1996).

Power, Frank. *Letters from Khartoum* (Sampson Low, 1885).

Robson, Brian. *Fuzzy-Wuzzy: The Campaigns in the Eastern Sudan, 1884–85* (Spellmount, 1993).

Schmidt, Alvin J., and Marvin Olasky. *The Great Divide: The Failure of Islam and the Triumph of the West* (Continental Sales, 2004).

Slatin, Rudolf C.; Translated by Major F. R. Wingate. *Fire and Sword in the Sudan: a Personal Narrative of Fighting and Serving the Dervishes, 1879–1895* (John Wilson and Sons, 1896).

Spencer, Robert and David Pryce-Jones. *Islam Unveiled: Disturbing Questions About the World's Fastest Growing Faith* (Encounter Books, 2002).

White, Stanhope. *Lost Empire of the Nile* (Robert Hale, 1969).

Wingate, F. R. *Mahdiism and the Egyptian Sudan* (John Wilson and Sons, 1891).

INDEX